GEORGE CLOONEY
A Biography

Jeff Hudson

For Abigayle and Harriet

This paperback edition first published in Great Britain in 2004 by
Virgin Books Ltd
Thames Wharf Studios
Rainville Road
London
W6 9HA

First published in 2003 by Virgin Books Ltd

ISBN 0 7535 0872 9

Plate section designed by Anita Ruddell
Typeset by TW Typesetting, Plymouth, Devon
Printed and bound in Great Britain by
Mackays of Chatham PLC

CONTENTS

ACKNOWLEDGEMENTS

This book would not have been possible without the advice and co-operation of many people – some who would prefer to remain anonymous, others who would wish to have every attention drawn to them. Mention first of all should go to the good burghers of Augusta, Kentucky, for putting up with the comedy phone calls, and to the many people from George's past and present – actors, agents, girlfriends, teachers – who have given me invaluable insights into just how powerful the man has become. And to George himself, without whom there would have been a lot of blank pages.

Thanks go to my editor at Virgin, Mark Wallace, who identified an interesting subject before I did; to the marketing department at Fox for their mail-order service; to the staff at the BFI for the grapes and chocolates; and to all the café owners in W1 who have kindly hosted me and my laptop for hours at a time, and all for the price of a cup of Earl Grey.

On a personal note, I am indebted (literally) to the captain and crew of the good ship Wyldwood for their unstinting hospitality and breathtaking support over the last few years. Very much appreciated.

Also, the team at insidearts.co.uk (for covering for my book-enforced absences); Jo and Aaron (for roasts and rum); internationally renowned short-storyteller Ben Worthington (for legal aid and videos, but mainly the videos); the Sawbo collective, Roo, Miguel and Marigold; Dave and Caroline, Dredd, Nan and Frank, Dale and Babs – thanks to one and all.

And, finally, to Angela. The only reason I do anything. Thanks for coming on my boat . . .

INTRODUCTION: IT'S A GUY THING

A few years ago, George Clooney was driving home from his office at the Warner Bros lot when a pile of rubbish at the side of the freeway caught his eye. He swung his grey BMW over to the curb and walked back to the mound of litter. Pride of place on the trash heap was a gaudy old oil-painting of a fat Mexican woman. Nude. It was horrible, an unpleasant piece in every way. 'The ugliest painting you've ever seen,' George says. Whoever had tossed it onto the street should be commended for their good artistic sense if not their community conscience. Unperturbed, though, he picked the painting up, put it in the back of his car and drove home, a plan already hatched in his fecund mind.

Over the next few weeks, George's friends noticed that he started to cry off their Monday-night poker games and the occasional round of golf. 'I can't, I've got art class,' he explained. 'It's great, really therapeutic, you should come along.' There were no takers. But as the months passed, his buddies began to gain an insight into his new hobby. Days out would be punctuated by George dragging his pals into nearby craft shops to pore over different density paintbrushes. 'Oh, feel these, they're camel hair.'

For six months this behaviour went on until one day George presented his close friend Richard Kind, who plays press-secretary Paul in *Spin City*, with a special gift. It was George's first piece of work from his art class, and he wanted Kind, as one of his oldest and dearest friends, to have it. He had even signed it, in the bottom right-hand corner. Kind was honoured, touched even. And then he saw it. 'Gee, George, that's . . . great. She's . . . beautiful. Who is she?'

Just a life model at the class, George explained, his dark brown eyes studying his friend's face for signs of the slightest negative reaction. But it didn't come. After admiring the painting for a respectful amount of time Kind placed it gingerly against a wall. The next time George visited, he promised, his work would have pride of place in his home.

Kind was as good as his word. Visitors who entered his living-room were greeted by the swarthy señora's lusty pose and hideous composition. It was a talking point, at least, and, although it was not strictly to his taste, how proud Kind was to have his superstar friend's first artistic endeavour.

The next few times they met, George pestered Kind for news of his 'girl', visibly puffing up with pride on the outside at his friend's increasingly rambling compliments, but craving inwardly to burst out laughing. It was several weeks before he caved in and let Kind in on the joke.

Another friend, actress Bonnie Hunt, is still amazed at how well the sting worked. 'Richard had to hang the thing up because he wasn't going to tell George it was horrible,' she recalls. 'And George let it hang in Richard's house quite a while before he finally said, "I didn't paint that. I found it." '

Six months of planning went into this little stunt. Half a year of depriving himself of card nights and pretending to care about canvas tensions, just for a joke. And it could so easily have backfired. George was gambling that Richard Kind would be too good a friend to hurt his feelings. And he was spot on.

When George debouched to Los Angeles in 1982 with just a couple of hundred dollars, no job and nowhere permanent to live, it was more in hope than expectation. He had not been in town long before he bumped into others like him, all of them decent enough guys chasing the Hollywood dream. Shared experience brought them closer; they went to the same auditions, drank in the same bars, chased the same girls. They played basketball together, put a roof over each other's heads when one of them was down on his luck, and generally provided the support that, for whatever reason, their blood families could not bring themselves to give. George's father had been apoplectic when George dropped out of college to go to California, and they did not speak for days; his relatives in Beverly Hills were equally underwhelmed at the prospect of another 'wannabe' coming to stay and they made their feelings clear. No, when he was down on his luck and alone in that mercenary city for the first time, it was Richard, Thom, Matt, Waldo, Tommy, Ben and Grant – 'The Boys' – who got him through. More than twenty years later, they remain his closest friends despite all the success, all the premieres, all the adulation – and all the practical jokes.

George's sprawling eight-bedroom mansion in the Hollywood Hills is the focus of The Boys' social diary. Most Sundays they all convene at 'Casa de Clooney' (as the handwritten sign on the gates announces) and go riding their Harleys or the identical

Indians that George bought them all for Christmas one year. Then they come back and swim, play some basketball, fix taco-heavy barbecues, watch a movie in the house's giant screening room and just hang out with everyone's partners and kids. It's a fun place to be.

George is never happier than when looking after his friends. 'He likes to be the caretaker,' Ben Weiss, one of The Boys, says. 'He doesn't like to be the one with the problems.' He prefers to be in control. Always. Whether it's on the baseball field, on a film set in the middle of nowhere or just planning a holiday, George needs to feel in charge of his own actions, if not anyone else's. He has a fear of being a burden and a pathological hatred of other people making his mistakes for him, both of which make him seem like a control freak – but in the nicest possible way. He is actually the best team player in the world, as long as it's his team. If The Boys are a modern equivalent of The Rat Pack, then George is definitely Sinatra.

In the moral-free area of LA known as Hollywood, George is something of an oddity. He plays the game – he plays it very well in fact – but he has never looked close to being taken in by Tinseltown's bewitching smoke-and-mirrors artifice. After two decades of living and working at its heart, he is the same person now as the day he arrived. How is it that a village hick from the tobacco fields of Kentucky can withstand the cynical ways of the world's entertainment capital when so many who were born and bred within the system have gone under?

In many ways, George is a throwback to another time, arguably one that never really existed. Blessed with the looks and charm of Cary Grant and Clark Gable, he has an approach to life that can be summed up by his worship of another screen idol, Spencer Tracy. 'He's a guy,' George says. 'You always wanted to go, "Spencer, what should we do here?" You felt comfortable with him because he was comfortable with himself. And that's what I strive for, which is: just let me be the guy.'

And it works. *From Dusk Till Dawn* director Robert Rodriguez remembers the impact George made on a daily basis – just by turning up for work. 'He's red-blooded and it shows,' he says. 'When he used to roll up on the set on his big motorbike, everyone used to stop and watch. He has that effect.'

'He knows what kind of persona he wants to present,' his *Perfect Storm* co-star, Mary Elizabeth Mastrantonio, agrees. 'He acts like a man. He has the opinions of a man. He thinks like a man.'

'He's what we used to call a "ride-back guy",' *Three Kings* producer Paul Junger Witt adds, 'the one in Westerns who would ride back and get you if you were shot off your horse.' As if to prove it . . . 'We lost a lot of crew members to cancer,' *ER* star Julianna Margulies recalls, 'and George was the first person there by the family's side with money, if that's what they needed, or to help the children through school.'

In George's world, this is how men behave. Did you know that this guy refused to quit *ER* before his five-year contract expired? Were you aware that he never once asked for an increase in his $42,000-a-week salary on the show, even though Anthony Edwards and Noah Wyle had renegotiated their take-home amounts almost tenfold? How many people realise that he risked his career as a young actor by standing up to one of the most powerful producers in TV to defend a co-star? Or that he got into a punch-up with another director over a similar incident a decade later?

Real men stand up for their principles even if it means getting a bloody nose. They look after their friends. They open doors, pull up chairs and stand when a lady enters the room. And they always pay the bill on a date, regardless of how much their partner earns. It is not a position that impresses everyone in the 21st century but George is unrepentant. 'I don't apologise for it,' he says. 'It's a guy thing.' And it's what Spencer would do.

As his friend Brad Pitt says, 'No one saw George coming.' So how did he get where he is today? How did he rise from college drop-out and self-confessed 'hair actor' to quietly become one of the most powerful men in Hollywood today?

It all started one spring day in Kentucky . . .

1. I GREW UP IN TELEVISION

Lunchtime on 17 March 1966, St Patrick's Day, in a television studio in Cincinnati, Ohio. It's business as usual for the crew working on set and the viewers tuning in, as the live show runs through its comfortable routine, serving up the usual mix of interviews, humour and opinion. In charge of the whole circus is amiable host Nick Clooney, communicating – connecting – with the unseen thousands watching at home, as effortlessly as though they were there in the room with him. Topical gags, local references and more than the odd knowing look to camera – it's another virtuoso performance from a broadcaster at the top of his game.

But the comfort zone in the world of entertainment is a dangerous place to inhabit. What audiences lap up with relish one minute they tire of the next; stars feted one day can be greeted with indifference soon after. Ideas, innovation and inspiration are the industry's lifeblood. Trafficking in the new, the newer and the newest is what keeps show business's financial heart ticking. As a shark needs to swim to avoid death, the failure of an entertainer to maintain career momentum can, in professional terms, be fatal.

The ability to stay fresh will sustain a career far longer than talent alone. Decades before Madonna and her contemporaries turned reinventing themselves into an art form, the showbiz world knew to be wary of serving the same dish too often, however popular at the time. The freshest food on the table is always the most desirable.

Keeping his show as pacey and as unpredictable as possible was one of the reasons Nick Clooney had survived as long as he had in the notoriously cut-throat and short-memoried broadcasting business. Although formulaic at heart, quirks and surprises had become a mainstay of *The Nick Clooney Show*. It shouldn't have been a surprise to many viewers, then, when the host announced that, to commemorate St Patrick's Day, they had a special guest, all the way from Ireland itself.

Cue music, trail-light and a camera directed at the incoming 'guest'. To the studio audience's applause and laughter, a small figure, less than half the interviewer's height, clad in green and chewing on a cigar, traipsed onto the stage. Students of European myth would recognise the visitor as a leprechaun, that native Celtic sprite. Workers on the show, however, would identify the guest as someone from closer to home, Nick Clooney's home to be precise.

And so it was that George Timothy Clooney made his television debut. The caricature beard may have itched, the Robin-of-Sherwood green tights may have made him self-conscious, but young George carried off his part with aplomb. Well prepped before the show, although probably too young to appreciate his family's Irish-American heritage, he trotted out the scripted answers to his dad's questions like a true pro. Not bad for a five-year-old leprechaun.

But George had long been familiar with his father's work. Like any child growing up in a close family, he didn't know any other way. Didn't all dads have TV shows? The answer, of course, was no. In fact, as Nick Clooney would be the first to admit, he was lucky to have his show. Not that there was any reason why he shouldn't do it; but with so many people in his profession having to work sedentary day jobs to fund their existence 'between shows', Nick knew he was blessed with good fortune to be able to earn a living – and a good one – doing what he wanted to.

In fact, a measure of Nick's gratitude at being in employment was the fact that chat show host was not his first-call career choice. As a trained journalist he had set his sights on becoming a newsreader in the style of his hero, Edward R Murrow. By way of compromise, his TV network, WRW, allowed him to read the nightly news as well as front their midday entertainment show. Consequently, he became the true definition of a 'household' name: housewives and children saw his shows during the day; in the evening, Nick would bring the menfolk of Ohio their news bulletins.

The Clooney clan had arrived in Cincinnati from Lexington, Kentucky in the mid-60s when WLW radio had hired Nick to replace the outgoing Bob Braun, who was moving to front *The 50-50 Club* variety show on WLWT-TV. Braun soon asked Nick to help out on *50-50* and so his career in variety began. Nick's own entertainment show followed soon after. It was a far cry from his original ambitions as a newscaster.

Nick's workload did not end there. As well as juggling TV and radio commitments, he also began to act at Beef'N'Boards dinner theatre in nearby Harrison. Although not his intended profession, Nick did have a little acting experience. As an eighteen-year-old on a visit to his sister Rosemary in Hollywood, he had been spotted by legendary film director Cecil B DeMille and asked to audition. He read the scene with actress Amanda Blake seven times before DeMille called a halt. 'He said, "Mr Clooney, we like the way you look," ' Nick recalls, ' "and we like the way you sound. But we do not like the two together. You look like you're eighteen and you sound like you are forty. When those two functions meld, we hope you will come back and see us." ' His son George would later suffer the same fate.

As a result of his personal market penetration, Nick became a major star in and around Cincinnati. From Ohio to Kentucky to Indiana, he was a recognisable 'face', likely to be chatted to in the streets any time he dropped by.

'My father was as big a star as you could be,' George recalls fondly. 'He was very popular and a really respected citizen in the town. He was God. Everybody everywhere we walked would stop him.'

And little wonder. WRW's *Nick Clooney Show* regularly earned sixty/seventy share figures. In layman's terms, it meant that for every person watching television during the host's air time, sixty to seventy per cent of them would be watching him. To put it into perspective, Clooney Jr's award-winning show, a certain hospital drama called *ER*, would only score in the low forties during its peak.

But that's now. In the 21st century, TV stars are two a penny. Thanks to the proliferation of channels and the modern thirst for 24-hour entertainment, you can't pick up a stone without a celebrity of some demarcation (and categories currently go as low as D-list) crawling out. In the mid-60s, though, to be a 'star' meant something. If not to the star himself, then to everyone else.

While NBC pumps out *ER* nationwide, from East Coast to West, WRW was a network broadcasting restrictively to the Cincinnati area. Although in the top twenty of broadcasting territories, Cincinnati had yet to register as a major player nationally when Nick was working there. Consequently, his fame, although intense, was restricted to the immediate area. If it was a drawback, nobody told his children. 'I loved being Nick Clooney's son,' George says. 'I loved the things that it got me to do.'

While being known as 'Nick Clooney's son' opened doors throughout his childhood, once George left the confines of Kentucky it would be another relative's name which would prefix his: that of his aunt, Rosemary. Despite the fact that her singing and acting career pretty much began and ended in the 50s, to be known as 'Rosemary Clooney's nephew' was good for generating a few column inches if not opening one or two doors. George may not have realised it as a child, watching his father interview national celebrities or seeing pictures of his aunt in the newspapers alongside presidents and world leaders, but the Clooney family wasn't like other families. In truth, it hadn't been for some time.

Nick would later try to quell his son's taste for performing, but he, too, had experienced the same career-lust as a child. Like his sisters Rosemary and Betty, he had been raised to believe that a career as an entertainer wasn't just possible, it was normal. On top of that, it offered the only escape from the often-unbearable suffering of their childhood.

Growing up in the small north Kentucky town of Maysville in the 30s, the Clooney children's early lives fell apart when their parents, Andy and Frances, divorced. It was not a clean break. Between their father's alcoholism and mother's constant travelling for her work with a chain of dress shops, the children were dragged – physically and emotionally – from one town to another, by one parent or the other, or often left with relatives for weeks on end. The worst was to come in 1941 when Frances Clooney decided to leave Maysville once and for all and start a new life with a sailor in California. Somehow it was decided that Nick would travel with her; the girls would stay with their father. The siblings were distraught at the separation but, as children are often forced to do, they tried to stay strong for their parents. According to Rosemary, their father tried his best to look after them, but in 1945 it all got too much for him. He went out one night to celebrate the end of World War II – and never returned. He took all the family money with him and left a string of bills for the teenagers to cover.

Directionless and in danger of losing trust in all adults, the girls looked for help from others in their family. In particular, they gravitated towards their Uncle George; and he to them. George Guilfoyle was a natural with children, and with adults, too. A celebrated B-17 bomber pilot in World War II, he returned to Maysville in the 40s a war hero before building a successful career as a raconteur and radio personality. 'He was an all-star basketball player, a good-looking, witty guy who dated Miss America,' his great-nephew and namesake reminisces. 'He was on fire with life.' Uncle George's talent for communication meant that he soon became a star in his bluegrass hometown. More than that, he became a surrogate parent for his disenfranchised nieces and, during his infrequent visits, for Nick.

One of the ways in which Uncle George buoyed the young Clooneys was to encourage their pursuit of the arts. Perhaps he was just being a good uncle; maybe he genuinely saw something in them. Either way, with this young trio he struck lucky because each Clooney child had a talent which, George realised, could be nurtured. Nick appeared to have kissed the Blarney Stone, as his Irish ancestors would call his gift of the gab; there was a career in radio for this young man as soon as he was out of short trousers. As for Betty and Rosemary – they had voices which could be exploited in the here and now.

One of the first things Uncle George did was to encourage the girls to enter an open audition on his radio station. They were an immediate hit, snapped up by the channel for a regular $20 weekly stint – at last, the domestic bills could be taken care of. Seizing the opportunity, Uncle George helped them build a proper career for themselves, and in 1945 they started performing in earnest as The Clooney Sisters. That same year, bandleader Tony Pastor was taken by one of their performances and promptly asked them to join his orchestra. It was too good a chance to turn down. For the next three years, Rosemary and Betty toured the region as featured singers with Pastor's band. With Uncle George travelling as their manager and guardian, things were finally turning out OK for the put-upon sisters.

There is a saying in the entertainment industry that you can't please all of the people all of the time. Normally this is directed at audiences, but occasionally it can be true of the stars themselves. Just three years after making her radio debut, Betty Clooney announced she was tired of life on the road. Yes, she enjoyed the attention; yes, she loved performing. But like another famous little girl taken out of her Midwest world, most of all she just wanted to go home. In Betty's case, it was to Kentucky, not Kansas. After discussions with Rosemary and Uncle George, she clicked her red heels and returned to Maysville. Aged seventeen, she retired from public life.

Rosemary had two choices at this stage. In retrospect, it wasn't even a close call: she would continue to sing without Betty, although with changes. She, too, was beginning to tire of life with Pastor's troupe, and so with Uncle George she began to look for fresh challenges for her prodigious young talent. In 1949, aged just 21, she arrived in New York. Before long she had recorded the song that was to become her calling card: 'Come-On-A-My-House'. If she had known fame before, this blew it out of the water. With that track, 'Rosie' announced her presence on the international stage – and the world listened. Hit followed hit, gold records began to cover her apartment walls and fans queued for hours in the hope of catching a glimpse of their idol. Throughout the 50s there wasn't a bigger female star in America: magazines vied with each other to entice her onto their covers; stars like Frank Sinatra and Bing Crosby asked her to duet with them; and, of course, Hollywood came a-beckoning. A lot of singing careers don't necessarily translate to movie success, but Rosemary acquitted herself well in *Here Come the Girls* and *Red Garters*. Above all, there was that perennial classic, *White Christmas*. The girl from Maysville was sure making her mark.

While Uncle George shepherded his elder niece around the globe, his young nephew was also fulfilling the prophesy made for him. Nick had seen his sisters take to the heady heights of showbiz like naturals and he'd watched as one of them returned back to earth, embittered by the experience. Nick wasn't the jealous sort – they were his sisters, after all – and in any case, his heart lay in more serious work. Inspired by his admiration for the wartime broadcasts of his hero Murrow, he had decided at an early age to try to become a newscaster. Showing the tenacity that would become a staple of his professional repertoire, he had pursued doggedly any opportunity that might help his dream job become a reality, and it had worked. Nick was still a junior at Maysville High School when he got his first break, contributing newscasts to local radio channel WFTM. He had built on this experience during his stay on the West Coast, but now was the time to return to his roots and carve a career for himself. Returning to Kentucky, this time to Lexington, he concentrated on making it as a journalist. The move paid off and he soon became a successful journalist, presenting the news for WLAP radio as well as hosting a teen bandstand programme on WKYT-TV. His appointment as president of the Bluegrass Press Club was the public icing on the cake.

If only his personal life was as straightforward. To paraphrase Jane Austen, a young man in the 50s in possession of a decent job and a good salary, must be in need of a wife. Nick Clooney was no exception to this universal truth. As a fledgling star around Lexington he was something of a catch. Not only was he famous, successful and attractive, he was good company. His ability to put new acquaintances at ease, so useful as an interviewer seeking answers, meant he had the requisite tools to become a natural born lady-killer.

If proof were needed of the silver-tongued Clooney's charmed life at that time, one episode supplied it in spades. A particular perk of his new-found celebrity was that he was entrusted with MC duties at the annual Miss Lexington beauty contest. The Bluegrass Press Club sponsored the event and naturally, as president of the Club, it was only right that he should take a leading role. Many red-blooded men would have been grateful for that coup alone. But Nick's interests in the competition did not end when the pageant did; once the jury had returned their votes, it was his solemn duty to escort the newly-crowned winner to her official appointments. As with most things, Nick threw himself into the role with gusto, squiring 1959's Miss Lexington to half-a-dozen functions and leading her through her token duties. It was his job to put her at ease, and he used all his powers to do so. Some might say, he tried a little too hard.

'By about the fifth or sixth of those chicken-and-peas dinners, I said, "Would you please pass the butter and would you marry me?"' Nick recalls. 'She picked up the butter, looked at it for a second and said, "Here's the butter and OK."'

Not quite the behaviour of a chaperone, but Miss Lexington – Nina Warren – forgave him. They were married two months later in Lexington.

Despite the rough ride he'd had as a child, Nick refused to believe that marriage wouldn't work for him. He'd seen the pitfalls from close hand; he knew the danger signs. He was determined that his own life would not follow his parents' course. To an extent, he would be successful in that pledge. But a man can only fight the battles he sees. No child is immune from the influences of his parents, however subliminal or insidious they may be. And Nick Clooney was no different. Given his experience of being shunted from one relative's house to the next, like an unwanted gift in a game of pass-the-parcel, the notion of having one place to call 'home' was almost an alien concept to him. His mother had travelled for her work; his father had just travelled. Nick himself had spent so much of his early life on the road that he probably didn't appreciate the joys of finding a base camp. If Nina had a taste for comfortable stability rather than an itinerant's wanderlust, this could prove tricky.

Those worries were for another time, however. Life for Nick and Nina in the early 60s could not have been sweeter. Nick's career went from strength to strength, picking up lucrative radio and television contracts. Nina, meanwhile, became pregnant with their first child, Ada. A year later, on 6 May 1961, Ada was joined by a little brother, George, named after the uncle who had played such a guiding role in Nick's life. The Clooney unit was complete and, until the last breath in his body, Nick was going to keep it that way.

Anyone who has seen a recent picture of George Clooney won't be surprised to learn that he was an attractive child. All smiles, with two goofy teeth dominating his ever-present grin as a youngster, he had a mischievous twinkle about his eyes and was always ready with a cheeky remark – not always appropriate from a three-year-old. Early portraits of him show a happy, tousle-haired scruff, obviously photogenic even then despite a tendency to find dirt wherever it lurked and (often) ill-fitting clothes. He wasn't the fastest growing kid in town, that was for sure. Even today, he appears a lot larger on screen than he is in real life.

Keeping true to his pledge to raise a better, more integrated, family than the one he came from, Nick devoted every spare moment to his wife and children. Unfortunately, because of his profession, those moments often came at unsociable hours, when his young family was safely tucked up in bed. So he hit on a compromise.

'I was determined that my kids shouldn't suffer the way that I and my sisters had suffered,' Nick explains. 'That's why I took them to work with me all the time. I couldn't stand to be away from them for any length of time.'

Given the capriciousness of his industry, Nick considered himself fortunate to be in steady work at all, so when a contract with one network was terminated, he tended to take the next offer he could get, whether it be presenting the lunchtime news on TV or hosting a radio talk show late at night. Security for his family had to come first. Each new job brought with it the possibility of upheaval, but for Nick that was normal – you travelled where the work was. It became normal for Ada and George, too, as did pottering around a radio control booth or fiddling with the latest new TV recording equipment. When you hired Nick Clooney, you got two little apprentices.

By three and four respectively, George and his sister were as familiar with the production rooms and backstage areas of half-a-dozen local networks as they were with their own home. With another two years' experience behind them, they had been promoted to helping with weather reports on their dad's show, operating the mikes and holding up cue cards. 'When I was six I could work the control booth and pipe in with the temperature when my dad read the weather,' George recalls fondly. He took it seriously, too. Nick placed great store in teamwork and everyone pulling their weight, and George didn't let him down. He didn't stomp around the set like the star's petulant offspring. He contributed in whatever way he could, and was happy to. Being part of a team, part of a shared experience, meant the world to him even at that early age. And he knew his chance would come.

But while George would rush to entertain the audiences and act as warm-up before the programme went live, even going so far as to chip in with the occasional song or two if guests were running late, Ada's fascination for the family enterprise was beginning to wear thin. 'Ada passed out coffee and doughnuts but she never really cared for show business,' Nick reveals. 'But George revelled in it. He made friends with a lot of the guests, including Kenny Rogers. George was always full of questions.'

As Ada gradually elected to sidestep the magnifying glass of celebrity, just like her Aunt Betty had done a decade earlier, George became free to hog a little more of the spotlight than usual. Like most backroom staff, he just wanted to be the other side of the cameras, entertaining. Sure, just being part of the show was great in itself, but to actually perform – in front of people – that was something else. Growing up with Nick, Rosemary and Uncle George as your role models, it was a natural reaction. Like a sports manager nursing a promising talent into his first season, Nick cut his son more and more slack until he thought the boy was ready. At the ripe old age of five, George's opportunity arrived and his leprechaun brought the house down.

He had seen audiences applaud him before, but not on screen, not on television. It doesn't take much to get a taste for acclaim and George knew he wanted to come back. Fortunately his father, and the audience, agreed.

'I grew up in television,' George recalls. 'I put on the little green suit and stuck a cigar in my mouth and they interviewed me as the leprechaun and then later as the Easter Bunny. By about seven I played characters in a commercial for potato chips.'

It was true. On the strength of his stints as seasonal make-believe characters, commercial directors thought he would be perfect to endorse their products in the slots between programmes. Soon George had completed his first wage-earning engagements: for Husman's crisps and Green Magic floor cleaner.

Between the paying commercials and spots on his dad's shows, the youngster's taste buds for a life in show business were being well and truly whetted. And who could blame him? His mother was a beauty queen, his father was 'the Johnny Carson of Cincinnati' and Aunt Rosemary was tearing up Hollywood. Was he going to dream of becoming an accountant?

2. I TALKED LIKE AN ANCHORMAN

Hollywood is a funny old town. It does strange things to people. Makes them act in odd, often illogical, ways. It entices otherwise rational people to give up perfectly good, safe and comfortable homes elsewhere to migrate to LA with no job, no contacts and nowhere to stay. And for what end? For the very slim chance that one day they might see their own name up in lights alongside – or instead of – that of Harrison Ford or Angelina Jolie or Brad Pitt. Ethel Merman hit the nail on the head when she sang 'There's no business like show business', but she wasn't telling the whole story. Not everything about it is appealing, far from it.

In September 2002, it was reported that *Gladiator* star Russell Crowe had threatened to get a waiter the sack if he didn't stop interrupting him. The Beverly Hills Hotel employee's crime? Asking the Oscar-winning diner for advice, against hotel policy. His defence? He was an actor 'trying to break into showbiz', according to a hotel staff member, and he was looking for pointers.

While Crowe's reported put-down – 'If you don't stop bothering me, your only question will be "Is there going to be a sequel to my job?" ' – got most of the room laughing, the episode highlights the sad truth about the Los Angeles catering industry: most of its employees, from chefs to waiters to bar staff, are only in town for one reason – and it is not to wait tables. The majority of the workers are from outside the area; a lot of them do not even speak English. But they have given up everything to get to Hollywood. They want to get connected, to become a player. To become a Somebody.

Another thing that the foghorn-voiced Merman conveniently overlooked was that show business is exactly what its name says: a business, and a cut-throat one at that. Like the Ford Motor Company or Microsoft or any other manufacturer, its sole aim is to produce a product which consumers will pay good money to acquire. It exploits talent the way other industries exploit oil or cattle, and for the same end: financial gain – and lots of it.

Nick Clooney never made it to Hollywood (his encounter with DeMille aside), but Hollywood made it to him. The media business in Cincinnati and its neighbouring cities was ruled by the same orthodoxy as LA, the same obsession with market forces and the pursuit of profit. Even in local television and radio in the 60s, entertainment had to equal money. If it didn't, then change the entertainment.

Like a lot of his contemporaries, Nick was exposed to the caprice of his audiences. If his share started to wilt or his approval ratings looked like they might be about to slide, he could expect a visit from the network controller. If the controller was strong, then between them they could make changes to coax back the missing viewers. But if the controller cared more about short-term figures than long-term results, then Nick could expect to be shown the door. And he frequently was.

While George and Ada were young, going to work with their father offered the perfect solution to his professional dilemma. As far as the children were concerned, one studio was the same as another. Even the constant upheaval of moving house to be near the new job failed to impact on their young lives.

That all changed, of course, when Ada and George came of school age. Suddenly their lives began to be affected by the career quirks of their father, and it was not for the better. Most noticeably, they were forced to enrol in five different primary schools in eight years as Nick chased the rainbow that was employment. For all the best reasons, Nick was subjecting his own children to the almost picaresque lifestyle that he had been forced to endure as a boy. What we learn as children . . .

Nick was acutely aware of the impact their carousel life was having on his family, but to his mind he had to chase the work while it was there – wherever 'there' was. The consequence of not doing so was too grave to bear. He only had to look at his elder sister for proof of that.

The whole world may once have known Rosemary Clooney, but by the time her nephew was ready to start school, the singer's day in the sun had passed. From being one of the brightest stars in the American firmament at the start of the 50s to a washed-up has-been by the end of the decade, her fall from the top of the entertainment pile was spectacular by any standards. The worst thing about it was that it was not even her fault. There were no ill-conceived career gambles, no image-busting diversions; she wasn't caught *in flagrante delicto* on camera, she didn't swear live on a talk show. The world just moved on.

'By 1955 it was all over for her,' her nephew George reflects. 'She was 24 years old and all washed up because rock'n'roll had started and popular music and jazz just went away. She did not become less of a singer.'

George is slightly off with his dates, but spot on in essence. Aunt Rosemary had had her moment. It was as simple as that. Her fall was all the more jaw-dropping because of the level of her prior success. Through the early 50s she clocked up fifteen gold records, with number-one hits including 'This Ole House' and 'Mambo Italiano'. One of her hits, 'Man', featured a B-side called 'Woman' sung by Oscar-winning actor José Ferrer. This was no coincidence. Despite a publicised affair with her frequent co-star Dante Di Paolo, she surprised everyone in 1953, at the height of her fame, by eloping with Ferrer, sixteen years her senior. They set up home in a Beverly Hills mansion once owned by George Gershwin and became Hollywood's golden couple, regularly in the gossip columns thanks to their celebrated pool parties and lavish lifestyle. The marriage lasted for eight years, slightly longer than their careers. A solo television programme, *The Rosemary Clooney Show*, was launched in 1956 to try to capitalise on her earlier fame, but it ended a year later. The writing was on the wall.

With her popularity waning and her marriage crumbling, Rosemary turned to tranquillisers and sleeping tablets. As her life disintegrated, her addiction worsened; like most sufferers, she found it was the drugs that gave her the will to face each new day. The final straw came when she witnessed her close friend Robert Kennedy's assassination from just yards away. It triggered a mental breakdown that saw her storm offstage at a Reno engagement, cursing her audience and her life. After a few more public collapses, she checked herself into the psychiatric ward of Los Angeles's Mount Sinai Hospital. It would become her sanctuary, on and off, for the next two decades.

George is flippant about her breakdown – but only outwardly. He is bitter about show business's brutal treatment on his aunt, and he cannot stand the thought of it happening to others – or himself. 'She didn't understand it,' he says of the waning popularity of jazz, 'and she became a nut for twenty years, took every drug known to man and had nervous breakdowns until she finally got her act together.'

He blames the business for her health problems.

'She had believed them when they said how brilliant she was in 1950,' he says. 'So that meant automatically that she was an idiot in 1955. Of course, neither was really true. I've had that a lot with my father and with various members of my family.'

Rosemary's main problem, as George rightly surmises, was that she equated her own personal worth with the volume of applause; when it dried up, so did she. Considering she was an eighteen-year-old when she first found fame, who could blame her? It still happens today. As she discovered, even if you do get that lucky break, unless you are very, very fortunate, there will always be a long line of temporary waiters and kitchen staff poised to take your place at the first sniff of failure. It is not a business for the faint-hearted.

Nick Clooney's career never scaled the heights of his sister's, but nor did it plumb her depths. He had witnessed and cried for Rosemary's plight and it only made him stronger in his own life. He crystallised the main problem for his son. 'Dad taught me not to believe people when they say you're a god, or to believe them when they say you suck,' George recalls.

Considering the amount of jobs Nick went through during his children's early years, more than a couple of know-nothing network executives must have suggested he 'sucked' at one time or another. When they did, it was up sticks and off, the whole family uprooted if necessary.

And so it was that, after a lengthy run, *The Nick Clooney Show* was considered to have outgrown its audience and was dropped. Suddenly, after several years of security, prosperity and respect around Cincinnati, the Clooney family – because it had become very much a family show – was told it was no longer wanted in that town. Unless Nick could find employment with another local channel, there would only be one outcome. A new start. Again.

Although Nick's next job was for another Ohio station, it was still too far to consider commuting from Cincinnati. Once more, the removal wagons were called in and the family decamped further north, to Columbus. The new job carried less kudos than the last, but with two young children to feed, as usual Nick felt he had no choice. Financially, it was a sound move and his young family could still live in relative luxury. And that is what mattered.

Columbus was a large town, like Cincinnati, and had a lot to offer a cash-rich young family. Nina dutifully set about home-making while George and Ada fitted into their new school as best they could. They were becoming quite adroit at dealing with the stigma of joining a class part way into a fresh term, although Ada found it harder to deal with than her more vivacious brother. Both children knew to their cost that life-long friendships were not going to be found in these classes. How could they be, knowing that at any moment the pair of them could be whisked out of the class to move to a new state?

With that possibility always in the back of their mind, the children were still surprised – and shocked – when the news reached them that their time in Columbus was up. Sadly they were the last to know. Nick had not found the right time to tell them before a local newspaper ran a story with the headline 'Clooney Canned'. The news became the talk of the school and George and Ada endured a harrowing time as the butt of their classmates' jokes before Nick arrived to pick them up.

Worse was to follow. Despite Nick's best efforts, another job failed to materialise and so costs had to be cut. Starting with the house. As soon as they could, the Clooneys vacated their luxurious town house and moved into the local trailer park. From mansion to mobile home in a matter of weeks. What show business had done to Rosemary Clooney it was doing to her brother.

Christmas that year was a lean affair but everyone enjoyed it as best they could. Importantly, Nick did not let the situation get to him. He kept himself busy, devoting a lot of time to finding new work as well as taking the occasion to help out more around the home, such as it was. There would be enough times when he was too busy to join in the evening meal at the family table or to help Nina with the groceries, so for now he was happy to embrace the opportunity he had been given.

Nick's diligence and his family's forbearance were rewarded when a new contract materialised. As ever, the job required a change of home. For once, as the Clooneys waved goodbye to their Columbus trailer park, they had no regrets.

Mason, Ohio was the new destination, but it, too, proved only a temporary move when the chance to work in Cincinnati again came up. After years of rootlessness, the family was heading back to the scene of Nick's greatest success to date. The kids, especially, were looking forward to it. The opportunity to be known by sight as 'Nick Clooney's son' was particularly appetising. Even Nina could not wait to get back to the city where they had had so many good times as a family.

It came as a shock to everyone, then, when Nick announced that he had other plans. The guilt he felt about putting his young family through the painful upheaval finally caught up with him. What Nina and Co. needed was a base camp, a permanent pitch to call home. If it meant passing on jobs to keep the family together now that George was old enough for high school, then so be it. A worthy sentiment, his family agreed. What caught everyone out, though, was Nick's preferred site for their new home. Not Cincinnati, not even somewhere in Ohio. No, the place he had in mind was considerably quieter.

Augusta is a small town on the Ohio River in Bracken County, tucked away in the northern part of Kentucky. The first settlers began arriving at the turn of the eighteenth century and in 1862 the town's riverbanks were the site of a Civil War battle. It is the sort of place that location managers spend thousands of dollars researching for big budget films if they want to show the America of yesteryear. Friendly, slightly behind the times in a non-cosmopolitan way, full of attractive late-nineteenth-century architecture – and small. Very small. Between 1990 and 1998, the population of Augusta rose by just ninety, to the grand total of 1,434. Cincinnati it is not.

The key factor in Nick Clooney's decision to move his family to Augusta was the fact that it was just seventeen miles from Maysville, his childhood home. Compared to city life, Nick felt it offered a haven to his family. The only problem was, Nina, Ada and George all liked city life. The idea of holing up in the heart of Sticksville was as desirable to the kids as going back to the trailer park.

'It wasn't a popular idea with them, or my wife Nina,' Nick says. 'But gradually they admitted it was a wonderful place to grow up.'

There was only going to be one winner in this argument, and in 1974 the Clooneys rolled into Augusta. Their new riverside home was a two-storey house dating from the 1800s, tucked back from the road and nicely hidden from casual view by a phalanx of trees. The privacy may have been a happy coincidence, but as Nick became a household name (again) through presenting the nightly news for WKRW Channel 12, it proved a handy security measure for his family.

The drive from Augusta to Cincinnati is just 45 minutes, so Nick was able to commute to work, safe in the knowledge that his children's school was comfortably within walking distance from their home. Augusta High School is a red-brick, proud-looking building, with an imposing bell-tower and, like many of Augusta's structures, a history dating back to the Civil War. Since George Clooney became a star it has acquired extra historical significance, of course, although it is not a place he recalls with fondness. Young George, it seems, had many talents. Unfortunately, schoolwork was not one of them.

Ada, however, showed little sign of having had her schoolwork disrupted by the years on the road and easily qualified as a National Merit scholar. She still liked to help out on her father's shows, but more through a sense of being useful than wanting to immerse herself in show business. Her brother, on the other hand, was prioritising his time in the studio over his studies. If his parents were aware of this, they were not able to prevent it. With shows like *Money Maze* and *Bowling for Dollars* complementing Nick's newscasting duties, George was helping out more than ever. He still enjoyed performing in front of an audience, and began to front local film-theatre presentations as well as racking up more screen time in a variety of roles on his dad's shows. For a while it looked like there could be a competitor to Rosemary in the family as George made his singing debut, performing the wartime knees-up anthem 'Straighten Up and Fly Right' as part of a nostalgia event. He followed this with a rendition of The Carpenters' 'Sing'. Both songs are sadly unpreserved on videotape today.

Thanks to his sideshow-performing habits, coming to grips with the ways of Augusta life took a little getting used to. Just as his father had confounded Cecil B DeMille decades earlier, George found himself sticking out in the local high school because of his accent. 'Everyone had a very thick Kentucky accent,' he explains. 'You couldn't understand a word. There I was, in this small town where everyone talked like a bunch of hicks, and I talked like an anchorman.'

Newscaster-style enunciation was not the only thing that got George into trouble with the locals. Again, it was Nick's influence that was the cause; again, it was something that George himself totally endorsed.

'There was a lot of bigotry around when I was a kid,' George recalls. 'Kentucky was not really the South, but kind of. When I heard someone say the word 'nigger', I got in a fight with them. Unfortunately, I wasn't a very good fighter and I usually got the shit kicked out of me.'

'I remember that we would be out to dinner or somewhere and if somebody said some kind of racial remark we knew my dad would take the family and walk. When you are a kid, you think, "Dad, you don't have to agree with them, but don't walk, please!" But my dad would always say to us, "If somebody says something racist you have to fight them . . ." The upshot was that we would learn to eat very quickly!'

It was not just meals that Nick was prepared to sacrifice in support of his morals. His 'guy thing' went deeper and took more risks. There was one instance when a station tried to force his hand and he resigned rather than be bullied. Faced with an embargo on working in the area for a year, Nick bought out the contract. It used up nearly every penny of their savings but he kept his integrity and his freedom.

Just as George and Ada wished Nick would bite his tongue when faced with racism – if just to let them finish their meal! – it was natural for the children to wish their father would keep his job. But Nick believed that material worth is nothing to the riches of personal beliefs. Some things just do not have a price, and a man's integrity is one of them. How could he look his family in the eye if he did not follow his own preachings?

Within a few years, faced with a similar proposition, George would behave in exactly the same way as his father, although he plays down his circumstances.

'My dad is a lot smarter than I am and his line of integrity is to a fault,' he reflects. 'I've quit jobs for the right reasons before and I've gotten into fights. But it was easy because I had money in the bank. People go, "Oh, you were really brave." But I think to myself, "It's brave if you are my dad and you do that when you have two kids and no money in the bank."'

Nick's Channel 12 colleague Dennis Janson sums up the Clooney ethos: 'I've always said, "Integrity is doing the right thing even when no one is watching." And that's pretty much Nick.'

More than once, George would demonstrate it was pretty much him, too.

3. SHE WAS OLDER THAN ME

Apart from instilling into their children a sense of right and wrong, Nick and Nina also fought to protect them from the usual baggage that goes with growing up in the celebrity spotlight. Drew Barrymore, Liza Minnelli, Michael Jackson – the list of casualties among child stars or those with famous parents is a long one. The one thing they all have in common is growing up in a goldfish bowl. It cannot be healthy: look at The Osbournes.

While Nick was never a national figure, he was exceedingly famous in his hometown, wherever that town happened to be. In Augusta, he was just about the most famous thing to happen to the place since the Civil War. While not as big as Cincinnati, for example, where Nick was also famous, there were fewer places to hide in Augusta, so the family was constantly on show. It could have affected some kids badly. Not George. He enjoyed the attention. In fact, he would go out of his way to gain it.

'I don't mind the recognition,' he admits. 'You can't mind it. That's part of the reason you do it. If I'm going to be honest, you know, there were kids who got up in the middle of the room and put the funny hat on and told bad jokes – and that was me. So yes, I think that I sought some of that attention.'

Aunt Rosemary agreed. The family occasions when her five children and Nick's two were thrown together often turned into verbal bun-fights, with the oldest naturally holding court. 'He was the youngest of all the children,' she recalled, 'so he had to work a little to get the attention, which was his main goal in life.'

Sometimes his ambition was sorely tested. 'My dad did about two hundred personal appearances a year at public functions, and we were part of the act,' George says. 'We'd be fighting in the car on the way over, but when we'd get out of the car and people would shout, "Nick!" and ask for autographs, we'd have our arms around each other, smiling. After the show, we'd get back in the car and sulk all the way home.'

George's desire to please an audience was at the crux of one particularly embarrassing moment. Barely into his teens, he was preparing himself to reprise his annual role as the Easter Bunny for his dad's TV show when disaster struck – literally.

'I think I was thirteen one Easter and I was at home trying on the costume in Kentucky where I lived,' he recalls. 'Suddenly the ground started shaking. It was the first earthquake Augusta had had in 150 years, things were flying and I was running out in these giant feet and full bunny outfit on a Sunday afternoon yelling, "What the hell's going on?" That's humiliating.'

Rabbit costumes aside, the Clooney children were encouraged to grow up as 'normal' as possible. They had the same problems and got into the same scrapes as other kids. George, in fact, became a familiar face at the local emergency rooms.

'I've been plenty of times,' he says. 'I'm a klutz. The first time I went to an emergency room I was fourteen years old. I had hair down to here [he points to his shoulder] and the Elton John shoes and my hands cranked down in my pockets. I'm walking about fifty feet behind my dad in Cincinnati and I step off a curb. I start to fall off my shoes and I can't get my hands out of my pockets because they were so tight. I hit a raised mantle cover with my face, broke my nose and knocked out my front tooth.'

This was not the first time George had experienced the delights of hospital treatment, only the first time he had been at fault. A year earlier, just a couple of months after the family had settled in Augusta, he had contracted Bell's Palsy, a debilitating illness which can have the same symptoms as a stroke. It struck just after George and his father had watched The Pride of the Yankees, the film about baseball player Lou Gehrig and his fight against the disease that would be named after him. As he sat in the stalls at the Saturday matinee, tears rolled down George's cheeks as he watched actor Gary Cooper suddenly unable to hold a bat. The next day in church, George thought it was happening to him.

'I was convinced I had Lou Gehrig's disease,' he says. 'We were up in the balcony, and suddenly my tongue got numb. It scared the hell out of me.' As the family made their regular post-Mass stop at fast-food eatery Frisch's Big Boy, it got worse. Like a patient fresh from the dentist's chair, just drinking a glass of milk was impossible – and messy. It was as though his entire mouth was anaesthetised. The problem was soon diagnosed and over a year it gradually healed. But starting out in a new school with the left side of his face partially paralysed, George was the butt of a lot of jokes. He responded by giving as good as he got. With knobs on.

Joking was a mainstay of George's early life. While Ada went quietly about completing her studies, George went noisily about avoiding his. Ever the ringmaster, he often went to elaborate lengths to make his classmates laugh. 'George had an incredible sense of humour,' a slightly biased Nick Clooney remembers, 'and was the funniest kid in town. He was clearly developing his skills as an actor even in high school.'

Aunt Rosemary had also picked up on his natural way with wit. 'More than anything else, I thought he was a funny kid,' she said. 'He always had a smart answer and a kind of skewed look at the world. I thought he'd probably be a comic. I thought he was going to be Don Rickles, and he turned out to be Tyrone Power.'

If he had learned anything from watching his father's shows, it was how to work with an audience. And George loved an audience, even if it meant stealing the limelight from his teachers. Tales have emerged from his high school pals of George playing ventriloquists with a shark's head in a dissecting lesson, faking his own suicide for the benefit of his maths class (and nearly giving his teacher a heart attack) and generally clowning around. Just your everyday schoolboy behaviour, in fact. Thirty years later, myriad actors, directors and film crews can testify that the pranks have not improved – they are just a little more expensive.

Another part of his repertoire was a talent for caricatures, and he would entertain his friends with sketched attacks on various teachers and Augusta townsfolk. In fact, to this day, a cruel but lifelike image of Nick that George painted at sixteen hangs in the Clooney house. (He inherited this gift from his mother: on the same wall is a painting by Nina, of George and Ada.) He also developed a talent for impersonation, another staple of a class wag's weaponry. Not only could he sketch his teachers in a most unflattering light, he could put words into their mouths.

When he was not kidding around, George found another outlet for his excess energy, one that would also allow him to play to a crowd. He took up sports. Basketball was a big favourite, football less so. The one he really excelled at, though, was baseball. Could that boy slug a ball!

As a diversion from his schoolwork, baseball proved a great pastime. There is little more satisfying for a natural show-off than having an audience see you do well, and in the diamond of Augusta High George did very well. As he worked his way through various school teams, scoring regularly against challengers from all over the state, he gradually came to realise that it could become more than a hobby. His dreams looked set to come true when he reached sixteen and was asked to try out for his beloved Reds following good reports from the club's scouting staff. The Cincinnati outfit was George's local team and he regularly spent his weekends watching their home matches. Now he was being given the chance to play with them.

The big day came and a nervous George set off for the Reds' Cinergy Field stadium. Undaunted by the business-like professional set-up, he acquitted himself well and struck ball after ball, just as he did on the practice field. Sadly, though, while good hitting was enough to win matches at high school level, success in the Major League requires more rounded players and George was told, in no uncertain terms, that his throwing and fielding were just not up to scratch. And that was that. He was crushed. He had never auditioned for anything before. He had never failed so publicly in his life. More importantly, he had never wanted anything as much as he had wanted this. He was sixteen and this was the end of his world.

Looking back, George accepts it was never meant to be. 'I'd been in a world where I was the best around,' he explains, 'and then I went into a camp where all the best around met, and I was nowhere as good as those guys. They threw rockets. When I realised I was never going to be those guys, I could walk away because I'd at least given it a run. My greatest skill is probably understanding my own limitations.' Maybe his second greatest skill is being able to laugh at himself. 'I only lacked skill,' he adds. 'That was the only thing holding me back.'

From an onlooker's perspective, missing out by a whisker on the chance to become a professional sportsman is no mean achievement. How many sports fans even come that close? When you are in the eye of the storm, however, and it is the only thing you can ever imagine forging a career from, that is little consolation. For weeks afterwards, George was difficult to live with and moody. As well as the humiliation of failure, he genuinely had no Plan B as far as his future was concerned. With decisions needing to be made soon, he had some thinking to do.

In the meantime, there was fun to be had. You do not wander around a small high school being funny, good looking and a natural at sports without picking up your share of admirers. George, of course, denies any such accusations of being anything out of the ordinary.

'I graduated with twenty-three people in my high school class so it's automatic,' he demurs. 'Everyone is popular.' He even plays down his appearance. 'I looked like I look like now, but I wasn't quite as grey.'

He means that to sound self-deprecating, of course, but perhaps he did feel he was average-looking at school; his future co-star, Michelle Pfeiffer, after all, famously claims she looked like a duck as a teenager. Maybe George does think his looks are over-rated today – his prominent jawline, exaggerated eyebrows and big, cow eyes are almost cartoon-like in their proportions – but thousands of fans and an increasing number of casting directors would disagree.

According to his childhood friends, George was a late bloomer with regards to chasing girls, although they seemed interested in him, as high-school baseball coach Bill Case recalls. 'Girls would line up on the street just to watch him walk home,' he says. One high-school date lucky enough to walk with him for a while was Debra Fraysure-McCormick. 'He liked to play Nat "King" Cole music and sing "Walkin' My Baby Back Home" to me,' she says. 'It was awesome.' Universities one hundred miles apart would eventually end the teen relationship, but they made a game effort at keeping in touch. 'He would send the sweetest cards,' Debra recalls. 'Really funny, bizarre ones that no one else would get. One had these two little snails on the front and said something like, "I sure do love you, my escargot." '

One of the reasons for George's appeal was that he did not appear to be looking for a girlfriend, a trait still true today as director friend John Bowab elaborates. 'George is a sexy guy because he doesn't try,' he says. 'If you name him "Sexiest Man Alive" he'll giggle about it for days – then he'll put on his sweaty basketball shoes and go shoot.' When he was not sending snail-mail to one lucky belle he was fine with his own company. More precisely, he was too much of a lad to be pinned down by a single date when there was fun to be had hanging with the boys and hunting with the herd. Clinches came and went, but if they didn't that was cool, too. 'It wasn't that he was a shy boy or anything,' school friend and Augusta neighbour Laura Laycock explains. 'George always liked to go to parties and be with his friends. He didn't have many girlfriends at all, he was just friends with everyone.'

It is easy to point out that he would go on to make an art out of running with a pack of friends, but obviously camaraderie was as important to George the teenager as it appears to be today. For all his reputation as Hollywood's leading Lothario – and there is plenty of evidence to back this up – he has always found great security and pleasure in the company of a group of like-minded cohorts, arguably more so than in individuals. Looking back on a lifetime peppered with brief, intense relationships with women, one cannot help but note how the time spent with his friends – his pre-fame friends – has been the one constant in his life. There are not many major stars who can say that.

Like a lot of George's current behaviour, cause-and-effect experiences that took place in his adolescent years have shaped his adult actions more than perhaps even he realises. Certainly some of his recent girlfriends might be interested in a story he tells of his life as a young roué finding his way.

'I used to be a DJ at a bar in Cincinnati,' he says. 'I'd watch the guys go up and hit on a girl and say, "You want to go out to dinner?" And I watched the girls take those guys' egos and just pummel them, and I realised I was never going to give any girl that kind of power. I was never going to go up to a girl and say, "Here's my ego, just throw it on the ground and stomp all over it." '

It is probably a little harsh to pin all of George's failed relationships on that early experience, because there are enough stories to show he is as ready to put his ego on the line as the next guy. (Admittedly, the chances of a world-famous actor being knocked back are probably few and far between, but it is gratifying to know that it does happen – and once in front of a pack of press men, as George would find out at the Cannes Film Festival . . .) But that he recognises the Cincinnati dance-floor moment as an epiphany of sorts means it plays a part in his make-up to some extent.

Revelations about George's early days as a handsome young buck do not come around very often. When the tough questions need to be asked, though, there is really only one man up to the task. In 1998, George Clooney was the mystery guest on self-styled 'shock jock' Howard Stern's show. No one goes into a live event with Stern with their eyes shut and George was primed for the line of questioning that he would doubtless face. He was not disappointed. Neither were his fans. In a conversation that mostly focused on which of his co-stars he had slept with and how good his then girlfriend was in bed (plus, did he think Kelly Preston regretted marrying John Travolta after being with him?),

Howard got down to the nitty gritty. Did George 'get laid' at high school? Embarrassed pause. 'Er, yeah.'

A lot of interviewers would have stopped there. One or two might have gone on to ask who George's girlfriend was. Only Howard would demand to know ages. Visibly squirming (the Stern show is broadcast in a highlights package on TV as well as going out live on radio), George finally gave in to the testosterone-ridden studio atmosphere. 'I was fifteen, I guess,' he admitted, to Stern's great amusement. 'I think she was older than me, seventeen I think – which was a score.'

Follow that.

In May 1977, George graduated from Augusta High. Before he could get down to his future, he had some serious partying to do. As an adult (almost). The highlight of any American graduation is the high school prom, and George and his friends threw themselves into it. Pictures of the night show his bouffant hair straining to steal the show even then, while his dress sense had patently not improved since the bang on the head in Cincinnati as a fourteen-year-old, although fashion has to take some of the blame – this was the 70s after all. Adorned in a fetching silver-grey three-piece number, complete with Elizabethan ruff-styled shirt and the mother of all bow ties, George looked quite the dandy as he squired neighbour Laura Laycock to the dance. Typically it was not strictly a date: George made sure to hook up with a bunch of his equally daftly attired mates beforehand. The team-player ethos of the baseball wannabe still prevailed.

Nick Clooney was happy to let his son enjoy the prom festivities and he and Nina lined up with all the other parents to capture the coming-of-age ceremony on camera. But after the hangovers had cleared and the borrowed suits were returned to their real owners, he wanted to know what his son planned to do next. In the absence of anything sensible from George, Nick made the decision for him: he would go to college, study journalism and follow in his, Nick's, footsteps like a good boy.

On paper, the plan was not a bad one. At sixteen George had already spent more time in a studio than some professional broadcasters. He had certainly exhibited a proclivity to court attention and a talent to amuse, so he had the foundation skills. A few years at a decent college would hammer his undoubted natural gifts into employable shape.

A lot of people who have decided to get jobs after finishing school view seats of higher learning as little more than playgrounds for rich kids who want to avoid the real world. To be fair, a lot of degree students themselves agree. George Clooney may well be one of them. Northern Kentucky University offered him some breathing space while he plotted his future. Sure, broadcasting was an option but, to be honest, he had not quite got over missing out on being the next Willie Mays for the Reds. Nothing else really excited him, not yet.

Still, city life had its compensations and George and his posse were the guys to find them. Bars, dance halls and other teenage hang-outs became his regular fixtures; lecture halls and libraries took a back seat. 'To George, school was a very large restaurant and night club,' says his disapproving mother. She still hoped the work was being done. After all, she and Nick were paying a lot of money for George's privilege.

Who was she kidding? George took to his studies like a duck to concrete. 'I would visit class every once in a while and stop by and go, "How's everybody doing?"' he laughs. 'I was still a responsible kid, but I didn't take school seriously.

'In college, I basically partied a lot,' he admits. 'You gotta understand. We're a very strict Catholic family. Curfew was at nine p.m. when I was a senior in high school. So I got out of the house and thought, "Oh my God!"'

Being allowed to stay out later than nine is one thing, but a man needs something to fill his time. He recalls a favourite drinking spot in the Covington area of Cincinnati. 'I was nineteen the first time I went to the Conservatory, which was underage,' he says. 'You had to be 21. You could go to the Lighthouse when you were eighteen and drink 3.2 beer, but the Conservatory had older women there, like 22. I remember going there and trying to act old.'

Illicit drinking was not his only vice, as he admitted in an interview with *Playboy* in June 2000. 'People don't ever really like to talk about this anymore,' he said, 'but there was a period of time when blow was considered OK, like it won't hurt you at all. It was almost mainstream. All the designer drugs were OK – quaaludes and blow. So that was the time in college for me: drugs and chasing girls.'

What frustrated his parents most was that George did not even dislike the subject he had enrolled for. 'The most important job we have in the world is journalism,' he says. 'It's more important than government. It's the watchdog of government, the watchdog of ethics.

'When I was growing up it was in the heart of Woodward and Bernstein, and before that Murrow and Cronkite, and the people who we didn't just look up to, we looked to them, the journalists, for information and leadership.'

No, it was not the subject matter that turned him off college. He objected to being told things he had learned as a kid from watching his dad. 'Tell me something I don't know,' he seemed to be saying. He was Nick Clooney's son – didn't that count for anything?

Looking back, George admits it was arrogance that was his downfall. 'I wasn't very good,' he says, 'but I thought I was – that was my biggest problem. I thought I was interesting. But nobody said I was smart. Just because you know about journalism it doesn't mean you're smart.

'I could be funny, you know, but that's not necessarily enough. It took someone who could be very quick on their feet and ask the right questions.'

After three years, George was still in his freshman year. Realising he could be stuck at college forever, he decided to augment his learning with a part-time job on a local TV channel, much to his dad's pleasure – and partly thanks to him.

'Being Nick Clooney's son in Cincinnati, where my father was very big, I knew I could get my foot in the door right away,' he admits. 'The problem was that then they'd expect me to be as good as my father and I was never going to be that good, ever. But my father wanted me to go into broadcast. He wanted me to be an intern. I tried it for a while but I wasn't very good.'

He plugged away though. Hosting local evening programme *PM Magazine* was his goal, but for now he contributed reports on a freelance basis. As a kid in his early twenties, he took everything in his stride. He was now a player, in his mind anyway. Interviewed by a news programme in 1982, aged 21, he was confidence itself.

'People keep coming up to me and saying, "Isn't it awful being known as Nick Clooney's son?" ' he said. 'You know, five years from now they'll go up to my dad and go, "Aren't you George Clooney's father?" '

It was said tongue in cheek. Wasn't it?

4. GEORGE, YOU STAY HERE

In 1976, the United States of America celebrated its bicentenary. It was not a quiet affair. At a local level, street parties and festivals swallowed up the lion's share of many towns' annual budgets. On a national scale, the entertainment business pulled out all the stops and hours of TV programming were given over to making sure no one missed out on this anniversary.

As a writer, James A Michener provided a tribute in the only form he knew: as a book. That book was turned into a TV programme and that programme was filmed in Augusta, Kentucky. The fact that Michener's project was called *Centennial* betrays its period: it focuses on just the first hundred years of US existence, centring on the indomitable spirit and the pioneering achievements of that century. Where else to shoot a film set in 1876 than in a Rip Van Winkle town that on the surface seems more centred on its past than its future?

Augusta offered the perfect location for the film. Everything the director needed was on hand. As well as the majestic Ohio River, it benefited, if that is the right word, from a riverfront devoid of power cables, energy centres or other totems of modern innovation. It also retained a lot of the period housing crucial to the tale. On top of that, it had a very willing youth population desperate to take part in the filming. The script's demands for hundreds of extras would not be a problem.

Seventeen-year-old George Clooney was one of the first in line for his tricorn hat and other period garb. He had been involved with radio, TV and theatre before, but this was big-budget stuff – this was drama, and a mini-series at that. He was as blown away as every other teenager in town, all of them vying for the most 'walk-by' parts.

It was not just the film itself that excited George. He was particularly looking forward to the arrival of its lead actor: Raymond Burr, star of the Clooneys' favourite show *Perry Mason*. While George had met countless celebrities, those encounters had always been under the guise of 'work'. Helping out on his dad's shows he had met them almost as equals and studio etiquette dictated he keep a professional distance. When Burr came to town there was a marked transformation: goodbye hackneyed TV professional, hello George the fan.

'This was an event without precedent for the people of this place,' George recalls. 'I chased him all day and every five minutes I grabbed his jacket and just said, "You are Perry Mason." '

Enjoy it as he did, when the *Centennial* crew left town, so did George's thespian aspirations. He may have had a privileged background by some standards, but even he knew that movie acting was beyond normal people. It was not even worth wasting his hopes on because things like *Centennial* were once-in-a-lifetime opportunities, and he had had his.

Or had he? In 1982, while George was half-heartedly attempting to carve out a career as a TV reporter, he learned through his father that some of their relatives were coming to town. José Ferrer and his sons Miguel and Rafael – Rosemary's now ex-husband and children – were arriving in nearby Lexington to shoot a movie about horse racing called *And They're Off*. George called cousin Miguel and they hatched a plan for George to go along and cover production for his programme.

As soon as he arrived in Lexington, all thoughts of news-making left George's mind. He was smitten by the buzz around the set and enjoyed milling among the film workers. Memories of those days spent stalking Raymond Burr came flooding back and he was sold. This was what he wanted to do. But how?

As he would learn again, there is no point having famous relatives if you do not use them. No sooner had he arrived than Miguel informed George that he had a small role in the film. Of course, that was what he was going to do with his life. He was going to be a movie actor!

The fact that the Ferrers had turned up for the shoot meant that there were serious hopes for the film. In March 1982 the *Hollywood Reporter* carried a full-page advertisement announcing the start of production. According to the ad it was going to be about 'a young jockey's struggle to attain love, power and wealth in horse racing's exciting world of high stakes and violence'. Neither George nor his family was mentioned, although cameos were promised from the likes of equestrian legends Willie Shoemaker and Eddie Arcaro.

Billing did not matter to George or his cousin. They were too busy having fun, as Miguel recalls. 'He came and camped out in my room for about three months. We played practical jokes, we drank too much and we slept with about a million women.' Real student behaviour, in other words, exactly what George had been rehearsing for at Northern Kentucky. What he was only just discovering, though, was that actors got to goof around, too – and they had better perks. He watched open-mouthed as attractive make-up girls tended to the needs of their male stars and made a decision that was to alter his life: 'I was seduced,' he says. 'I fell in love with the whole industry.' He decided to join it, whatever the cost. 'I never thought I'd make any money at it, but I just loved doing it.'

Love conquers all and, to prove it, George refused to be put off by the fact that *And They're Off* was never given a commercial release. Bullishly, he also made light of the fact that he lived in Kentucky when the place to be was LA and that he had no money to do anything about it – he would get some. But he did not budget for his father's obstruction. Nick was disappointed that George wanted to give up on a burgeoning broadcasting career; after all, it had been good enough for him. He was also concerned that the partying habit that his son had got into at university would swamp him in Hollywood, and God knows there had been enough casualties of the good life in his family already. Most of all, though, he feared for his son's feelings. He did not want to see George ripped apart by the heartless vicissitudes of casting fashion. Rosemary's fate was still a sore point.

'When George said he was planning to go to Hollywood to be an actor, I told him he was crazy,' Nick understates. 'The rejection you suffer is cruel and very unusual. You're either too short or too tall, too this or too that. It's asking for a lifetime of rejection. But like most kids, he ignored his dad completely and did what he wanted to do.'

George knew that his dad had his best interests at heart, but that did not stop him feeling frustration at the interference. 'At times my dad's my hero, sure, but at other times he's a pain in the butt like everybody's dad,' he says. This was one of those times. The atmosphere at home deteriorated to the point where they were hardly talking.

By becoming an actor, George could see a way of stepping out of his dad's shadow, which he could never do if he stayed in local TV. 'I was going to be Nick Clooney's son for the rest of my life,' he says, 'and I was never going to be as good as him. Although

Rosemary had done *White Christmas* and other films, she was known as a singer, so I decided I was going to find something where I wasn't going to be compared to anyone. I followed my cousin Miguel's footsteps and decided to become an actor. At least you don't get compared as often until you make it.' George Clooney was going to Hollywood.

It was a good plan in theory, but moving west required money. Without a cent to his name, George threw himself into a series of body- and spirit-sapping jobs to earn enough for the journey – he would worry about accommodation later. At first he set himself up as a cartoonist in the local mall, offering caricatures of passing shoppers, but that was not lucrative. Insurance selling came and went, too. As it was summer, he signed up for some back-breaking work cutting tobacco on his uncle Jack Warren's farm, as he had done before in summer holidays.

Despite the physical pains of tobacco cutting, it was not the worst job George took on. That accolade must go to his time spent as a salesman in a ladies' shoe shop. It was not particularly arduous work, but it had its own horrors.

'I worked at a store called McAlpin's in Kentucky,' he says. 'We'd be selling shoes for old people. It was a horrible, horrible, horrible job to do. All women lie about their shoe size, let's face it, and there was a group of women that had had a toe cut off for their pumps. There are these eighty-year-old women who would wear pumps and they would have a toe cut and they'd be like, "That's a hammertoe." And you'd go, "Well, that sure is." And then you'd try to jam a six on their foot.'

At the end of the summer George had amassed enough savings to get to Hollywood. He spent some of the cash on a car, a 1976 Ford Monte Carlo and was left with $300. It was a start. After an interesting journey that led him to christen the Monte Carlo 'the Danger Car', he arrived in Beverly Hills outside the home of Aunt Rosemary. Dear, sweet Aunt Rosemary. She was family. She would look after him.

Of a fashion, she would. Rosemary was still only just getting her life back together in 1982. The years of drug dependency had taken their toll, the death of her sister Betty (from an aneurysm) in 1976 had shaken her badly, but finally she was taking control of her affairs again. As much as she loved her nephew, she had not planned on his gate-crashing attempts to rebuild her relationship with her five children. More importantly, she sided with Nick Clooney in thinking it was a bad career move for the boy. She was still feeling the negative effects of her own brush with stardom, as George let slip in a 2000 interview. 'She is now seventy and still trying to pay back all the cattle investments she made then,' he explained. 'I'm kind of scared about that stuff.'

George stood his ground and Rosemary relented. What woman could refuse his dark, pleading puppy-dog eyes? She was won over, although the Danger Car had to go – it was an eyesore. 'She made me get rid of the car,' George recalls. 'Didn't want it parked in her driveway.' He moved his few possessions in and, with Miguel and his brothers, picked up his life of carousing and womanising by night. By day he attempted to piece together an acting career. That was trickier, despite what others might think.

'I was doing the Merv Griffin show,' George recalls, 'and he said, "Well, it must have been a lot easier for you being Rosemary Clooney's nephew. You get off the plane and they go, "Rosemary Clooney's nephew, come with us, we got a series for you."'

Nothing could be further from the truth. The work just was not there for an actor with no union card and an acting résumé which began and ended with blink-and-you'll-miss-it appearances in one mini-series and an unreleased film. 'Your aunt's who?'

It was Rosemary who came to George's aid, although not in a way he had hoped. She was rebuilding her career and was about to tour the region as part of the show 4 Girls 4 with fellow singers Margaret Whiting, Martha Raye and Helen O'Connell. The 'girls' needed a driver and George needed a job. So . . .

He was not in a position to refuse, even if at times his days at McAlpin's shoe emporium for the bewildered must have flooded back to haunt him. 'I remember once that Rosemary and Martha were in the back and my cousin Rafael and I were in the front,' George recalls. 'Martha was drinking as Martha could do and at one point she made us pull the car over so she could hang one leg out and go to the bathroom. There ain't enough cash for that gig – you turn round and you learn a little too much about the ageing process! I took her back to the house and she passed out holding onto this dog. The next morning she somehow misplaced her dentures so there were all of us looking for them because otherwise she couldn't do the show. Nobody really wanted to find them, but eventually we did.'

A downside of working for Rosemary was the fact that she appeared to treat him more like an employee than a family member, and his cousins accepted it. It was not unusual for the Ferrers to go out for the night and leave their country cousin behind. More than all the rejection he felt as an unemployed actor, this behaviour from the people closest to him wounded George. It still rankles. 'I will never really get over how humiliated I was,' he says. 'We'd all be sitting around and they'd go, "OK, let's all go to dinner. George, you stay here." '

If this treatment was designed to make George go running back to the I-told-you-so arms of Augusta, it did not work. He was not afraid of hard graft, he never had been. Even when he was treated, quite literally, as the poor relation, he still found room to have a little fun occasionally as Rosemary admitted soon after he joined ER.

'George said, "The next road trip that you're on, I'm going to paint that fence," ' she recalled. 'So I got home and I was in my room upstairs. I went in my bathroom and I could see the tennis court and said, "Gee, George painted the fence, what a wonderful thing." And then I happened to walk out and he had just painted the part I could see from my bathroom!'

For all the hardship, George remains grateful to his aunt's hospitality, such as it was. 'There are two ways she helped me,' he says. 'She gave me a place to live for a year, without which I couldn't have made it. And I got to see how to avoid certain mistakes in my life by watching things that had gone wrong for her. She didn't cope a lot of the time. It nearly destroyed her and my advantage is that I got to see how that worked.'

Apart from his debt to Rosemary, George was also grateful to Nick. The day he set off for LA marked the lowest point in the father-son relationship. But distance and time calm the roughest waters and Nick's anger soon turned to concern. George had only been away a couple of weeks when they had a particularly poignant phone call. Nick was almost pleading with his son to return to Augusta before he got his spirit trampled on. 'Come back, finish school, and when you're finished you'll have broadcasting to fall back on,' he recalls. 'There was this long pause. Then George said, "Pop, if I have something to fall back on, I'll fall back." '

If Nick and Nina had worried that George did not have a thick-enough skin to tough it out in show business, a year spent living with the Ferrers proved them wrong. Demonstrating the hide and stubbornness of a bull (he is a Taurean, after all), he determined to stay for as long as he could get away with it if it meant advancing his cause in Hollywood. After a year, though, his credit was up and it was time for George to move out. Carrying even less money than he had arrived with, George was forced to call in favours once again.

The sum success of George's first year in the showbiz capital of the world was a series of soul-destroying cattle-call auditions, where vast numbers of hopefuls parade like show dogs in front of a bank of unimpressed casting directors. George approached them all with the same wide-eyed enthusiasm that had made him a hit on his dad's shows, believing each time that this would be the one. They never were, of course, and he left dejected, but only temporarily. He had too much of an instinct for self-preservation to dwell on what he saw as other people's shortcomings: it was the directors' loss, not his. He would show them.

As one bravado-driven performance melded into another, George got to know his fellow strugglers. They could not avoid noticing him. With a confidence quite at variance with his experience, he breezed into each ego-testing session with the air of someone who expected to get the gig, head held high, hair bouncing off his shoulders and voice booming. His gregariousness paid off and he made some firm friends during that time. One of the firmest was Thom Mathews.

Thom gave his homeless friend a roof over his head. He also gave him walls, a floor and his own door – everything you would expect of a closet, in fact. It is true: for eight months, George Clooney, future film star, slept in his friend's admittedly large cupboard space. Anything to stay in LA.

To sustain even this meagre living, George was forced once more into the free market to find temporary work. The old staples of insurance selling, cartooning and shoe selling – this time for men – were all tried again before he hit upon construction work as a decent compromise. At just under six feet he had the physique to carry off manual labour while the physical exertion kept him in shape for possible parts. There was enough flexibility in his day to scoot off to auditions on his bicycle and he earned enough to contribute to Thom's bills and still be able to party. That, if nothing else, was working for him, as Mathews marvels. 'I could never understand how he got girls in that closet with him,' he says. 'What could he possibly say to get them in there?'

The answer is probably not what he said, but how he said it. When George is happy, he shows it. When he is annoyed, you get to hear about it. When he is interested in a girl, he makes her aware of it, without pretence, without showboating, without graces, just the good old Clooney charm. Just like his father, he connects with people, effortlessly putting them at their ease. It is a rare talent.

Girls were not the only people to fall for George's patter. After eighteen months in Hollywood he finally got his first call-back. A day later he got his first job. George announced his presence at the casting session for a Panasonic stereo commercial by cracking open a round of ice-cold Sapporo tinnies with the question, 'Anyone up for a beer?' To this day he is convinced that it was this, rather than his acting, which got him the job.

More stunts were to follow. Trying out for the role of a rock singer in a small theatre production, George delivered the read-through until the name of his character's band was mentioned. Then he whipped off his T-shirt to reveal the name – Body Fluids – tattooed on his chest. Again, 'You've got the job, Mr Clooney.'

Pulling off such bluffs was down to his healthy self-belief. With a little encouragement from cousin Miguel, he translated this chutzpah to paper and constructed a new résumé for himself, citing all those out-of-town plays and foreign commercials he had starred in. He also enrolled for acting classes at Milton Katselas's school of arts. The combined effect was that agents started to notice him. Now he was able to turn up at auditions in the knowledge that they were expecting him. It didn't necessarily mean he would get the jobs, but he was moving up the ladder. Slowly.

5. THE BRAVEST THING I'VE EVER SEEN A VEGETABLE DO

It is amazing what agents can do. After months of scraping by with a mixture of unpaid theatre productions, construction work, acting classes and unsuccessful auditions, George's luck changed. He got his first movie role on merit.

As a concept, *Grizzly II – The Predator*, was as awful as its name was clumsy, and for a lot of reasons. Interestingly, if you want to blame anyone, start with Steven Spielberg. The staggering success of his 1975 film *Jaws* drove a lot of film-makers back to their school nature books to find another fearsome creature to exploit. Ants, piranhas, killer whales, bees, spiders, snakes – they all became the stars of various monster movies in the late 1970s, as producers scrabbled around for each year's new 'shark'. The first of these catch-up productions was delivered as early as 1976, just a year after *Jaws*. Carrying the tagline 'the most dangerous jaws on land', Film Ventures International released *Grizzly*, the horrific tale of an eighteen-foot bear's murderous rampage through a national park. The combination of its knowing references to the shockbuster of the previous year, William Girding's astute direction and the marketplace's hunger for another when-animals-attack-type horror all worked in the film's favour. By the end of its box office run, *Grizzly* had earned $40 million.

In 1978, Universal Pictures released the first of *Jaws*' three sequels, the accurately titled *Jaws II*. Roy Scheider reprised his role as the fin-phobic, water-hating Amity police chief Martin Brody. Not to be outdone, *Grizzly* producer David Sheldon produced a script for a follow-up to his ursine nightmare. Just when you thought it was safe to go back in the woods, there came *Grizzly II – The Predator*.

Sequels in the horror/monster genres rarely win much acclaim and their box office seems to be governed by the law of diminishing returns. Nonetheless, until a series actually begins to make a loss, movie companies continue to churn out new episodes until the franchise has nothing left to give. The downward spiral of *Friday The 13th*, the market leader for follow-ups, was on a seriously precipitous plunge until number ten, *Jason X*, started to attract anything like the acclaim of the original. While *Jaws II*, remains the exception to the rule, building on its earlier success, *Grizzly II* had no such kudos.

While $40 million represented an impressive return for the first film, little of that appeared to be invested in its sequel. Certainly the cast was not going to push proceedings over budget. Of the three main leads, only one had been in a proper production before. That said, there was a definite pedigree to them all, as a glance at their background revealed. Joining Nick Clooney on the set's famous-parents roster were Hollywood big shots Bruce Dern and Martin Sheen who turned up to watch their kids Laura and Charlie cut their big-picture teeth (like George, Charlie was making his official debut). Someone on *Grizzly II* obviously had an eye for talent, if not for a surname.

For all the project's overriding flaws, 22-year-old George Clooney was ecstatic at the opportunity to appear in it. As far as he was concerned, this was what he had been working towards: proper work on a proper film, proper lines in a proper script. The pain of all those rejections disappeared as he embraced his future. This was the beginning of something big. This is what he had come to Hollywood for. Except . . .

The first disappointment for the young actor came when he saw the production timetable. Despite the film's being set in California, financial stringency meant its shooting locations were more Eastern Bloc than West Coast.

'We shot *Grizzly* in Budapest,' George says. 'It was supposed to take place in northern California, but it was cheaper to film in Hungary.'

Once he was over the initial shock, George adapted to the news well. He became one of the 20 per cent of Americans to own a passport and looked forward to being paid to spend a couple of months in Europe. It sure beat sleeping in a closet and, after all, they had women and beer over there, right? And co-star Charlie Sheen looked like he knew how to have fun.

Although George mocks the project for dressing up Budapest as California, filming in Eastern Europe is a tactic still employed today by big-budget outfits. In 2000, Johnny Depp led the cast and crew of *From Hell* to Prague rather than try to film his Jack The Ripper Victorian drama in London's authentic, but prohibitively expensive, East End. As the end result proved, the Czech capital delivered a convincing English impression, showing what can be achieved when cost-cutting is carefully marshalled.

The same compliment cannot be paid to David Sheldon's production of *Grizzly II*. With a budget apparently suffering from the same indiscriminate slashing as the great bear's victims, the shortfalls presented by the local – cheaper – options showed themselves at virtually every turn. Trying to coax Hollywood-standard FX from the local crews was one area of deficiency. 'They had nothing but horrible effects,' George recalls. 'In Hungary, it's cheaper to kill a couple of Hungarians than to get fake blood.'

There were similar problems trying to eke American-looking performances from the star-struck rentacrowds. 'We filmed a rock concert scene with twenty-thousand Hungarians who'd never been to a rock concert in their lives,' he says. 'The assistant director would go, "Okay, everybody wave your arms!" and everyone would go [George adopts a Frankenstein monster scowl, arms stiff out front]. Mmm. It was awful.'

George was not the only person to think so. With the budget in disarray and each day's roughs highlighting the financial shortcuts, production was eventually cancelled. A disaster from start to end, the film was never finished, although George remains surprised that no one has ever tried to capitalise on its cast's later success. 'As big stars as Charlie and Laura have become,' he says with trademark modesty, 'the movie has never come out – not even on video – because it's so bad.'

George's CV now had another unreleased film to go alongside *And They're Off*, but at least he was going in the right direction. He had been paid for his time on *Grizzly* and, although it would never make him a star, it had given him valuable on-set experience. He knew from cousin Miguel how movie sets worked, but now he had first-hand familiarity with the procedures and jargon. When the call came from Hollywood again, he would be better equipped than ever.

While he waited for the word, George returned to his programme of theatre and auditions. October 1984 saw the mini-breakthrough he was looking for. The long-running drama *Riptide* was advertising for someone to play a criminal in one episode. With his healthy physique and beach-bum good looks,

George walked the audition and, for the first time, a TV show carried his name. The episode was called 'Where the Girls Are' and he played a villain called Lenny Colwell. Dressed in a smart hooped shirt and white shorts, George's hunk credentials were exposed at large for the first time, as was his impressive Hasselhoffian beach hair. Not only was it a paying gig, but it qualified George for his union card. 'I played a bad guy, holding three girls hostage,' he recalls. 'I didn't have any transportation, so I rode a ten-speed from my aunt's house.'

He was also offered a role in the implausible daytime soap opera *Santa Barbara* for $1,400 a week. In a show of commitment to his long-term future, George's agent said no. 'He was convinced there was better work around the corner and there was,' George says. 'But it was hard to turn that money down when I didn't have any.' Other small parts followed. *Crazy Like a Fox*, *Street Hawk* and *Hotel* all carried his name for one episode, but anything longer term than a guest spot stayed out of his reach. All that looked like changing, however, when he landed a part in a show centring on the emergency room of a Chicago hospital. That show was called *ER*.

Before Clooney aficionados rush to check whether some pages have fallen from this book, read on. Although this TV show was indeed called *ER*, it presaged its more celebrated namesake by a decade. And George Clooney starred in both. What are the odds? This *ER* was a vehicle for actor Elliott Gould, Oscar-nominated star of *M*A*S*H* and *Bob & Carol & Ted & Alice* (although for a younger generation he will only ever be Dr Geller, Monica's dad in NBC hit *Friends*). Alongside Gould's Dr Sheinfeld, Jason Alexander, later to evolve indubitably into George from *Seinfeld*, played Harold Stickley.

George had never played a comedy role before – he had not had many roles, period – but his innate sense of humour and gift for timing came across to whomever he met. Years spent as his father's comedy foil and revelling as the high-school prankster had honed his talent to amuse to the extent that no casting director would forget him, even if he did not get the job. He had that kind of bravura, that kind of engaging confidence. Who else would brandish a six-pack of Japanese beer at a commercial audition?

The part of Ace in *ER* did not tax George unduly. Dress as an intern, look cute, walk around the hospital wise-assing the other characters: he could do this in his sleep. For eight weeks, he did. After just one season, the show was canned.

Although disappointed at the loss of income and exposure, George was not overly concerned at losing the work. This was TV; he wanted to work in film. For now, though, it would do. Enough major names had started on the small screen and look at them now. John Travolta, Robin Williams, Tom Hanks, Michael J Fox – even Dirty Harry, as George rationalised to himself. 'TV is not the kiss of death,' he says. 'Most of them, starting with Eastwood, had television series. It's just finding the right one . . .'

With George's recent workload upping his cachet in town, he was able to move out of Thom's closet and into his own pad. Size-wise, there was not too much in it, but at least he had his own front door. He also invested in some new wheels. Since Aunt Rosemary had ordered him to scrap the Danger Car, he had been on the look-out for the right vehicle at the right price. With his new income, he found both: a 1960 Oldsmobile Dynamic 88. A few modifications in the shape of internal carpeting and a pair of fluffy dice hanging from the rear-view mirror personalised the car as his. Who's the daddy now? he seemed to be saying.

Cruising around LA at the wheel of his dream car, George thought he knew the answer – it was him. And why not? He was getting work – regular, contracted work – casting directors knew his name when he arrived and he had money in the bank. Not much, but some. Enough to ward off the trailer park, should things start to unravel. The only element of his life that did not change was his luck with women. That was still dauntingly impressive. From a nobody who got all the girls to a somebody who got all the girls, life was sweet. And it was about to get better.

In 1979, the then-struggling NBC ordered a spin-off series from the hit comedy *Diff'rent Strokes* as a way of maximising their limited resources. With the Drummond family locked integrally into the show, producers looked to the household's excitable housekeeper, Mrs Garrett, for their development. The result was *The Facts of Life*, a comedy about life in a private girls'-school, with Mrs Garrett ensconced as the housemother/dietician. After some major restructuring, the show established itself as the big hitter for its time slot – 9 p.m. on Wednesday night – positioning NBC as a force to be reckoned with.

By 1985, the school premise had been superseded by a gourmet emporium, which in turn became a malt shop, but still at the core was Charlotte Rae's Mrs Garrett. Following another round of cast changing and upheaval, actors Mackenzie Astin and George Clooney joined the all-female cast, the latter bringing with him 'the worst combination of over confidence and bad acting you've ever seen in your life'.

While Astin's Andy the errand boy would remain until the programme was cancelled, Clooney's George Burnett, the show's macho carpenter and love object for the girls, appeared for just one full season. As much as he respected TV actors and for all the fun he was having being part of a funny hit show, the last thing George wanted was to be typecast as a piece of meat in a chick-com. In the end, after apparent differences with the new *Facts* producer, he was as good as fired at the beginning of his second season, 'rehired' as he was still under contract, and ended up leaving of his own volition, point made, ego intact.

Nick Clooney had prepared his son for principled stands like this. 'It's the right thing to do' was a recurring phrase in the Clooney household and if it meant missing out on a main course to escape dining within earshot of a bigot, or downsizing house-wise, then so be it. One of George's heroes, for this reason, is former President Jimmy Carter. 'This is a man whose character should never be questioned,' he says. 'Remember the handshake between Begin and Sadat? Then he sacrificed his presidency for the hostages. And remember the debate with Ford, when they asked Ford about Watergate and how much he knew, and when it came time for Carter's rebuttal he said he had no rebuttal, Jack.'

Although he was able to walk away from *Facts of Life* with his head held high, George was aware that he had reason to be grateful for his time on it. For the first time in his life he had been in a popular show, the number-one programme in its time slot, and audiences had begun to notice him. Reviewers pointed out how he could deliver a punch line with the best of them. He even started to get fan mail from women wanting him to bring his 'tool kit' to their homes.

The Facts of Life took George Clooney into a new realm, career-wise, but once again it was a case of luck as much as judgement which saw him get the chance. Early in 1985 his agent had secured him a try-out in front of ABC's head of casting John Crosby. This could be the start of something big, he reasoned, if only he could make an impression. Not a problem. George had been undergoing something of a professional epiphany with regards to auditions and he thought he had them worked out. No more Mr 'Please-Like-Me' for him. He was going to take each opportunity by the scruff of the neck and make people remember him, if nothing else. Like defending a principle on *Facts of Life*, it was another part of being true to your own beliefs.

'I'd been out here about a year and a half, and I couldn't get a part in anything,' he says. 'Then one day I decided to audition the way I played baseball. I decided to go in and read for parts not like "I hope, I hope, I *hope* I get the part", but like I was the best thing that ever happened to them. I mean, I figured they didn't want me to fail. They wanted me to be the guy, right? So I started acting like I was the best actor they'd ever seen.'

This *carpe diem* moment produced instant results, starting with the Panasonic six-pack and the Body Fluids tattoo stunts. This would be a new George who auditioned. 'I started to come in selling confidence, not even my acting skills,' he explains. 'I thought, "From here on out, I cannot lose a job. I'll do whatever it takes." So I'd come in with a dog under my arm for some scene. I'd pull a champagne bottle and phone out of my jacket and do the scene. People were like, "What the fuck is that?" I just thought, "Fuck it. It's *where* I'm going to hit the ball, not *if* I'm going to hit it." '

George was in one of those big-hitting moods when he read for Crosby. When his spot was called, he introduced himself to the casting panel and hollered, 'OK, let's do it.' From the ante-room a posse of 'roadies' (so it said on their T-shirts) appeared and set about erecting bunk beds, replete with small mattresses. Grant Heslov, the guy who had lent George money for his first publicity shots, appeared and took over the bottom bunk; George clambered up to the top. Their joint reading of the scene from *Brighton Beach Memoirs* lasted fifteen minutes instead of the allotted three. Someone must have been impressed.

'It was pretty calculated,' George says. 'The secretary was going crazy and yelling, "You can't do this, you can't do this," but I just told her, "Don't worry, we can pull it off." And John Crosby loved it.'

The bunk bed set-up had only ever been a gimmick to win attention. George knew that it would take more than comedy props to impress a hard-nosed casting executive, but he had enough conviction in his own talent to believe that, if could just find a hook, something to make him stand out from all the other wannabes showcasing that day, he would be OK. It worked. When he had finished shaking his head in disbelief at the cheeky actor's cajones, John Crosby offered him a four-month contract with ABC. This young man was going places and Crosby wanted a slice of it.

With a studio contract under his belt, George knew it was only a matter of time before his big break came. Studios do not invest in unknown actors for the fun of it and Crosby would be working as hard as he was to find the right vehicle. Enter *The Facts of Life*. Until then, though, there was boredom and frustration. One of the conditions of a contract is that you do not attend other studios' auditions. This is fine when you have a job, but liable to drive anyone to distraction in the downtime, as George found out.

'I love being busy,' he says. 'I'm either really working and have no time at all or I have so much spare time because unlike other actors I can't go on interviews. And when I'm working I go nuts because there is no time to get to all those stupid, regular things you have to do between nine and five.'

Earning his chops as an actor meant more to George than getting a few laughs on a popular sitcom. 'It's more what I can do with comedy that got me the job,' he says dismissively. 'In *The Facts of Life* I'm just the guy who comes in and hassles people and leaves.'

Despite the fact that the show gave him a healthy income and something like a national profile, he never saw it as anything other than the piece of fluff, albeit quality fluff, it was. As far as George was concerned, TV was a means of getting to films, nothing more. If it paid the bills and helped him on his journey, then great. Eastwood and Co. had used the small screen as a stepping stone, and so would he.

George's next screen project after *The Facts of Life* was somewhere between the two, a movie made for TV. Written by Paul W Shapiro, *Combat High* was about two juveniles sentenced in court to a year in military training school, low on laughs but big on sentiment. Or, as *Variety* put it, 'Try to imagine *Police Academy* done with none of the gross, sexist or explicit humour, and written so that everyone ends up learning a lesson. That's about what you get with *Combat High*, a film with no reason for existence.' The film went out on 23 November 1986 as part of NBC's 'Sunday Night At The Movies' series and George's name as Major Biff Woods earned third billing in a cast which, according to *Variety*, 'reads like a season's worth of *Love Boat* performers. Though some of these names brought a lot of talent to the project, there was scarcely a decent role to be found for any of them.'

It is safe to say that *Combat High* was probably not director Neal Israel's finest hour, and George's neither, but at least it was a step closer to proper film-making. A year later he got nearer still with another school-based movie destined not to set the world alight, *Return To Horror High*. He is open about his reasons. 'I took those roles to survive because I was trapped in sitcom hell,' he admits. 'But from looking at my father's career, I knew that if you survived long enough, your career would eventually take off.'

From an outsider's perspective, George had a funny way of going about surviving. He had thrown in the towel on a hit show for roles in dodgy comedy and horror pastiches, but at least he had a plan. 'When you're starting out as an actor, those are the things you do,' he says. 'I did a lot of cheesy, funky films.' The man does not lie, unfortunately, and he has the CV to prove it. But let's start with *Horror High*, a cliché-by-numbers attempt at recreating the slasher pix of the early 80s.

A movie company embarks on a film about a real-life serial killer set in the actual high school where the original murders took place. Unbeknownst to the film-makers, the murderer is still inhabiting the now-abandoned building and, you guessed it, one by one the cast and crew begin to disappear. Neither his good looks nor *Facts of Life* credentials is enough to save George from a bloody end, although it would have helped the budget if he had survived. Despite the film being shot in LA, its effects allowance rivalled that of *Grizzly II* and only some inventive thinking meant audiences got to see the full 'horror' of George's character's vile decapitation. 'They didn't have enough money to do a good prosthetic head,' he recalls, 'so they stuck my head through the trash can and put this piece on my neck to look like it's been cut off.'

Thoroughly unimpressed by the whole affair, George's life was further complicated by his other commitments. 'It became the bane of my existence to do that movie,' he says. 'I did *Return To Horror High* as a favour to a friend of mine, Greg Sims. I would fly out on weekends from Chicago where I was doing a play at the Steppenwolf, and shoot my scenes.'

Shuttling between a day job in Chicago and various film sets would become a recurring feature of George's professional life, but not yet. Right now he was trying to contribute to a mate's movie as well as hold down a job with America's most prestigious theatre project. Chicago's Steppenwolf company was formed by an actors' collective including John Malkovich, Gary Sinise and Laurie Metcalf with a view to putting on challenging and risqué work. To win a role at the Steppenwolf was to get a serious pat on the back.

George's role as a drug dealer in the play *Vicious* certainly lived up to the company's liking of non-comfortable work. As its name suggests, the play focused on the controversial and seedy life of Sex Pistols guitarist Sid Vicious. George has nothing but pride for his chance to appear in it. 'It's the only play I've done that was really worth seeing,' he surmises. 'It was dirty and it was nasty, but there was a certain energy about it and it was chic so everybody was coming to see it.'

Part of the enjoyment of theatre is the chance of unscheduled mishaps. *Vicious* suffered one or two but George's experience of live TV as a child and his readiness with the perfect quip saw him through. 'Things don't always go right,' he admits, 'so you have to be prepared to roll with the flow.' One time in particular he found himself the wrong side of a locked stage door. Bemused audience members watched as he made his ungainly entrance via a bathroom window. 'I just started singing "He Came In Through The Bathroom Window",' he laughs. 'But it's that kind of stuff that keeps you fresh, and it's also the stuff I love.'

A year earlier, George had appeared in another theatrical triumph, this time a two-headed show co-starring his cousin in crime, Miguel Ferrer. Riding high on his *Facts of Life* success, George was a shoe-in for one of the two parts in Bill Davis's *The Wrestlers*. Ironically, although it was originally Miguel's idea to do the play (he had first wanted *Hardy Boy* Sean Cassidy to accompany him), the show's backers considered him too much of an unknown quantity to stump up the finance. But that was before they saw his new, improved and Clooney-tweaked résumé. It did the trick and the pair of them were suddenly faced with three weeks to learn their parts and get the show on. It premiered during Thanksgiving 1985 and ran until the New Year with decent reviews in the LA press.

Although happy to put *Facts of Life* behind him, George was still pursuing TV as a backdoor route into motion pictures. In 1987, he was busy again juggling his workload between two projects, one for each medium.

The Bennett Brothers was billed as a buddy comedy about two brothers with different personalities who move in with each other after one of them suffers a marriage break-up; a sort of *Odd Couple* update. A Double-L production for NBC, the script was put together by the show's executive producer Lloyd Garver. In the lead roles were George Clooney as the womanising, good-looking rogue and Richard Kind as his straight-laced emotionally torn-up fraternal foil.

TV works differently in America. In some ways it is a lot smarter than in Europe, in others aspects it seems over cautious. One example of this is its tradition of relying on pilot shows. Rather than invest in an entire series of a show, most studios develop tester episodes that allow them to gauge public and network reaction without having to commit to long-term contracts. Other countries do things differently. The UK seems to take the in-for-a-penny approach and either produces an entire series or nothing. Given the parlous state of recent BBC and Carlton sitcoms, audiences can feel aggrieved that the pilot system is not favoured here.

The Bennett Brothers was one such pilot. It was aired on 22 July 1987 on NBC after which the network sat back to analyse the response. *Variety* was blunt as ever: '*The Bennett Brothers* isn't bad, just probably not good enough to go to series.'

The magazine was right and the series option was not picked up. Another knock-back for George Clooney, but did he really want to follow *Facts of Life* with another sitcom? In fact he did. The producers had gone some way to shaping the programme around his own life, especially with the set's apartment including a basketball backboard and hoop – it would become a *de rigueur* feature of any movie set he later worked on.

There was one benefit to come from the show, however. Richard Kind and George hit it off at once and became close friends. Kind would eventually secure a fame-winning part in the political comedy *Spin City*, but their relationship really grew when neither was known. Thanks to *The Bennett Brothers* Richard Kind had just become one of The Boys.

While *The Bennett Brothers* showed that a major TV network had faith in him to 'carry' a programme, George's reputation in the film business was less hardy. At the same time as he was filming the abortive comedy, George was also taking part in his latest movie, which began shooting in San Diego on 22 June 1987. Not only was he not the lead actor, he got to deliver the worst line in the movie. But what a line: 'That must have been the bravest thing I've ever seen a vegetable do.'

The vegetable (or is it a fruit?) in question was a tomato; the film was *Return of the Killer Tomatoes*, John DeBello's sequel to his 1977 underground hit *Attack of the Killer Tomatoes*. Sporting a towering mullet haircut that surely no hygienic restaurant would allow in its kitchens, George plays Matt the pizza chef who comes up against the scientifically enhanced danger foods. Kubrick it is not, but George was hell bent on furthering his big screen image and this film certainly had potential – at least at the script stage.

'It's one of those movies where you read the script and it's hysterically funny,' he says. 'When you first start out, you read every script as if Barry Levinson is going to direct it. You think, "God, this is going to be great," and then of course it's done for $500,000, it looks like shit and it's badly directed. *Return of the Killer Tomatoes* was campy as hell. It was such a horrible movie, but it was fun to do and it still kind of works in a sad, embarrassing way.'

'More calculated than the original but fun nonetheless' was *Variety*'s verdict, and as a bit of fun it certainly did not hinder George's career, nor those of other bit players Gary Condit (yes, really) and Rick Rockwell. But surely he could do better than this?

6. THIS SHIT I WILL NOT EAT

As a wise man once wrote, it's amazing what agents can do. As well as lining George up with work, his representation also ran a neat sideline in supplying new partners. 'I just looked down their client list and picked my next girlfriend from there,' he joked back in 1988. He was not so far from the truth on one occasion, though, because it was his agency that suggested he and fellow client Kelly Preston should attend the same party. George picked Preston up and within weeks they were living together. What woman could resist that car and hair?

That is not as spurious as it sounds (although Kelly Preston drove a better car, a Jaguar). By the mid-80s George was cutting quite the figure in Hollywood. He had never been short of female attention and as soon as the money had started coming in, he proved more of a catch than ever. The sports car, the corny chat-up lines, the basketball player's physique and of course that charm put him at least equal with all the other good-looking men in town. With a hairstyle for any occasion, maybe he was slightly ahead.

When Hawaiian-born Kelly Preston met George Clooney, shortly after separating from husband of two years Kevin Gage, her career was at a more advanced stage than his. After the familiar bout of dues-paying on fairly forgettable flicks like *Mischief* and *Christine* she had taken the next step, filming *Twins* with Danny DeVito and former Mr Universe Arnold Schwarzenegger. George had had his fair share of press, but Kelly was suddenly in demand from the international media, a new experience for both of them. The fact that they moved into a new house together just 23 days after meeting only fuelled the tabloid intrigue.

When she wasn't being quizzed on what it was like to kiss her Austrian co-star ('Arnold's a great kisser but not as good as my man') Kelly was being interrogated about sharing a house with a pig. For once it had nothing to do with George's hick upbringing ('I'm just white trailer trash,' he has deadpanned more than once). As a birthday present he had surprised his girlfriend with a gift that resurrected memories of his high school career as a practical joker: a tiny Vietnamese pot-bellied pig named Max. Not everyone's cup of tea, but Kelly was not fazed. 'When I saw Max I screamed,' she confessed, 'but I loved him.'

Photos of the happy event show a cat-sized Max and a frizzy-haired Kelly, both sporting matching red bows. As the proud 'father' George is most remarkable for the length of his droopy curtain fringe. But at least the mullet had gone. In fact, as an up-and-coming actor he was really beginning to look the part – even if he was not getting them.

The chances were still coming, though, and that was the main thing. And looking good counted for a lot. 'The best actor never gets the job when they audition,' he insists. 'Especially in television. The guy who gets the job is somebody who comes in and delivers every day. It's often looks more than anything.'

Ironically, while his looks would go some way to shaping his career, for a while George was convinced they were holding him back. A 1985 audition for the teen flick *The Breakfast Club* went well acting-wise, but the directors thought Judd Nelson had the more authentic look. A pattern began to emerge.

'I was in the wrong place at the wrong time for so long,' he says. 'I was too old for the Brat Pack parts, when everybody was getting work. And then when that ended, they said: "We don't really want your kind of look. You've got that old Hollywood look. We want a raspier look, a rugged look." And then I got kind of beaten and ragged, and they said I was looking a little too old.' It was Cecil B DeMille and Nick all over again.

These things have to be taken in context, of course. He obviously had the look that some casting directors in 1987 were searching for or he would never have won guest spots on shows such as *Hunter*, *The Golden Girls* and *Murder She Wrote*, playing Matthew Winfield, Bobby Hopkins and Kip Howards respectively. He was playing characters with names and their own plot arcs on major series. Financially, it certainly could not be called a barren period: George was paid well. But then money had never been the issue. 'I was the highest paid unknown actor in Hollywood,' he says with some embarrassment. It was nice, but not what he wanted.

If George appeared a man in a hurry it was because of what he had witnessed happening to his aunt. 'Most people have about a seven-year career realistically,' he says. 'And it so easily goes away. There is no way to avoid it. The most important thing is to understand it and know it's going to happen. And then enjoy the ride. Rosemary was as successful as she could be and then unsuccessful. And it had nothing to do with her. When you see that, you have a better, clearer understanding of how little it has to do with you.'

Despite his frustrations with his career trajectory, he was still a seize-the-day, glass-half-full type of person. He had seen too many other people not enjoy the ride and then regret it. One such example is Joshua Logan whom he met shortly before the legendary screenwriter/director died in 1988. Logan used his Pulitzer Prize as a doorstop and had his haul of Tonys and other awards similarly deployed, but George sensed a feeling of underachievement in the man behind classics like *South Pacific* and *Mr Roberts*.

'It breaks your heart because you're looking at this man who has accomplished so much,' George explains. 'What seemed important to him were these satellite moments: the premiere, the winning of the awards. What I learned is I can't rely on those moments – a premiere or your big episode of the TV show – seven days a week. Coming to work every day has to be those moments. Coming to work and saying something that makes everybody laugh. You've got to live for each day.'

Saying something to make everybody laugh has certainly become George's stock in trade, along with on-set practical jokes and general good-natured tomfoolery. Another reason for enjoying each day, he had learned, was to pre-empt a show's sudden cancellation. How many pilots had he made that had not been picked up? How many walk-on parts in a TV production line series had he contributed?

In 1988 *Killer Tomatoes* was released, a year after George had finished work on it. It did not set the world on fire and a lot of industry insiders agreed that it seemed an odd move for the actor to make. Was he really that desperate for film work? He certainly didn't need the money by this stage. And now that he was dating Kelly Preston, his movie career looked comparatively shabby. George held onto the belief that the transition to film would happen for him though.

'It's this giant chasm you have to cross,' he says, 'but it certainly can be done, especially if you get a point where you have a lot of clout as a TV actor, you're front-and-centre in a hit show.'

As if to prove his commitment to the medium, George signed up for another pilot with a series option. The show was called *Roseanne* and it was a comedy based on the dysfunctional family life of a sassy waitress played by loudmouth comedienne Roseanne Barr. Not only was the pilot a success but the show went on to become one of the biggest hits in American TV history, making its controversial star one of the richest and most loved/loathed people on the planet for a few years. George sums her up perfectly: 'She was hysterical,' he says. 'She was the foulest woman I ever met, and I thought *I* was foul.'

George played Roseanne's boss Booker Brooks, an unpleasant male chauvinist who was the foil for the show's star, but the job came about by accident. 'I actually read for the wrong part,' he admits. 'But I ended up getting the job because I was funny.' Unfortunately, the intrinsic nature of Booker was far from funny. He was unpleasant – a characteristic that George had never before been called upon to play, especially in a comedy. It is to his credit that he pulled it off week in, week out, but it was a strain and he never really got to grips with the role in his own mind. He was much more comfortable off camera, larking with co-star Sara Gilbert, pretending to vomit or suffer joint dislocation for the crew's general amusement.

It was probably in one these lighter moments that George made a decision that, if it didn't change his life, certainly dominated conversations. One scene in the factory called for a rat to scurry behind the machines. For reasons best known to them, the show's producers 'employed' a tiny black pig to play the rat – maybe porcine actors learn lines quicker? George fell in love with it immediately. 'I saw him and said, "I want that," ' he recalls. He may have given the pig – Max – to girlfriend Kelly as a present, but it was really his pet, although he doesn't think the studio were absolutely honest with him about Max's future. 'I took him home because they said he was a miniature,' George says. 'Now he weighs 150 pounds. Man, I love him, but you learn as you get older to be more careful about impulse buying.'

Pet rescues aside, George's dissatisfaction with his own on-screen efforts marred what should have been a happy time, as his personal stock grew with the success of the show. By the time it hit number one in the ratings, he was pretty much a household face – but it would take a while longer for his name to sink in, too.

Aside from his concerns over his own career path, George was beginning to tire of the on-set atmosphere. 'It was a nightmare,' he says. There were daily arguments between Roseanne and the show's executive producer Matt Williams and filming was fraught with network politics. There were even suggestions that it was only a matter of time before the axe fell on his character. '*Roseanne* wasn't much fun,' he admits. 'They didn't want me there in the first place, but they were stuck with me because I was under contract.' As with *Facts of Life*, George made his move when it suited him. After *Roseanne*'s inaugural season, during which time it reached the top ratings spot in the country, he quit. It was not the first time he had walked and it would not be the last. But he did not need the hassle. Life is too short.

Although the move threw her plans for the second season into turmoil, Roseanne Barr has nothing for respect for the way George handled himself. 'Everyone in Hollywood is scared and they'll totally compromise themselves to get ahead,' she says. 'But George is his own man. He's not for sale.' She is an astute woman, that Roseanne. 'I'm an actor, but I'm also a businessman and a bit of a hothead,' George says. 'This town is run by fear, but I've always had a line that I would not cross. It may have cost me some jobs, but at least I can look myself in the mirror every morning.'

On a professional footing, the face staring back from that mirror was as conscientiously unblinking as George could wish. If only he could say the same for his private life. By the end of his stint as Booker, he had realised that life with Kelly Preston was no longer what he wanted. 'I felt sort of cornered,' he says. Not only had he rushed into co-habitation – Kelly was the first woman he had lived with outside his family – but he had also tied himself down to an ever-expanding pig and a sizeable mortgage on their house. On top of that, the stress of going to work on *Roseanne* every day, even for a happy-go-lucky guy like him, had contributed to a painful stomach ulcer and one unhappy actor. Something had to give.

The split with Kelly was relatively painless if a little sudden; neither party has been willing to discuss it, even years later. One minute in February the doting couple were inviting *People* magazine into their lovely home to see how happy they were, even bandying around the 'M' word. Two months later it was goodnight Vienna. George won custody of Max and sold the house. While he was soon seen in the company of Dedee Pfeiffer – Michelle's younger sister – Kelly ended the year, with almost 'Hamlet's mother-like' haste, engaged to George's co-star on *Grizzly II*, Charlie Sheen. The relationship would be tempestuous, to say the least, and on one occasion Kelly was taken to hospital after Sheen accidentally shot her in the arm. Marriage to the more stable figure of fellow Scientologist John Travolta, her co-star on 1987's *The Experts*, would follow on 5 September 1991.

If Preston seemed a tad disrespectful for becoming engaged so soon after splitting from George, he went one better. Maybe it was the macho competitor in him, but by the end of 1989 he had traded one live-in partner for another. Only this time, she was his wife.

George had first met Talia Balsam in 1984 when they worked on the same play. She was going out with someone else at the time, but George had come as close as he gets to chasing her. It paid off and they had dated for eighteen months before splitting up. At 23, George admits he was too young for a proper relationship. Five years later, however, it seemed the most natural thing in the world when they rekindled their love. 'Talia and I were together for a long time,' he says quietly. 'She was the girl I chased and was in love with, the girl I always wanted to marry.' In autumn 1989 they set off for Las Vegas with Talia's mother and two best friends in a 33-foot Winnebago. 'We got married in the Chapel of White Lace and Promises,' George recalls with sadness. 'They play "We've Only Just Begun" on this rotating log that goes, "Ting-ting, Ting-ting," [he begins singing] "White lace and promises . . ." It was horrifying.'

The daughter of Martin Balsam and Joyce Van Patten, Talia was an actress in her own right, appearing in numerous unmemorable films and even more TV series than her husband, from *Love Boat* to *Happy Days* to *Magnum PI* and *Hill Street Blues*. Her career was certainly more on a par with George's than film star Kelly Preston's had been; cynics would suggest that this was easier for him, as a man, to cope with now that he was a 'star' thanks to his time on *Roseanne*. Whatever his inner motivation, Mr and Mrs Clooney appeared very happy. He even got his ulcer seen to.

'I grew up with a very meat-and-potatoes kind of upbringing in Kentucky, so I'm not Mr Hocus-Pocus,' he says. 'I don't believe in ESP, or ghosts, or literally anything. I tried acupuncturists to get rid of things, and it didn't work. Don't believe in chiropractors, either. But I went to this guy who does herbs and he looked in my eyes and told me what I'd had wrong with me over the years. Okay, I was a little bit impressed by that. Then he gave me these herbs and about three months later I got rid of an ulcer I had for two years. I figure, "Good enough, I'm a believer." I still take them.'

The newly-weds soon settled into a comfortable life of trying to pursue their individual careers while juggling their domestic commitments. Talia got to grips with living with Max, George returned to his hobby of messing around with car parts and generally trying to build things. He attributes this talent to his mother, Nina. 'My mom taught me how to be scrappy,' he explains. 'My mom buys a table saw and goes out and builds a bar in the house. My dad couldn't possibly do that. She doesn't do it the right way, but she does it. She taught me that by example. I can take my motorcycle apart and put it back together again. It keeps you feeling like you're still a guy.' And we know how important that is to him.

Knowing his way around a steel horse may have played a part in landing George his next big job. Patrick Hasburgh, producer of *21 Jump Street*, the series that gave Johnny Depp his big break, was putting together a new show along the same lines and he wanted George Clooney to take the lead. If anyone was built to be 'Chic', an undercover motorcycle cop who combines crime-fighting with playing in a rock'n'roll band, babysitting teenage runaways and delivering sententious anti-drug messages, all from beneath the comfort of a *Mad Max*/Aunty Entity-scale mullet haircut, then it was the man Clooney. He strode into the part and the cool dude threads like a man born to the role. Unlike his spots on *Facts of Life* and *Roseanne*, this was a part he would not be embarrassed about being known for. It was a guy role. If the series took off, he could be the next Don Johnson.

Unfortunately, *Sunset Beat*'s similarities to *Jump Street* were so striking that accusations of Hasburgh over-milking the idea cow were rife. When the show's two-hour pilot finally debuted in April 1990, critics were unconvinced. *Variety* found the action convincing and 'George Clooney is likeable enough', but the show's social responsibility was overcooked: 'laudable, yes, but such an obvious public-service announcement that you half expect a phone number to follow.' But ABC felt the programme had done enough to warrant a run and they signed up for a series. Was this the vehicle George had been waiting for? The short answer was 'no'. The series broke domestic television records by being cancelled after just two shows. It was back to the drawing board again.

George took the death of *Sunset Beat* well, but then he was used to it by now. Less than a year earlier he had been promised that *Hot Prospects* would be the show to make him a star. The CBS project did not make it past the pilot stage. Who wants to be a TV actor, anyway?

It could all have been so different. When George got the call to audition for the part of a drifter in a new Ridley Scott film, he was convinced his time had arrived. He did not even let it bother him that, as a vehicle for Geena Davis and Susan Sarandon, the film was essentially another female-friendly project. Scott's earlier films included *Blade Runner* and *Alien* and, having read the script to this one called *Thelma & Louise*, George was convinced of its potential. The audition went well and he got the call back. And another one. 'I read about five times with Geena Davis,' he says. 'It was down to three actors at one time and I thought I was going to get it.' It was not to be. The part went to another of the three, a young-looking guy called Brad Pitt. 'The part catapulted him,' George admits with some envy. 'I wouldn't see that movie when it first came out,' he acknowledges. 'I was just so mad. And Brad just kept going and going and going. I finally saw it a year later when it came out on tape. I sat there with my mouth open, saying, I would never have thought of doing things the way he did them. Suddenly I realised how right Ridley Scott was. When you don't get a part, you think, "The director's just an idiot." Truth is, he couldn't have been more right. Brad couldn't have been more perfect for the role.'

There were other film opportunities, albeit smaller scale ones. In May 1989 *Variety* had announced that 'George Clooney will head the cast of Arrowhead Entertainment's feature *Red Surf* now lensing under the direction of H Gordon Boos, according to Arrowhead's executive producer Greg Sims.' It was Sims who had persuaded George to appear in *Return to Horror High*. After the hell of commuting between LA and Chicago for that shoot it was now payback time and Sims delivered. The *Variety* piece goes on to explain that 'Clooney, best known for his comedic role in the sitcom *Roseanne*, appears in a dramatic role'. Not exactly the career credentials he was hoping for, and one of the reasons he jettisoned the role at the first opportunity.

Red Surf was released in May 1990 with George in the lead role as Remar, an ex-champion surfer gone to pot (and other drugs). For the first time in his life, his name was carrying a movie. Fighting off the dreaded comedy-actor tag, 'he brings some charismatic fire to his performance as the self-indulgent, self-loathing Remar', *Variety* was forced to admit. The magazine also singled out his on-screen chemistry with co-stars Doug (*Masquerade*) Savant and Dedee Pfeiffer, the latter pairing 'reinvigorating their hackneyed dialogue through sheer force of persuasive acting'.

The fact that Dedee and George had fallen for each other during filming may have added the 'reinvigorating' frisson to the film, but it was not enough to invigorate major box-office activity and the film went straight to video, like *Tomatoes* and *Horror High*. As a sidebar, George was beginning to realise that co-star romances were an occupational hazard. Talia Balsam the first time back in 1984, Dedee now and others since. 'They can become a nightmare,' he says. 'If you're doing series television and you have to go to work together every day for nine months, what happens when you break up? What the hell do you do? At least in a movie, it's four or five months and you're gone.' Such pragmatism offers an interesting insight into George's expectations of relationships. He seems resigned to affairs being brief; but was this based on experience or desire? Was he capable of sustaining a romance past a few months? Did he have the maturity to stay with a partner once the initial allure dulled? These are questions he would soon be asking himself.

Meanwhile, there was work to be had, and from an unlikely, if circuitous, source. The power of Hollywood to distort reality is well known: actors look taller, actresses look younger and singlet-wearing cops single-handedly thwart armies of terrorists. Everything is bigger, faster, stronger – even karmic truths. In Tinseltown, the Six Degrees of Separation theory is seen as at least three degrees too many. Hollywood's a small town and everything and everyone is connected. Holistic theory rules.

John Travolta met Kelly Preston in 1987 when they were shooting *The Experts* and in 1991 he married her. Two years earlier, he had made the first of his famed comebacks with *Look Who's Talking*, a comedy about a single parent and her 'talking' baby. Kirstie Alley played the mother, Travolta played a lumbered cab driver and Bruce Willis voiced the kid. The film's success led to a sequel and an ABC spin-off TV series. No prizes for guessing who got Travolta's cast-offs on the small screen. Small world.

First, though, it was pilot time again. Despite the almost certain feeling that *Baby Talk* would be another aborted effort, George duly pitched up to play Joe the handyman opposite *Hotel* star Connie Sellecca's rendering of the Kirstie Alley character in the September 1990 trial run. Supplying another floppy-haired cartoon creation that didn't exactly tax his retinue of funny faces and hand gestures too much was easily within George's capabilities, and if the show took off it was good money. But, surprise surprise, there was a hitch. The show's executive producer Ed Weinberger, a veteran of *Taxi* and *The Mary Tyler Moore Show*, thought improvements could be made, notably to the lead actress's part. Sellecca was summarily dropped and *Newhart* face Julia Duffy drafted in as a replacement. Six months later, in March 1991, the revamped show debuted for real.

George was now in his third major series, a fully-paid-up member of sitcom hell. There were reasons for staying, of course, and the $20,000-per-episode fee was one of the main ones, plus the obvious fact that being on a regular show put him in the shop window for other parts. He never let up remembering how his heroes McQueen and Eastwood and many others had built their movie careers from successful TV roots. If he worked hard and kept his nose clean, it would work out.

The only problem was that George was a Clooney through and through. He had walked from *Roseanne* as a protest at the atmosphere on set and dumped *Facts of Life* after his integrity was called into question. As Barr says, he is not afraid of the system; he is not for sale. If there is a fight to be had, he will have it, regardless of how it affects him. On the set of *Baby Talk*, there was a fight to be had.

Ed Weinberger was in the same position on *Baby Talk* that Matt Williams had suffered on *Roseanne*. It was his job to pull the show in on time, on budget and on target laughs-wise. Unfortunately, in George's eyes, he went about it the wrong way. Weinberger is dismissive of the contretemps today, as he might be considering George's global standing – but he deserves to be heard. According to him, George resented Duffy's arrival at the expense of Sellecca. Weinberger's treatment of the show's stars –

the baby actors – was similarly unpopular: 'The audience hated those first babies,' he says. 'We had to get cuter ones. The babies didn't know they were being fired. But George blamed me.'

According to George, Weinberger ran the set like his own personal fiefdom, dropping actors without having the courtesy to tell them first. The majority of the crew and cast were aghast but inactive; they had livelihoods to protect. That has never been a Clooney's first instinct. That's not how a real guy behaves. One day, as another actress was publicly relieved of her duties, George snapped. It was game on.

'Ed Weinberger was a bad guy who intimidated everybody,' he says. 'There comes a point where you go, "I've got to draw the line; this shit I will not eat." It was my *Network* moment.' In front of his colleagues, George tore into the producer, putting him straight on a few matters and quitting the show in the process. 'There is the moment where you are two men sitting in a room. Now do you want to fuck with me? Forget that you're the executive producer who could fire me, because my job is already out the window. You have nothing over me now. I own you. I am bigger than you.' Weinberger gave as good as he got and the last word, as far as he saw it, was his. 'You'll never work in this town again' has become a Hollywood cliché. But blacklisting was the risk George was up against.

Nick Clooney remembers his son's actions with pride. 'I remember him calling up and saying Weinberger warned him he'd never work again,' he says. 'And George said, "Pop, maybe he means it."'

'It was very dangerous for George to quit *Baby Talk*, but I told him it was the right thing to do. No matter how frightening it feels to jump into the void, you keep your integrity and eventually something even better comes along.'

Integrity-rich, George called his agent for words of solace. There were none. 'You maybe blew it, but maybe not.' It was a case of waiting to see how far Weinberger's alleged threat, if he made good on it, could carry.

As it transpired, it was not very far at all. Less than a week had passed before Gary David Goldberg called with a job offer: he had a pilot called *Knights of the Kitchen Table* and George was his new first choice, once they had adjusted the character's biog to fit George's age and build. Why? Because it would piss a certain producer off. 'I asked them why they were doing this and they said for the simple reason that it would be fun for them to do that to Ed Weinberger,' George says. 'So that was fun.

'What Ed lacked in couth, he made up for in pure anger,' George reflects. 'It was the first time I ever thought of doing something else with my life. When I quit, I thought I'd be fired for good. But the minute I stood up to this guy, who was a jerk, things changed. Actors always come from a place of fear that they're never going to work again in this town. Like there's this little club where they sit around and say, "You know this guy Clooney? Let's never hire him again." The truth is the opposite. Suddenly, I could make balky decisions, take falls.'

Knights of the Kitchen Table was not picked up but at least it was a public statement that George Clooney was still a player, despite the exaggerated rumours of his commercial demise. And there was always another pilot around the corner. *Rewrite for Murder*, about a prim television-mystery writer (*Mork and Mindy's* Pam Dawber) and her love-hate relationship with a new blood colleague, also came and went in 1991. There were even a couple of auditions for major-budget motion pictures that year.

Between them, Francis Ford Coppola and Quentin Tarantino have seen and done most things in the film industry. Neither, though, had ever seen anyone read for them quite as badly as George Clooney did in 1991. For a part in *Bram Stoker's Dracula*, George unfathomably rediscovered his roots and read like a Kentucky hick: 'This goddamn Dracula thing's comin' in here, comin' down this here slide and blowin' up like a ball-a-fire!' In fact, he was so appalling that Coppola called George's agent and asked if there was something mentally wrong with him. At least Tarantino kept his own counsel. George was no better when auditioning for *Reservoir Dogs*, despite the fact that the young auteur had actually requested he try out.

'Quentin had seen some horrible movie that I had done and he liked me,' he says. 'So I was walking into that audition from a good place. But I did a really horrible, horrible audition. I remember walking out and saying to myself, "Well, I blew that."

'I read for the Michael Madsen dancing-around scene. I probably would have been horrible and I thought he was so great in it. It's the best thing I ever saw Michael do.' When they finally worked together years later on *ER* and *From Dusk Till Dawn*, Tarantino would remind George on a daily basis of just how much he blew it by.

Professional disappointments George could cope with. Personal ones were harder to deal with. In 1990 he was rocked by the death of his Uncle George. The man who had taught him about humour and encouraged him to pursue his acting desires had died of lung cancer. George was at his side when the end came. Uncle George had had it all: he'd dated Miss America, been decorated for his war exploits and built a career on radio, but his last words summed up his life: 'What a waste.' It was like seeing Joshua Logan all over again. Uncle George had never married, he had been an alcoholic and unreliable, but he was good fun, charming and handsome. 'He was a guy who never lived up to his potential, but he could still walk into a room and light it up,' his young namesake says. 'He was the guy you wanted to teach you how to throw a baseball when you were little, the guy who could captivate you with a story and teach you some sort of moral. He was everything you'd want from a man except success.'

Shaken by the comparisons, George declared at that moment that he would double his efforts to eke out opportunities. 'In my world, meanwhile, everything seemed insurmountable,' he recalls. 'But I went home and thought, "Let's change things. It's time." I didn't want to wake up at 65 and say, "What a waste." '

One of the things he changed was his marriage. After less than a year, it was clear that George and Talia were not destined for the happy-ever-after ending. If George had been too immature to cope at 23, he was no better equipped five years later. 'I was 28, and in Kentucky, when you get to be that age, you're supposed to get married,' he says. In hindsight it is obvious that he wed Talia on the rebound from Kelly; it is also obvious that whatever they had – and had ended – in 1984 should have been left alone. Furthermore, now in his late twenties it was obvious that George did not have the capacity for a long-term relationship. He wanted to be a 'guy' but suddenly he was behaving like a teenage boy. The problems he was having on the *Baby Talk* set did not help. Problems at work became problems at home. Suddenly there were better things to be doing than going home to his own house.

'George spent more time with his friends than with me during our marriage,' Talia says. It is a fair point. Speaking to *Playboy* in 2000, George revealed how he felt 'sort of cornered' by marriage. Once the initial thrill had worn off, he was left with a feeling of claustrophobia. 'George is not the sort of person to play by other people's rules,' Richard Kind explains. 'And marriage is all about that.'

Although not mature enough to do anything about it at the time, years later he is grown up sufficiently to take the blame. 'I probably – definitely – wasn't someone who should have been married at that point,' he admits. 'I just don't feel like I gave Talia a fair shot.' His 'Kentucky wedding' ideal did not help. 'I had this image of marriage and when ours didn't exactly fit that image, I thought it didn't work,' he says. 'I wasn't very bright about it. We had to reconstruct our marriage a little bit, and I wasn't willing to do that. I walked away. I could have been scared. Maybe I wasn't ready to be married.

'I married a terrific girl, a great lady, and it didn't work out. I don't take full responsibility for that but when things started to go wrong I wasn't willing to try and fix them. I just wanted to chuck the whole thing. The biggest part of why the marriage didn't work was my fault.'

The Boys are less critical of their buddy. 'I think he really made an effort in his first marriage, and it really hurt him that it didn't work out,' Matt Adler says. 'And he'll tell you, he wasn't very good at being a husband.' Richard Kind agrees. 'I don't think when he divorced Talia he divorced the woman,' he insists. 'He divorced his "wife". It may have been a lifestyle that didn't jibe with him.'

After a period of estrangement, the couple divorced in 1992. Coming on top of everything else, having to watch his private business dragged through the courts did not sit well with George. 'I would say to Talia, "You tell me how much. What you think is fair. I won't negotiate,"' he says. 'Instead, I paid $80,000 in lawyers' fees and that makes me angry.'

The net result was one desperately unhappy and poor divorcee. Once the cheques had been cashed, he was effectively homeless. But at least he had The Boys. 'I lived at Richard's place for nine months in his spare bedroom,' George recalls. 'I was stone-broke, and Grant Heslov, who's an actor as well, he'd take me to dinner and pay for everything. He took care of me.'

Clarity often comes from adversity and George used his time of suffering to concretise two life-shaping resolutions. One was that he would never again marry. He just wasn't cut out for it: he was too young, too selfish, too focused on his career. All these reasons flitted through his mind. The second was that while work would be his first love, his friends, The Boys, would be next on the list. Woe betide any woman who thought she could come between them.

There was still space for family. As distraught as Nick and Nina were about George's divorce (they were both very fond of Talia), their loyalties lay with their son. After a year of emotional upheaval, George could do with a little pepping up, Nick figured. And that Christmas he knew just the thing to do it.

'George always coveted my 59 Corvette, which I bought to court my wife,' Nick recalls. 'He always wanted to drive it, and I was reluctant to let him. I thought he might hurt himself or someone else, so it was a bone of contention throughout his adolescent years. Then in 1992, when things were not going well for him, I had the car refurbished and sent out to California. George said it was the best Christmas he ever had – and he had thought it was going to be the worst. He still drives it once a week – it's his connection to family and home. He calls it the gift that keeps on taking – he's getting it repaired all the time. It probably cost him four times what I paid for it.'

Try as he might to dedicate his life to guy pursuits with his male pals, George was still seen in casting land as the first-choice hunk for a number of girl projects. That's how he found himself on a show about four women called *Sisters*. To be fair, it was his choice. Warner Bros had him on a contract since 1990 so they were committed to finding him a show. He was presented with *Café Americain* and *Sisters*. He chose the latter on the understanding that other projects would be developed for him.

By now George was thinking more about his career than ever before, and not just his big-screen aspirations. 'I decided to stop thinking of myself as a movie actor working temporarily in TV and just try to do better TV,' he says. 'And at that moment, everything changed.' Things started going for him. Where *Café Americain* was canned eight weeks into its life, *Sisters* was a hit. And so was he.

George joined the show during its fourth season, in an episode called 'The Land of the Lost Children'. He stayed for a year and left in the third episode of season five, 'I Only Have Eyes For You'. His character, Detective James Falconer, was popular from the start, especially in his interaction with Sela Ward's character, Teddy. Fan mail to the show had always been from female fans, but generally identifying with the cast for various similarities with their own lives. When George arrived, there was only one topic people wanted to discuss. The mail rooms at *Roseanne*, *Baby Talk* and *Facts of Life* had seen it before, although not on this scale. Something about this guy Clooney connected with female fans.

A certain amount of pride had to be swallowed for George to accept that maybe his film career was on hold, but *Sisters* provided him with good arguments – about forty thousand of them every episode, in fact. But still he had to fight to allow his character any masculinity at times. 'This was a show for women,' he explains. 'And it was a great show. But there were times where I had to go back to the writers and explain to them, "Uh, straight guys don't talk like this."' For a real 'guy's guy', these details matter, but in truth the whole period was a good one for George and the money certainly helped.

Sisters marked the biggest success of George's career to date and he stayed with the show from 1993 to 1994. Although not exactly to his taste, its overriding constituent factor was quality, which was more than could be said of some of the work he had undertaken just before signing the contract. Another film was released in 1992 and again it went straight to video, again begging the question, why? (Considering he apparently turned down an audition for *Guarding Tess* in 1994 because the part was not significant enough, this is a dubious call at best.) Called *Unbecoming Age* (and later *The Magic Bubble*), it was the story of a man refusing to grow up. One can see why the eternal playboy George was attracted to it, but Alfredo and Deborah Ringel's production was cumbersome and uninspired. 'The spirit is winning but the inspiration is missing,' as *Variety* put it. As Mac, George offered little relief.

Another film, *The Harvest*, released in 1993, went equally unloved despite George's pre-*Priscilla Queen of the Desert*'s turn as a lip-synching transvestite. He was talked into the part once again by cousin Miguel, who played a writer involved in a kidneys-for-cash scandal in Mexico. Mrs Ferrer, Leilani Sarelle, plays the vamp interest, but she is given a close run by George who, in blonde wig, full make-up, false breasts and mini-skirt, camps his way through a playback of Belinda Carlisle's 'Heaven is a Place on Earth'.

George also tried his hand at another crime series called *Bodies of Evidence* in 1992, once again running an elite branch of law enforcement, as in *Sunset Beat*. And like *Sunset Beat*, it was a short-lived project. A year later, in 1993, he played Kevin Shea in a made-for-TV movie called *Without Warning: Terror in the Towers*, an eerily prescient tale in hindsight. The other project of note at this time was a role in the pilot of a show called *The Building*, produced by and starring his good friend Bonnie Hunt. Despite excellent reviews, audience figures were not great and the show died prematurely. But it got people thinking, and in hindsight one can see why. The building of the title was to be found in Chicago, where George's character arrives in town for a medical conference, having left his girlfriend Hunt there a year or two earlier. A doctor abandons his Chicago hospital and girlfriend for a new life? Sound familiar?

7. THIS IS NO PLACE FOR A PAEDIATRICIAN

When George Clooney's marriage to Talia Balsam fell apart in 1992, he turned to Grant Heslov, one of The Boys, for moral and financial support. Two years later and it was time to pay back the favour. In 1994, Heslov split up from his fiancée and George was there for him in his own inimitable style. Out came the Winnebago and off they went to play golf across every state line in America.

'We'd stop at each state line on the freeway and tee up a golf ball into the next state,' George says. 'It was just an idea. You know, let's go state to state, playing through the problem, so to speak.'

Typical big-hearted gesture. Typical George. At 33 he could certainly afford it financially and time-wise. Although it bugged him as a soubriquet, being 'the highest-paid unknown in Hollywood' had its compensations. As they drove east from LA, George did his best to distract his hurting friend. He also took the time to analyse where his own career was going. He had been in Hollywood for twelve years. In that time he had made fifteen pilots, most of which were not picked up, filmed eight forgettable films and played in four popular sitcoms, always leaving before he could become typecast. It was lucrative work but eye-candy comedy was not what he had set out to do.

As the golfing itinerants hacked their way through Arizona, George's cell phone rang. Heslov could tell from his friend's reaction that the news was big – George was driving, after all. Turning to Heslov, a stunned George simply said, 'I just got a career.'

George's star had been rising for a number of years although the hit that he hoped for had yet to materialise. 'I was making a living in an industry where 95 per cent are unemployed,' he says phlegmatically. 'So if you're making a living at all you're doing well.' Each new project brought the same assurances. 'This'll be the one, George.' But he was playing a long-ball game. More importantly, so were Warner Bros. The studio had had George under contract since 1990, convinced that if they could find the right vehicle they would have a major star on their hands. 'He's the greatest guy in the world,' says Leslie Moonves, former president of Warner Bros Television and current president of CBS Entertainment. 'The minute he walked into my office at Warner Bros we clicked, and I knew he was going to be a big star. There is, with George, this match of personality and talent. A lot of times you get one or the other, not both. With George, what you see on-screen is what you see off-screen.'

Warners had produced *Sisters* for NBC, which did nothing to dampen their expectations for their protégé. George had originally taken the role while Warners workshopped other vehicles for him. In summer 1994, Moonves and Co. came up with something a little meatier for their boy.

'I was doing *Sisters* on a week-to-week basis,' George says. 'It was basically paying off my holding deal while I was waiting for a project that was being developed for me. Then this script, out of the blue, came up, and one of the casting directors snuck it to me. I read it and called up the executive producer, and said, "I'm the guy for this job."'

The show being developed specifically for George's benefit was a cop series called *Golden Gate* where he would be undisputed top dog and not, as he felt on *Roseanne*, 'seventh banana on the number-one show'. The covert script he fell in love with, however, was for an ensemble-cast medical drama called *ER*. Placing strength of writing over vanity, George wanted *ER*. Badly.

The idea for *ER* had been alive for almost as long as George. In 1970, former medical student Michael Crichton had published *Five Patients*, a factual book based on his years as a trainee doctor in the emergency room at Massachusetts General Hospital. As Crichton went on to publish a series of science fiction novels as himself and, under the pseudonym 'Jeffrey Hudson' – never a name likely to set the publishing world alight – his medical career took a backseat to full-time authoring and film writing. In 1974, after a string of big-money pictures like *The Andromeda Strain*, *Westworld* and *Coma* had been made from his books, Crichton set about transforming *Five Patients* into a screenplay.

Even with his phenomenal track-record of mixing human drama with near-future science fact, Crichton had trouble selling *EW* (Emergency Ward), as it was now known, to the studios. The screenplay's structure was innovative to the point of intimidation as far as bosses were concerned. Multiple storylines, a large cast and a baffling dose of medical jargon were not what Hollywood wanted. Throw in uncompromising quick-fire scene changes more suited to 1990s pop videos than the average 1970s picture and the studios were running for cover.

'The screenplay was very unusual,' Crichton admits. 'It was very focused on the doctors not the patients – the patients came and went. People yelled paragraphs of drug dosages at each other. It was very technical, almost a quasi-documentary.'

Fast-forward fifteen years and enter a man whom Crichton had befriended as an aspiring director in the early 1970s. Steven Spielberg had already earned the tag 'director of his generation' by the time he decided, in 1989, to buy the rights to the admirable Crichton's script (now evolved into *ER*). *ET*, *Indiana Jones*, *Duel* and *Jaws* had established Spielberg as a clever and commercially-attuned film-maker, but now he wanted something earthier to get his teeth into, something more believable.

That was the plan, anyway. Unfortunately (for the project), during script meetings Crichton let slip details of his next novel. The words 'DNA', 'theme park', 'cloning' and 'dinosaurs' were all Spielberg needed to jettison thoughts of any other project. So much for more believable.

While Spielberg busied himself with *Jurassic Park*, *Hook* and *Schindler's List*, the treatment for *ER* lay dormant and unloved in the ideas tray at his Amblin production company. In October 1993, it came to the attention of Tony Thomopoulos, president of Amblin's television arm. He had one question: why is this perfect TV script in the film pile?

Michael Crichton was not convinced. The same problems that made so many movie heads think the script was unfilmable would be exacerbated in the puritan and conservative world of American TV. No network would cope with its disjointed and frenetic pace. Thomopoulos had this one covered. He introduced to the project John Wells, successful producer of the challenging Vietnam drama *China Beach*. If anyone could translate Crichton's vision into palatable TV while staying honest to the writer's intentions, it was Wells.

Production duties for the pilot were to be shared between Amblin, Warner Bros and Crichton's Constant Productions. Finances in place, a specialist pilot director was sought. With a track record of eleven out of thirteen pilots being picked up, including *China Beach*, *The Equaliser* and *The A-Team*, Wells wanted Rod Holcomb to make sense of the mammoth 157-page preliminary script. With him on board the next stop was the cast.

From the moment George Clooney had been slipped the advance copy of the script, he wanted in. He had been in enough ignored pilots to know not to get his hopes up, but even if this one did not take off, just being involved would be a boost to his résumé. 'I wanted to do it because it was Spielberg, because it was Michael Crichton,' he says. 'Up to this point, you have to remember, my career had not really been known for doing great television. So I needed some camouflage, and a two-hour movie of the week that a lot of people would see, written by Michael Crichton and produced by Steven Spielberg, would make a lot of difference. That's a coup for an actor coming from the place I was coming from, which was *Return of the Killer Tomatoes*.'

No sooner did he hear that the pilot had been green-lighted than George was on the phone to John Wells begging for a try-out. What he did not know was that he was high on the producer's list anyway because of his strong Warner connections.

'As soon as the show got a pick-up, George called me and said, "Doug Ross is my part," ' Wells recalls. Rod Holcomb was hired on a Thursday and George read the next day. 'He was terrific. Rod gave him a couple of adjustments which he did beautifully and when he walked out of the room I said, "Boy, he's great" and we hired him right away.'

Within Warners, there was surprise that George had favoured this ensemble role rather than his own show. 'George went in to John Wells and sold himself,' Les Moonves recalls. 'I give him a lot of credit because he saw that being one of six or seven in a great show was better than being the star of a good show.'

George occasionally claims he originally read for the Mark Greene part (Dr Ross is certainly not the star of the pilot) but that went to ex *Top Gun* actor Anthony Edwards who was felt to have a better affinity with the morally defined resident surgeon. Paediatrician Doug Ross, on the other hand, makes his entrance in *ER* requiring treatment for self-inflicted inebriation, he hits on a young female trainee and tries to get Greene to admit to adultery. Of the two parts, one has Clooney written through its core like 'Blackpool' through a stick of seaside rock.

Three of the four other main characters were easily cast. Sherry Stringfield had impressed on *NYPD Blue* and was poached to play

Dr Susan Lewis. Noah Wyle joined as wet-behind-the-ears trainee John Carter and Julianna Margulies was secured as Nurse Carol Hathaway. Peter Benton's part remained uncast until shooting had begun, when Eriq La Salle finally became free to audition. He walked it. Two days later he was filmed giving rabbit-in-the-headlights protégé Carter the grand tour of the department, a complicated-enough scene even without the short notice. As an omen, getting this shoot right offered favourable portents for the rest of the show. With another 85 speaking parts to cast and manage, John Wells and his team needed every assistance they could get.

Remaining true to Michael Crichton's original script, the ER pilot tells of a day in the life of a Chicago hospital emergency room. Entitled '24 Hours', the day it chooses to focus on is 17 March 1994. Twenty-eight years to the day after making his TV debut dressed as a St Patrick's Day leprechaun, George Clooney was taking the biggest step forward of his career.

As Crichton intended, the speedy interaction of a vast array of characters is the dominant aspect of the programme. The test episode is bookmarked by Dr Greene trying to catch a few minutes' sleep in an empty ward bed before his next eighteen-hour shift. But in between there are the beginnings, middles or ends of twenty plot lines. A lot of the story centres on the staff themselves: hints at a past relationship between Clooney's Dr Ross and Nurse Hathaway; suggestions of a dalliance between Greene and Susan Lewis; Benton's 'resident' antagonism towards the more qualified surgeons upstairs; the strain on Greene's marriage caused by his long shifts; his attempts to find a lucrative job at a private hospital; Dr Ross's drink problem; his proclivity towards hitting on cute trainee doctors ('I'm just being friendly'; 'I've got enough friends'); new boy Carter's naivety in all practical areas; Benson's implied God complex and intolerance of his new charge; Dr Greene's emotional control of the ward – 'You set the tone,' he is told by his boss, played by William H Macy. Oh, and a suicide attempt by one of the six main characters.

And that is before any patients enter the building. A major part of Crichton's 1974 screenplay, a local disaster involving a collapsing building, is ER's first emergency. In a *tour de force* of snappy camera angles, switched emphasis and multiple centres of focus, Rod Holcomb pulls off an invigorating sequence involving a dozen bodies arriving, being assigned rooms and medics and getting treatment. It is pacy, breathtaking stuff which sets the standard for the show. Busy, noisy, bloody, fast.

And true to life, according to John Wells. 'The life of a resident consists of tremendous boredom followed by bursts of extraordinary adrenaline,' he says. 'Residents face tremendous traumatic injuries. The rhythm is quick, with little time for each patient. You never know when someone will come through the door and how many minutes you have to treat him. The residents of ER are flawed but real. Each show is about how the resident makes it through the day. During the course of one day the resident will see 28 patients. They work long hours and their job can be overwhelming.'

For confirmation of this, George and the cast visited real downtown Chicago hospitals for a taste of what really goes on in what Wells calls 'the front line' of medicine. 'When we were getting ready to do the series, we spent some time in hospitals,' the actor says. 'What you find is it's a war zone in some of those inner-city places. A good two-thirds of the people who were coming in were handcuffed to the gurneys or were armed guards with twelve-year-old kids shot to pieces.'

It seems only fitting that capturing the essence of those real-life horrors in an entertainment show requires a greater stretch than most acting jobs, even if it is carried out in the comfort of the artificial Cook County set on the Warner Bros lot rather than in the hotbed of Chicago. 'It's a very tough show to do,' George says, 'because there are so many things you're doing. You're learning a dialogue – you're learning Latin basically – you also have to work a choreography out where you have to be a doctor, and you have to do the physical things.

'We have to perform medical procedures as if we were professionals, and we have to do that with fifty extras flying through on a Steadicam shot with no cuts, saying 'Super ventricular tachyarrhythmia' without screwing up.'

In the show's pilot, apart from a drunken rendition of 'Danny Boy' at the start, George's child specialist doctor flits in and out of the action, hitting on students, goading colleagues about their extra-marital inclinations and almost getting in the way during the all-hands-to-the-pumps mass-casualty entrance. As an elderly patient vomits blood over his night-on-the-tiles tie, he retreats saying, 'This is no place for a paediatrician.' A conversation between two orderlies encapsulates his character: 'He's very handsome.' 'He knows it.'

If the carousing, womanising, gossiping Dr Ross seems immature among his more earnest and similarly aged colleagues, he is every bit the conscientious adult with his own patients, the ones who cannot answer for themselves, the ones who need him. In the pilot's most chilling sequence, a terrified babysitter brings her tiny, battered charge to Ross's attention. The child has been systematically abused by its mother. As he confronts the affronted parent with threats of legal action, Dr Ross is appalled to learn that she is a lawyer. Disgusted with her and, we sense for a second, with all adults, he storms from the room. In one of the episode's longest scenes, George Clooney delivers the performance of his life, delivering the lines that blew John Wells away at his audition.

Despite being physically a largely peripheral figure in the scene-setting pilot, George Clooney's character hangs hauntingly over the show's largest plot line, emphasising his pivotal role in the show even when he is not on screen. When Nurse Hathaway is rushed into the ER having taken a drugs overdose, her recent break-up from Doug Ross is thought to have pushed her over the edge. As Anthony Edwards' Dr Greene battles valiantly to save Hathaway, it is Dr Ross engaging viewers' minds. What's the history? Why did she do it? What did he do to her? What's he really like? By the end of '24 Hours', Dr Greene may have won in terms of screen time, but Dr Ross is already confirmed as the spirit of the show. Advantage Clooney.

George had had too many knock-backs after strong pilots to think that this one would be plain sailing, even with Spielberg and Crichton on board. While NBC took the episode over the traditional assault-course of focus groups, committees and infernal numbers meetings, its star decided his nerves would be better served out of town distracting broken-hearted buddy Grant Heslov.

George had every reason to worry. The number crunchers at NBC could not see *ER* as a hit. It did not have the right profile. Most of the top shows in the 1993–4 season were half-hour comedies: *Seinfeld*, *Frasier*, *Home Improvement*, *Roseanne*, *Grace Under Fire*, *These Friends of Mine* and *Coach*. *ER* was one hour of relentless, challenging drama with the occasional laugh. Of the non-comedies doing well, each was traditionally structured: one or two, at the most three, story lines reaching a conclusion in one episode. *ER* had more than twenty plots, some resolved, some postponed, some never to be heard or seen again. Who would watch a show like this?

The members of the focus groups for a start. The lucky guinea-pig audiences returned one of the most positive verdicts in NBC's history. 'The powers that be at the time, even after they saw the pilot, thought it was far too complicated, because there were fifty story lines and they weren't tied up,' George says. 'They thought this was too complicated for the normal American citizen and that audiences wouldn't catch up. Then they tested it and it tested through the roof. And they thought, well maybe we were wrong. You look back at the television shows that have been successful over the years, *Cheers* and *Seinfeld* and *M*A*S*H*, and they are all very smart television shows, and so is *ER*. It just needs to be entertaining.'

Added to the fact that the controversial *NYPD Blue* and *Homicide: Life on the Streets* were also picking up viewers (the shows ranked eighteen and nineteen in the season's top twenty), NBC was won around. *ER* was go. And George Clooney, as he told Grant, had a career.

The same, sadly, could not be said for Julianna Margulies. Her character, Carol Hathaway, had been seen dying in the pilot; she ostensibly had no further part to play in the series except as a haunting figure in Dr Ross's future. Ever aware of his character's possibilities, George viewed the loss of Hathaway as a major blow to Doug Ross's chances of developing. George being George, he decided to do something about it. George being George, he was able to. Using a decade's worth of experience of NBC procedure (*Facts of Life* had been his first show on the network), he went straight to the top. 'I went to New York to talk to Don Ohlmeyer, the West Coast president, and Warren Littlefield, the head of entertainment,' George explains. 'I said, "It's too bad Julianna dies." In typical network fashion they then told me, "She's not necessarily dead." '

For the first and only time in *ER*'s history, writer Michael Crichton opted to put his entertainment sensibilities ahead of his medical responsibilities and Carol Hathaway miraculously recovered from her once-fatal suicide. George had the pleasure of telling Margulies herself. 'He called me just in time,' she says. 'I was just about to cut my hair, dye it red and straighten it for another part.'

The inaugural St Patrick's Day episode of *ER* was broadcast on Monday 19 September 1994. The official first episode went out later that week in NBC's traditionally prime spot, ten o'clock on Thursday, previously the domain of ratings giants *Hill Street Blues* and *LA Law*. From near-cancellation to cornerstone of the network's broadcasting strategy, this bold scheduling move announced *ER* as a contender, the one to beat.

Over 26 episodes in its first season, *ER* established itself as the show that took chances. Not only was its format revolutionary, but its off-hand, de-sensationalised treatment of illness was unlike anything seen since *M*A*S*H*.

As much as anything, the large ensemble cast gave the writers the chance to power through hundreds of storylines without any one actor burning out. Dr Ross got his share of juicy plots, mixing business with pleasure. In 'Into That Good Night' he steps in when a girl's family can't afford to cover her medication. In 'Long Day's Journey' he is up to his gills in a suicide, a child with cancer, parent abuse and a teenage prostitute with AIDS. By contrast, in 'Another Perfect Day' he kisses Nurse Hathaway even though she is about to move in with a new boyfriend. Things get more complicated in 'Sleepless in Chicago' when he invites Diane to dinner and Hathaway pays a visit. With the show's rapid-fire scene changes, viewers had to watch every episode in case they missed a titbit of storyline that would be crucial the following week. 'Sheer energy carries the show,' raved *Variety*.

Actually, in its review of the first episode of *ER*, *Variety* also looked at another medical drama set in Chicago. What are the odds on that happening? Former Steven Bochco apprentice David E Kelley had moved on to his own award-winning *Picket Fences* and was now presenting CBS with a programme revolving around the daily traumas of a Chicago hospital. Unlike *ER*, his *Chicago Hope* leant on a strong 'name' cast: Mandy Patinkin, Hector Elizondo, Adam Arkin and EG Marshall were big-show veterans. It also focused more on top-of-their-profession surgeons than the more junior Emergency Room residents, using fewer plot lines in the process. But otherwise the similarities were enormously coincidental, from both shows being filmed in LA (apart from outside Chicago shots), even down to Arkin sharing an uncanny physical likeness to rival doc Doug Ross. 'Both shows are riveting, superior TV fare,' *Variety* was forced to concede. But others would not sit on the fence. When CBS announced that *Hope* would go head to head with *ER* on Thursday evenings, it was a declaration of intent. There could only be one winner.

By the end of the first season, the name of that winner was clear. *ER* was in the top three shows of the year. *Chicago Hope* did not make the top twenty and the writing was on its pristine walls. By contrast, after less than a dozen episodes in series one, NBC commissioned another series. *ER* was going to run and run, along with George Clooney's career.

8. I ALREADY HAD A WIFE

Anthony Edwards' Dr Greene may have 'set the tone' in the pilot's Emergency Room, but off-screen the Warner Bros set was strictly George's domain. He had spent so many years there either working on bad shows or under contract that he was virtually one of the fixtures. He knew the names – first and last – of every security guard, secretary, executive or agent who passed through the studio gates and he was always available for a chat.

When the *ER* cast first assembled, George took it upon himself to ease everyone into the environment in his own way, either through on-set basketball bonding sessions or avuncular advice. Just as he had shaped co-star Margulies' career, he also gave novitiate Noah Wyle crucial tips on schmoozing and being seen with the right people. George was no brown-noser – as his common touch and stance against bully bosses had proved. But he knew how to play the game. As he says, 'When you've failed enough, you learn how to be good at the business. I'm probably better at the business side than I am at acting.'

George goes out of his way to make friends, it is a natural part of who he is. One example of his camaraderie-building is legendary. Within weeks of *ER* being signed, he instigated a movement to abolish the 'them-and-us' lunch arrangements at Warners. If it was good enough for the talent, it was good enough for the crew. How do you get the best out of people if you treat them like inferiors? Sensible, knowing, but most of all just plain decent manners.

On another occasion, when an *ER* carpenter was killed in a motorcycle accident, he helped set up a fund for the man's three-year-old daughter. He also stepped in when the show's Conni Marie Brazelton got into car trouble: 'One time they towed my car off the set, and I was crying,' she says. 'George just came up and embraced me, saying, "Here's the money to get it back. Do this, do that." '

When he was not playing big brother to the cast and crew, George could be relied on to keep the mood on the set light. They were not real doctors, after all. No one was really dying. During rehearsals he would play football with his doll 'patients', use the IV stand as a skateboard or use one of the electronic defibrillators as a telephone. Then there were the funny voices, the gurning faces off-camera while others were filming and, his *pièce de résistance*, the whoopee cushion. Many a scene had to be reshot as soon as a character sat on one of George's noisy little toys, most of them ending up on the show's Christmas 'bloopers' tape, often at great expense. He is unrepentant. 'Hey, funny's funny,' he insists. 'You can't put a price on it.' NBC's accountants might disagree. Every reshoot after one of his jokes cost a minimum of $5,000.

George is a naturally 'up' character, hence the constant clowning. With such a large staff on the set, there were occasionally times when his joking coincided with a sense of humour failure in one of his colleagues. He normally won them round, though. 'There are times when you just want to say, "George, take the blue pill," ' Julianna Margulies admits. 'But every now and then, to look over and see him with a urine container on his head, just makes you feel a little better about your work.'

As self-established daddy – or uncle – of the set, George was the natural first choice for the show's producers to front their publicity campaign in the early days. Magazine interviews, talk-show spots and public appearances were all crucial tools in whipping up interest in what was an expensive and ambitious show. Without doubt, the producers backed the right man. Whether it was Leno, Letterman, Oprah or Barbara Walters, George had the live audience, and the host, in the palm of his hand from the moment he approached the guest chair. If he had rehearsed the anecdotes, you would never tell. His natural charisma, his decade of experience on various comedy shows and his self-deprecating demeanour off-screen came flooding out through every appearance. As Les Moonves says, because George never pretends to be someone he is not, he has nothing to fear from being himself.

Viewers in their millions agreed and George's rising stock went index-linked with that of the show. At the end of the first season, *ER* was America's number-two programme, commanding $1 million in advertising per episode (by comparison *Chicago Hope* was struggling to attract half that), and also securing critical success via an Emmy nomination for Best Drama. At the same time, George Clooney was dubbed 'TV's Hot Doc!' by *TV Guide* and named as one of the 'Fifty Most Beautiful People in the World' by *People* magazine. He also had his own Emmy nomination for Best Actor (as did Anthony Edwards), he was earning $42,000 a week and NBC were receiving up to ten-thousand fan letters for him a month. In May 1995, thirteen years after arriving in Hollywood, he had made it.

'I love that no one saw him coming,' Brad Pitt says of the man he beat to the part in *Thelma & Louise*. 'He wallowed around for ten years on some absolute crap shows, which he'll be the first person to tell you about, and then he hit on *ER*.'

Boy, did he hit. Fame affects different people different ways and George had seen the best and worst of it within his own family. He was determined not to let success destroy who he was. To a certain extent, it was not his choice. 'You want to know what one of George's secrets is?' his friend Richard Kind reveals. 'He started out when he was 21, when he came to LA. When did he hit great fame? At age 33. Well, that's twelve years of struggling.'

George is the first to concur. More than a decade of rejection would keep anyone's feet on the ground, though the temptation was there. 'It's very easy to sit in a room at 23 and have everyone go, "You're the greatest," and believe it,' he says. 'Which I think I did for a minute, to be honest. I thought I was pretty happening because I had good TV hair.'

George has the utmost respect for *ER* colleague Noah Wyle, who was forced into the spotlight at 23. 'He's ten years younger than me,' George says. 'He's more successful than I was at his age, but he handles it with this great maturity that I don't think I would have had. I think I would've believed some of the hype.

'It's easier getting older, you calm down, you realise that fame isn't really about you. I was the same actor on television series like *Sisters* and *Sunset Beat* and horrible shows as I was on *ER*.

'I didn't get famous until I was 33,' he continues, 'so I had the opportunity to screw up a lot business-wise without really damaging anything. I learned about acting before I got famous. It doesn't make you a great actor, but it puts you in a position of understanding when you're a bad actor, and trying to avoid that.'

There were other things he was keen to avoid. By the time he found fame with *ER*, George was well into a financial game plan that he had formulated as a youth. 'We didn't grow up in trailers, although we did move around when the rent was due,' he recalls with some bitterness. 'The whole thing is about creating a foundation so you can't fall from here all the way down, so that as things start to fall, you have this great foundation of people and things. You don't spend your money like it's gonna keep coming in. You pay off your house.'

In 1995, he did just that. As soon as George realised that *ER* was a ratings stayer, he invested in a sprawling home in the Hollywood Hills, which once belonged to Stevie Nicks and had previously been rented by rapper Vanilla Ice. For a man not given to ostentatious gestures, the acquisition of an eight-bedroom, two-storey home raised eyebrows. It needn't have done. There was a good reason for his home needing so many rooms; seven reasons, in fact.

From the moment that George first landed, rootless, in LA back in 1982 he had been making friends. To this day, his closest relationships are those forged in the early years before he was famous. These are The Boys, seven men who keep him in a steady supply of bad jokes and reality checks. They are: Ben Weiss, a close friend of Miguel Ferrer's, who met George the day he pitched up at Rosemary's house and gave him the guided tour of Hollywood; Thom Mathews was the guy who lent George his closet as a base, for which George has said 'because of that, Thom will always be my best friend'; Grant Heslov gave George $100 in 1982 to pay for his first promotional head shots and helped him out financially following his divorce; Richard Kind, co-star on *The Bennett Brothers*, gave George a bed for nine months after the break-up from Talia. George met Matt Adler on a Hollywood basketball court in 1986. Actor Tommy Hinkley and stylist Waldo Sanchez complete the group.

'Probably the one thing I'm most proud of in my life is how hard I've worked at keeping everybody around,' George says. 'It can get tricky. Because when you start to get famous, people start to surround you and tell you how great you are; you get this whole crew of friends you don't know, and they're suddenly your best friends.

'But you have to keep the other people close, and that's work. So we talk to each other at some point every day. It's not like some sick, fucked-up thing. It's just like, "Hey, man, what's up?" It can be fucked-up if that's your obsession. But it's just friendship, The Boys. What it is is the greatest support group ever. That's what it's about when it all comes crashing down.'

Like George, The Boys mostly work in the entertainment business so they all understand the vicissitudes of each other's careers. More importantly, they operate as a unit, offering emotional and financial strength and generally hanging out together. Most Sundays they play basketball, ride bikes and have a barbecue – or 'taco-fest' – at George's house, with partners and children in tow. They also play golf and vacation together. And when the chips are down, they hide out at each other's houses. George had been in need of The Boys' hospitality more than once. Now his new house meant he could repay the debt as and when – all at the same time if necessary. 'We've all crashed on each other's couches over break-ups,' he says. 'The great thing is, we're all supportive of each other.'

Actor Matt Adler was the first to check in at Casa de Clooney. 'George did me a tremendous favour,' he says. 'I didn't know what I was going to do or where I was going to live, and George said, "I just bought this house, come live with me." '

Batman director Joel Schumacher sums the place up. 'That house is like a sitcom,' he laughs. 'He has these buddies who have recently gotten divorced, and they're all living there. George is like everybody's older brother. I'm 57, but if I was in trouble I'd go see George.'

Where his friends are concerned, there is no need to say you are in trouble. George would know. He recalls the occasion when Richard Kind's father died of a heart attack. Kind called to say he was going to Trenton for the funeral and that he was OK. George knew he wasn't. He rallied the troops, who were all working at the time, chartered a private jet and off they went. 'We sat in the back of the synagogue and Richard was in front with his back to us,' George relates. 'When he got up and started to talk about his dad, he saw us and started sobbing. He said, "I'm sorry, but I just saw my best friends back there." There was this amazing feeling that every one of these guys had dropped everything just to be there. That's what it's like. People like that keep you sane.'

'He really, really wants to be Frank Sinatra,' his old friend Bonnie Hunt, of *The Building* fame, says. 'He's the guy who takes care of everything, leads the pack, includes all the guys in his success. Success would be horrible for him without his friends around.'

The Boys are not just there for the bad times, of course. Apart from keeping George sane while the rest of the world itches to get a piece of him, they are all targets for his sense of humour. Richard Kind seems to be the particular butt of George's jokes – quite literally.

A framed picture inside Casa de Clooney shows a naked Kind screaming in pain with George creasing up behind him. It was taken during one of The Boys' Sunday get-togethers at George's. Kind was having a massage from one of the cute masseuses hired in for the occasion when George managed to step in and take over without his friend noticing. Banking on Kind not resisting 'her' wandering caresses, he edged the towel down and set to work on Kind's backside and inner thigh. As Kind slipped into a pleasured reverie, George gave his ass the biggest slap he could muster. The photo was taken at exactly that time.

On another occasion, there was a party at George's home. His friend Harry Hamlin left his camera by mistake. 'Hey, Richard,' George said to his luckless pal. 'Everyone's mooned into Harry's camera, now it's your turn, buddy.' As Kind duly obliged, George managed to get his friend's head in the picture along with everything else. A few day's later there was a call from Hamlin: 'Why the hell is there a picture of Richard Kind's ass on my camera?'

And finally in the litany of lavatory humour, there is the now classic (if you have ever seen any of George's US talk-show appearances) kitty litter jape. It's another ass story, of course, although not Kind's for once. When they lived together, George watched Kind look after his pet cat. After a while, George started to sneak into Kind's bathroom, where the cat's litter tray was kept and flush the day's mess down the toilet. He kept this up for about a week until Kind said, 'God, it's so weird. My cat hasn't taken a shit in forever.' The concerned parent, he took the cat to a vet who prescribed a laxative. Ben Weiss takes up the story. 'The poor cat is shitting and George is still clearing it up,' he says. 'And then finally George stood over the cat box and took a giant shit. Richard goes in there and says, "Oh my god! Kitty!" '

If being on the receiving end of his jokes is the downside, the upside of being George's friend is you get to share his success. What was the point of being a 'player' at Warner Bros if he didn't exert his influence every now and again? Viewers of the first instalment of ER will recall Dr Lewis breaking the news to a patient that he has cancer. It is a harrowing scene which contrasts sharply with the comic scenes either side. The actor informed that he has six months to live was Miguel Ferrer: payback for all those parts he had secured for cousin George.

It got better. Episode three featured an Alzheimer's patient wandering the corridors of the hospital, blissfully serenading all and sundry with numbers from the 40s and 50s. Playing Mary Kavanaugh was Miguel's mother, Rosemary Clooney. Another debt repaid as far as George was concerned, although Rosemary's character proved such a hit that she reappeared to deliver Christmas carols in the seasonal 'Gift' episode.

Tommy Hinkley and others would appear in due course.

That George had behind-the-scenes clout was never questioned. That his influence could extend beyond television, now that was a different story. Yet while he was providing showcasing opportunities for his relatives' talents, George was doing himself no disservice with other prospective employees. He had, as usual, a plan. And it involved Hollywood, where his heart still lay.

'When I was doing *Roseanne* with Laurie Metcalf, I'd watch her go off and do small parts in *Internal Affairs* and *JFK*,' he recalls, 'and I thought, "That's the perfect way to go, because eventually the TV series goes away." You need to fall back on something, and that's what my plan was.'

Of course, George had had his fingers burned by the big screen before. Just because he was suddenly in a hit TV show that he was proud of did not guarantee box-office appeal, or even decent parts. He only had to look across the networks to the plight of David Caruso for confirmation. Caruso had been the glue that held *NYPD Blue* together but he had succumbed spectacularly to the lure of movies and quit suddenly. In going, he burned his bridges with show producer Steven Bochco and, when his film career belly-flopped, he had nothing to fall back on.

Then there was the other possibility. George was on a water-tight five-year contract. There had been myriad occasions in the past when networks had refused to release actors for film parts. Most savagely Pierce Brosnan was handcuffed to his role as *Remington Steele* when the Bond producers came calling the first time. Tom Selleck was similarly forced to see out his run on cheesy beach-cop show *Magnum PI* before he could tackle such meaty roles as *Three Men and a Baby*. If the *ER* producers decided to play hardball, then George's movie resurrection was over before it had begun.

As he had done a year earlier, George put in a call to John Wells, executive producer. Wells is a practical man. He did not want to be obstructive for the sake of it, and since Dr Ross is only one of six main players and not the show's star, as was the case with Caruso, he gave his blessing. 'We have a large ensemble in which the work is evenly split,' he explains. 'If George is on a movie set Tuesday through Saturday, we can slot his stuff for Mondays, at least for a while. I think I'm more reasonable accommodating George because I was actually able to be more reasonable. George is not the central figure Caruso was for *NYPD Blue*.'

With the logistics out of the way, there was the small matter of finding a film, which was harder than it sounds. Although George was getting a script a day now that he was famous, he was conscious of the fact that there could be no more lip-synching transvestites in his future – and no more films with 'Return' in the title. And he knew he wasn't ready to carry a movie as Caruso or more recently Richard Grieco from *21 Jump Street* had tried to do. 'I didn't want anybody counting on me,' he says. 'I wanted to ease into something as an introduction.' Any bad choices he made now could punish his career for good.

It just so happened that the cast wasn't the only ensemble aspect of *ER*. It also had a raft of directors who alternated duties on each show. After all, no single director could cope with 26 episodes a series. As it was, Rod Holcomb, Mimi Leder, Charles Haid, Mark Tinker, Elodie Keene, Vern Gillum, James Hayman, Daniel Sackheim, Felix Enriquez Alcala, Anita W Addison, Christopher Chulack, Donna Deitch and Fred Gerber all helmed episodes during the inaugural season, most of them taking single shows. That left one episode, 'Motherhood', the penultimate one of the run. The director of that episode was Quentin Tarantino.

In 1995, fresh from phenomenal success with *Pulp Fiction*, what Quentin wanted, Quentin usually got. When Quentin wanted to shoot an episode of his favourite TV show, it was duly arranged.

Both Tarantino and George had come a long way since their first meeting during the latter's hideous audition for *Reservoir Dogs*. As the director took great pleasure in reminding George throughout the *ER* shoot, 'You really blew it.' But the two had remained friends and the Warner set was suddenly alive to two jokers instead of the usual one. Tarantino's best ruse involved his friend Rosanna Arquette dressing up as a Clooney groupie, much to the overdue amusement of the doc's long-suffering colleagues.

While 'Motherhood' is ostensibly a vehicle for the acting talents of Eriq La Salle's Benton, its impact on George Clooney was further reaching. While he was preparing to work on the episode, Tarantino played episodes of the show to his director friend Robert Rodriguez. Rodriguez was a newcomer to the series, but he was soon taken by it, in particular by the guy playing Dr Ross. It just so happened he was casting for a new movie.

'Quentin had shown me some ER episodes when he was thinking of directing the show,' Rodriguez says. 'A little later I saw George on an interview show. He was just sitting back and brooding. After that I saw him at an Academy Awards party and then I saw him on the cover of US magazine. I showed the picture to Lawrence Bender, the producer, and told him I thought he looked a little like Quentin.'

Although a stretch of the imagination to most minds, the similarity was important because Rodriguez was looking for someone to play Tarantino's brother. Quentin took longer to convince but he vouched for George's acting and general good-egg qualities. A call was made to George's agent and the deal was done. He had a summer project and they had the hottest TV actor of his generation.

The film was From Dusk Till Dawn, a road movie-cum-horror picture ('horr-action,' says Clooney) written by Tarantino in 1990, two years before he exploded with Reservoir Dogs. Special effects team KNB wanted to make their own horror movie and sought writers. They were impressed by screenplays for Natural Born Killers and True Romance, which were being hawked around by agents, and met up with the writer. They liked what they saw and commissioned a new script. 'It was the first time I had ever been paid to write anything,' Tarantino recalls. 'It was a measly amount, but I took that $1,500, quit my job and never took a day job again.'

Despite provisional commitments from genre leaders Robert Englund and Kane Hodder, the project fell into development hell for five years. In the meantime, its writer became the new king of Hollywood and suddenly his authorial trash can was being raided for shopping lists, credit card receipts – anything that could possibly be viewed as a script. From Dusk Till Dawn was unearthed and Robert Rodriguez, who had shot to prominence with his low-budget Mexican thriller *El Mariachi*, agreed to direct if Tarantino would rewrite. Tarantino would rewrite if his friend would direct.

From Dusk Till Dawn is not your average film. It is not even one film; more part road-trip, part *Night of the Living Dead*. 'It's like a big-budget drive-in movie,' Tarantino says. 'It's not even a serious take on the horror genre. It's a movie to drink beer to and to watch and hoot and holler.' The first section is as good as Tarantino gets, according to George. 'In the first half of that movie the dialogue is spectacular, it's *Pulp Fiction*,' he says. 'The second half is a much different kind of film, the kind I also enjoy. People who love that film absolutely love it. But the ones who hate it, wow!'

It starts with Tarantino's character Richard Gecko busting murderer brother Seth out of prison to flee to the safe haven of lawless Mexico. En route, they hijack the Winnebago of out-of-sorts pastor Jacob Fuller and his kids, Kate and Scott, and drag the terrified hostages at gun point over the border. With weapons permanently unsheathed, it is all Seth can do to keep his lascivious brother from raping the young girl before they reach their destination, the vampire-infested Titty Twister bar in Mexico. 'Quentin is very amoral,' George says of Tarantino's character. 'He rapes and kills and is basically like Lenny from *Of Mice and Men*. He touches pretty, shiny things and I go around saying, "Don't do that." I'm opposed to killing anyone unless I have to – only if they get in my way.'

Cussing, murder, hijacking, paedophile rape – not the behaviour of everyone's favourite TV medic. Which is exactly why Rodriguez thought George would be perfect for the part. 'This is an exciting actor in an exciting role playing something completely different,' he says. 'A complete scumbag.' People would pay good money to see Doug Ross turn shoot-em-up bad guy, he reasoned. 'It's not like putting Don Johnson in an action movie where you go, "I can see that on TV for free." ' There are parallels with the film career of Bruce Willis. When Willis played to type, the film, Blake Edwards' *Moonlighting*-esque *Blind Date*, was a flop. When he was cast as an action figure, people were suddenly willing to hand over their seven bucks for the white vest experience.

George would be the last person to pay good money to see himself, but the rest of the cast list had him chomping at the bit.

'Somebody comes up to you and says, "How would you like to do a Robert Rodriguez/Quentin Tarantino/Harvey Keitel/Juliette Lewis film?" ' he says. 'And you say, "Who do I have to blow?" That's the bottom line.' And that is even without mentioning Salma Hayek.

The downside of being among a stellar line-up is the possibility of falling short. While it did not seem to occur to Tarantino, George knew it would take all his efforts to keep up. 'I was scared to death,' he admits. 'I had to work with Harvey Keitel, and my character was supposed to dominate him. Now, nobody but nobody dominates Harvey on screen. I did my best, but when I look at the result, I can see him throw in a gesture, raise an eyebrow, or even take a pause, as he takes focus. That's why he's Harvey Keitel, and I'm just a lucky guy with the best job in the world.'

Filming of *From Dusk Till Dawn* took place on location in Mexico. Conditions did not exactly meet LA standards, but any set with George on soon begins to resemble his usual workplace: basketball, jokes, beers and laughs. 'Most actors you've got to drag out of their trailers,' says Douglas Aarniokoski, the film's first assistant director. 'George? You had to tell him where his trailer was. He's the only actor I ever worked with who could tell you every single crew member's name. He was like the camp leader.'

Even his co-stars' kids were included in the fun. Tom Savini, who plays bar hound Sex Machine, had ten-year-old daughter Lia stay with him throughout the shoot. 'One day she knocked on George Clooney's trailer door and squirted him with a water gun,' he recalls. 'He turned around and said, "Never come to a gunfight with a knife," and reached behind him, pulled out this huge super squirt gun and shot about two gallons of water on her – completely drenched her.'

A water battle ensued. The stuntwomen and the Twister's topless dancers sided with Lia and paid her $5 to lure George out of his trailer so they could soak him. Ever the smoothie, 'He gave her $15 to lure them someplace where he could get them,' Savini laughs. 'So there was this water war raging when I arrived on the set that day.'

Even the film's resident screen legend was roped into George's circus. Harvey Keitel, playing the preacher who has lost his faith in God, is not known for his sense of humour, or even for playing characters with a sense of humour. But George was not about to let a little fact like that stop him having some fun. On the first day of filming, as Keitel finished a particularly intense scene, the watching George was heard acclaiming, 'That was terrific, Harvey. Reminds me of my early work.'

'Fuck you, fuck you,' came the screen legend's response.

In revenge, Keitel dug out the most embarrassing head shots from George's pre-fame, bad-hair days and pinned them around the set. 'Jeez, I used to be pretty, too,' Keitel said, giving George some idea of what he could expect to look like in twenty years' time. Keitel got George to sign one: 'Dear Harvey, You show a lot of promise. Next time you get to LA, call me. I'll help you find an agent.' 'I don't think Harvey's ever laughed so much on a movie set,' the film's producer Lawrence Bender admits.

George's infectious humour spread throughout the set, just as it had done on ER and every other project he had settled into. Director Rodriguez went furthest by kidding his star to remove gradually every piece of padding for a particularly threatening stunt, 'because it was in the shot'. Then there was the day that the Emmy nominations were announced. George was on location with the film crew when he woke to find a note attached to his trailer:

TO GEORGE CLOONEY
EMMY SCHMEMMY
SIGNED
THE CAST AND CREW OF FROM DUSK TILL DAWN

Fun on the set was one thing, but by the end of summer George's ER commitments were returning. The only way to deal with it was to work round the clock. For most of the week he was on location, then for two days he would return to LA. Sometimes he was finishing with Tarantino at 2.15 a.m. then reporting for work at County General at 6.15 a.m. Reduced lines for the first few episodes of season two helped him partly, but the occasional aide-memoire pinned to the back of hospital furniture was always there as a fallback. There was no such corner-cutting on the film set. 'I grew up in television,' he explains, 'and if you were smart you never listened to the director.' Of the sixteen directors on the first season of ER, he says, they all wanted their episode to be the one where Dr Ross cries. 'They say, "Do this," and you say, "Got it," and then you do what you do.' With Rodriguez orchestrating proceedings, there is no such slack. 'You come in here and it's intimidating to me because you have to pay attention.'

Even so, working seven-day weeks for two months solid on two very different projects was very confusing. One day he was saving a dying child's life, the next he was having conversations with Salma Hayek's wondrously named Santanico Pandemonium along the lines of 'You'll be my slave, welcome to slavery'; 'No thanks, I already had a wife'. George admits there were moments of potential confusion. 'On the movie set I'd be shooting people then running to fix them up,' he says. 'And on *ER* I'd want to give a kid a lollipop and say, "Put this in your mouth, you little fuck." '

Just another day in the life of the world's busiest actor.

9. I AM SPARTACUS

Schadenfreude can be a very enlivening thing. As ER-mania threatened to take over Hollywood, there was some surprising news from the Emmy panel. At the final reckoning, the award for Outstanding Drama Series went to NYPD Blue rather than this much-vaunted newcomer. More amusing for Tinseltown-watchers was the recipient of the Best Actor In A Drama award. George Clooney missed out; Anthony Edwards was passed over. Picking up the trophy instead was Mandy Patinkin, hot-headed pedagogue on rival series Chicago Hope. So there was a god . . .

The respite from ER's onslaught was brief. The show still picked up eight awards (including one for Julianna Margulies and one for director Mimi Leder), and started its second season as favourite to take the number one spot from Seinfeld. George had also started the year, along with Noah Wyle, guest-starring as a doctor in an episode of fellow NBC debut act Friends (in 'The One with Two Parts: Part 2') and had hosted a special edition of Saturday Night Live where his talents for mimicry had made a victim of chat show host Jay Leno among others. Now, with a movie in the can, he stood every chance of making the transition from TV to film, following finally in the footsteps of his heroes Steve McQueen and Clint Eastwood.

Whether it happened or not would have to be seen. Television works differently to film. On a show like ER, each episode is recorded just a week before broadcast. There is very little margin for error but it does mean the writers can occasionally weave in topical references. The movie business, on the other hand, is a lumbering behemoth of an industry. Despite costing more money and having more personnel, From Dusk Till Dawn would not be seen by the paying public until the next year – at the earliest. But a few sneak glimpses of what was to come were inevitable.

Unlike most movie stars who customarily work on a film then disappear for a couple of months, George Clooney had the little matter of a TV series to work on throughout the last weeks of his film shoot. When he turned up to add his few minutes to the first episode of season two, George had the physical look of Seth Gecko. The tattoo running up his neck had been scrubbed off and the earring taken from its hole . . . but the hair. Gone was Dr Ross's trademark bouncy, light brown, side-parted style. In its place, a severe all-over crop, brushed forward and markedly darker. It was all about the *character*, darling.

'I wanted him to look like a guy who never had his hair cut,' George says. 'So I took a razor blade, and I cut off all my hair into this caesar haircut. I did it myself, with a razor blade. But because I was also doing this popular series at the time, the haircut ended up becoming something that I would get known for.'

It certainly would. George had long got used to the cut. During the summer, he and Quentin Tarantino had spent days socialising, both before and during production. Tarantino felt that the bonding would make playing the brothers more authentic, more instinctive. Many is the time they turned up to bars and restaurants, MTV awards shows and movie theatres with George still wearing his temporary tattoo and leather waistcoat and covered in dirt from the day's grind. And while Tarantino courted the attention, George fended off legions of admirers wanting to discuss – and even touch – his new hairstyle. The perils of being a 'hair actor'.

When he had the audacity to take the same hairstyle onto the set of his day job in September 1995, the press went wild. It did neither the programme nor the film any harm, but it put the actor firmly in the spotlight once again, as an appearance that month on Jay Leno's *Tonight Show* proved. As usual, George had all the answers. 'It's Frank Sinatra's toupée,' he said, pretending to align his wig. 'I got it at the estate sale.' As Leno mocked the brushed-forward nature of it, George added: 'You're gonna go for it. In a year you'll be like, "I am Spartacus!" '

Being the focal point for *ER*'s publicity agenda was one thing, but George soon learned the downside of putting himself forward as a public face. As the first season wore on, he became used to seeing his face plastered over the front of all manner of magazines and newspapers. Considering he was an actor working fourteen-hour days, six days a week during this period, he simply didn't have the time to do anything newsworthy. But that didn't stop the press seeking interviews with anyone who had ever met him. George was amazed at some of the people who complied: 'I said to my sister, "What are you doing?" ' he recalls. Ada, his family and those close to him, have since learned to speak only with his blessing.

National Enquirer and its ilk gained a new lease of life trying to keep up with George's mercurial love life, picturing him with one female after another on their front pages, regardless of any grounding in fact that the picture may have. It could have been George's sister, aunt, niece or co-star – as long as it was female, it was a scoop. George was obviously having sex with her. *Friends* stars Courteney Cox and Lisa Kudrow were two of his alleged conquests as they were snapped being friendly on the Warners lot where they all happen to work. Nicollette Sheridan's shared friendly goodbye hug as she exited a group dinner obviously meant she and George were having an affair. Models Cindy Crawford and Vendela were both said to be minutes away from receiving an engagement ring.

In a free society, there will always be a trade in information about celebrities and George, to his credit, appreciates this. But even he has his limits – and they were reached soon after *ER* started picking up momentum.

'I don't care about a man taking my picture in a public place, but I care if he comes into my yard and shoots in my bedroom window,' he says. It was such behaviour which forced him to invest in Casa de Clooney. 'The paparazzi found my old house,' he said in 1995. 'The house is on the street and they've been climbing the fence.' Photographers only climbed the fence once, thanks to Max, the Vietnamese pot-bellied pig. 'A few days ago I came out and some guy with a camera is cornered by the back wall,' he laughs. 'He's like, "Will he bite?" "Yeah, stay away from him, he'll bite." He dropped his flash and ran. I kept it!'

All good fun but annoying nonetheless. Unfortunately, another incident alerted George to the sinister side of fame; the celebrity set-up. Before the first season of *ER* was halfway through, he experienced trouble with an extra who insisted on talking while Dr Ross was trying to deliver his lines. Given the complexity of the hospital jargon, George felt that a bit of quiet was the least he could expect and so he asked the extra to be quiet. Twice. And then, as the script for *Dusk Till Dawn* noted when the vampires wake up, 'all hell broke loose'. Before he knew what had hit him, George was the proud owner of a defamation charge won by the African-American extra through the Anti-Defamation League of B'nai B'rith; she claimed he had racially abused her in public. To this day, he remains baffled about the motivation for the charge, which was summarily dismissed.

'She said I stood around the set in front of thirty blacks, including the ones I work with and am very close with, and said, "Let's go coon hunting some niggers," ' he says in disbelief. 'I said to myself, "OK, here comes the hell." '

Where celebrity-baiting is concerned, the truth is an irrelevance. George is no racist, far from it. When he was a young man, his dad would say, 'George, why don't you date black girls?' he recalls. 'Well, there weren't any!' That was not the case in LA in 1994. At the time of the racist accusation, he was happily dating black actress Kimberly Russell.

A lot of actors would have issued a flat denial and settled back to see the impact it had on their careers. Work-wise, it would probably not have affected him. 'This is a town and a business where a lot of bigotry and racism absolutely exist,' he says of Hollywood. But it was not something he wanted to be associated with – in any form. Not George, not Nick Clooney's son. His honour was being impugned and he was going to fight back.

No sooner had the charge been made against him than the Anti-Defamation League of B'Nai B'rith leaked the story to the *LA Times*. A reporter called George, who told him to ask any of the dozens of people on the set that day for the truth. The reporter promised to investigate. Unfortunately, the *Times* learned that *A Current Affair* was going to run George's side of the story and they refused to be scooped. 'They printed the story without ever investigating anyone,' George says. For a man raised on the principles of Edward Morrow, this was an unforgivable breach of professional responsibility.

As LA woke up to the news that their favourite TV doc was not the person they had thought, George acted. He anonymously called the Anti-Defamation League and lodged his own complaint. 'I'm an Irish-American,' he explained, 'I think I've been defamed and I need to know what to do.' He was asked for the facts of his complaint and they made shocking reading. 'Well, an employee that I work with has made some pretty terrible claims against me and gone to an agency, such as yours, designed to protect the rights of the individual. That agency first called up my employer and then leaked the story to the *LA Times*. And today I'm on the cover of the paper. I want to know if I've been defamed.'

The response he was expecting came back: 'Sir, you've been slandered. What organisation did this?'

'It's the Anti-Defamation League of B'nai B'rith. My name is George Clooney and I want to know what you're going to do about it.'

Wheels suddenly turned. The next day a 'star chamber' was assembled to hear evidence. George paraded a multi-racial witness team featuring every extra, background worker and crew member present on the set on the day of the incident. No one had seen any racism and they all said so. The League apologised and George won a full retraction in the *LA Times*. He refused to give an interview to support his action, however. Like trying to answer a damning question such as 'When did you stop beating your wife?', any dialogue on this subject would be open to misinterpretation at some point in the future. The truth would be his defence.

Sometimes, however, the truth does not seem to be enough. The attitude in the tabloid media is often that if a fire does not have any smoke, they will supply it and see what happens. Despite all evidence to the contrary, another insidious aspect of the press reaction to *ER*'s success was the continuing insinuation that the rest of the cast, and Anthony Edwards in particular, was jealous of George and that there was tension on the set. They all denied this. George publicly declared that he thought Edwards should have won the Emmy 'for captaining the show' and in particular for the episode 'Love Labors Lost' in which Dr Greene misdiagnoses a pregnant woman's illness then realises he can do nothing to save her. Edwards similarly denied any envy.

Professional feelings aside, how could he bear a grudge towards the man who saved his child's life? In 1995, the six leads were dining across the road from the soundstage. Edwards was proudly showing off his baby son when the child started choking on a chip.

'There's the six of us in our hospital outfits sitting around eating and his baby starts to choke on a french fry,' George says. 'The six of us jump up like, "Somebody do something!" and everybody's staring at us like, "You do something, you idiot! You're doctors."'

When he told the story on the Letterman show, George omitted to say that he stepped in. He held young Bailey upside down and smacked his back until the choking stopped. Edwards is not so backward. 'I thank God for George,' he says. 'Without his quick thinking, I'm not sure what I would have done. Bailey was turning blue and I just panicked. I jumped up and looked for help but another diner shouted, "You're a doctor, do something!" But despite all those lives my character saves every week, I had no idea what to do. I owe George everything.'

The real sign of friendship, of course, is when two guys can make fun of each other. When he appeared on the Howard Stern show, Edwards had his big-shot co-star banged to rights once Stern revealed that everyone on the show was getting an end-of-year something in their pay packet, even George. 'So apparently you don't have to learn your lines and you still get a bonus . . .'

As any musician will tell you, getting a hit is hard enough; repeating it is harder still. Following their amazing debut season would be tough for everyone involved with ER. The 'new' factor was no longer in their favour; audiences were used to the jerky action and zig-zag plot lines. The only way to sustain momentum was by quality of writing and character development. Audiences need to feel part of their heroes' lives.

Developing Dr Ross's character was never going to be easy. Handled badly, he could have become two-dimensional: there are only so many nurses he can hit on, only so many benders he can go out on, only so many children brought back from the brink. Fortunately, the writing for season two was as good, if not better, than season one. Yes, there were the sexual shenanigans – always the spectre of Hathaway in the background – and there were always going to be kid problems to make you weep – a child with AIDS in 'Do One, Teach One, Kill One' was the worst. But Ross's character undertook a major overhaul when viewers got an insight into his wayward, irresponsible behaviour. After a series of illicit phone calls, it is finally revealed that he has not seen his father for years; and he blames him for everything wrong in his life. When the father left Ross and his mother, he set in motion his son's journey to self-destruction. In 'Baby Shower', Ross pays a visit for the first time; by 'Fevers of Unknown Origin' three months later, he is getting too close to Karen, his dad's girlfriend. Could even Doug Ross cuckold his own father? After the decades of hurt and resentment, the answer is 'yes'. It is a low point in the character's history, but one well played by George in new territory.

More comfortable ground is covered earlier in the season when Ross's maverick attitude towards his work puts him in conflict with just about the whole department. In 'Days Like This', his job is threatened when he admits a patient against the orders of Dr Bernstein. In 'The Secret Sharer' he is dismissed by Greene after lying in a medical record and disputing his colleague's judgement on a patient.

Tucked away among the red tape-cutting procedures and amoral flirtations there was one episode in season two which served as a *tour de force* for not only Doug Ross but for the man playing him. When Ross has to save a boy trapped in a flooded culvert, *ER* suddenly turns into an action drama and George becomes an action hero. Cinema and TV are littered with career-defining moments involving wet leading men and women. Ursula Andress stepping out of the sea in *Dr No*; Colin Firth striding manfully from a lake in the BBC's *Pride and Prejudice*. In 'Hell And High Water', George Clooney gets wet. Very wet. It is his Bruce Willis moment and the first glimpse of his action hero potential. All in all, it was a strong season. That year's big opposition, ABC's *Murder One*, stood no chance.

Apart from his physical appearance, season two exposed a mechanical subtlety to George's acting that had not been there a year before. In the first season he is all movement: head bobbing, hair bouncing, all accompanied by a catalogue of facial twitches – an obvious by-product of those formative years lodged in sitcom hell. By 1995 he was a different performer, calmer and more restrained. With its new caesar cut, even the hair kept still.

Credit for reining in the puppy-like energy of his performances goes to Steven Spielberg who, on the first season of *ER* in particular, was forever floating around the set, checking how his first big TV hit was progressing. 'I remember once he came down on the set and was watching the monitor during a playback of a scene,' George recalls. 'He tapped on the glass with his finger and said, "If you keep your head still, you'll be a star." '

He was not wrong. The main difference to George's approach since those early episodes though, was 'The Look'. Patented by Princess Diana, self-styled Queen of Hearts and another fellow fan of hospital garb, off-screen George had developed the faux-coy habit of facing his head to the floor and only looking up with his eyes when he spoke. It was a trait he carried to the part of Dr Ross. One-on-one diagnoses and tense emotional scenes were suddenly delivered with a more polished mien. The transition was remarkable, the results superb. Dr Ross had always smouldered. Now he was on fire.

Before George left the *Dusk Till Dawn* set for the last time, Robert Rodriguez had promised to make him a film star. He had the form, he'd done the same thing for Antonio Banderas using the same tricks. 'You'll be a millionaire before the movie comes out,' Rodriguez had promised, having already paid the actor $250,000 for his star turn performance. 'All we have to do is send some bootleg footage around town so people will want to see you. I did the same thing with Antonio Banderas right after we wrapped *Desperado*, and that's how he got *Assassins*.'

He was as good as his word. 'While he was editing the film, Robert put together a trailer showcasing me, complete with fake reviews,' George elucidates. And it worked. Two months into the new season, and before his first film had been released, George got a call from Universal. How would he like to be the next big screen superhero?

The Green Hornet was not a superhero in the international league of Batman or Superman – and in any case the actors playing those characters were sewn into watertight long-term contracts – but his was still a charismatic name to an American public raised on radio heroes. With Alec Baldwin's *The Shadow* and Billy Zane's *The Phantom* also seeing the light of day, the major studios were frantically dusting down their old comic books to discover other filmable treasures. George could not believe his luck. He had been more of a sports jock at school, but every kid knew about the crime-fighting Green Hornet and his alter-ego Britt Reid. With horror director Sam Raimi on board, and star-in-waiting Jason Scott Lee lined up to play his sidekick Kato, George knew that Universal meant business on this one. He signed on the dotted line for a staggering $3 million and smiled at his luck. Come next summer, he would be playing a superhero on the big screen.

After a long apprenticeship, George's years spent working his way up from the bowels of TV-land had paid off. He was highly paid, internationally lusted after and about to release his first big(ish)-budget film with his second already arranged.

What a perfect time, then, for things to get messy.

It is typical of the run he was on at this time that George's bad luck would be the best luck in the world for any of his contemporaries. No sooner had he signed away his summer to Universal than he received a message from *ER*'s producer, that man Spielberg. It was short and to the point.

'He sent me a note,' George says, grinning. 'It said, "*The Peacemaker* is the first film from our new studio and I'd love you to do it." Of course,' he adds flippantly, 'you realise later that it was because I was cheaper than anyone else.' The fee on the table would still match *The Green Hornet*'s at $3 million. Cheaper than who?

The new studio in question was DreamWorks SKG, the brave new venture of three of the most respected talents in the entertainment business: Steven Spielberg, Disney's Jeffrey Katzenberg and music business guru David Geffen. Just working with these guys would be an honour; but to lead out their debut film? That was movie history in the making. But there was a fly in the ointment – a hornet, to be precise. Universal had just given George a perfectly sound deal on good money. He had been raised to honour a contract, and there was no moral reason why he should be allowed to renege on this one, even allowing for the debt he owed Spielberg for creating *ER*. Resigned to a feeling of 'the one that got away', he arranged to be measured up for his superhero costume.

While Nick Clooney's son might not have been brought up to treat contracts lightly, Steven Spielberg had been operating in Hollywood long enough to know such things were only a matter of positioning. Although strictly speaking he was now a direct rival to Universal, Spielberg called the studio with a few positions of his own. 'Remember *Jurassic Park*, the most successful film of all time? I made that for Universal. *Schindler's List*, the great Oscar-winner? I made that for Universal. I'm just about to begin production on *The Lost World* and I'd like to do it for you guys, too . . .' After a round of horse-trading, he also threw in the rights for Universal to distribute the new film outside the USA. The sweetener tipped the balance. By the end of November 1995, George Clooney was out of a contract and Sam Raimi and Jason Scott Lee were out of a job (Raimi would finally get his hands on a superhero in 2001, Marvel's webhead *Spider-Man*). *The Peacemaker* for DreamWorks SKG would begin shooting in summer 1996 in Europe, and George would be there.

By Christmas 1995, George Clooney was sitting on top of the pile and typically was looking to share his good fortune. He didn't have to look far. Matt, Thom, Richard and the rest of The Boys spent the holidays in Acapulco, no expense spared and with everything paid for by the movie star in the end cabin. A bit of golf, a few hoops, one or two beers and the company of some nice ladies. Now, that's success.

Before setting off, there was one more small piece of business for George to attend to. A producer from Fox Studios had called his agent. Did George fancy starring opposite Michelle Pfeiffer in a romantic comedy? He would, great. Would he be available for shooting in March? You're not sure? He's got a TV show? Can't he do a Caruso and get out of it?

Calling John Wells . . .

10. SHE HAS NO TALENT AND SHE'S KIND OF UGLY

When George returned from Acapulco, it was to face the opening of his first lead movie. *From Dusk Till Dawn* premiered in America on 19 January, topping the box-office charts with $10 million in its first week. Considering the entire project had only cost $12 million, it looked like being a success for everyone involved. Distributor Dimension Films, a subsidiary of giant independent Miramax, had a financial hit on its hands with an eventual $79-million take, half of that from overseas. Robert Rodriguez had confirmed his status as a director of imagination and economy. Quentin Tarantino proved that he didn't totally suck as an actor. And George Clooney? He showed that he could carry a movie.

'What demands attention by a wider audience is George Clooney's instant emergence as a full-fledged movie star,' raved *Variety*, comparing his looks, authority and action-film savvy with Clark Gable and even *Mad Max*-era Mel Gibson. 'Clooney is so commanding as an action hero that he often makes one want to forget that his character is a cold-blooded murderer. Even those not tuned into Rodriguez and Tarantino's gross-out trip might want to check this out for Clooney's star-making break-through.'

'Not many television actors make the transition to film easily,' the *New York Times* said, 'but not many look this much like Cary Grant.' The film's June release in the UK found *Empire* equally effusive: 'Clooney, in his first major role since hitting the big time with *ER*, proves why he's going to be huge.'

It was the consensus view: the film was good or bad, depending on your taste, but George was superb. He proved he could carry an action role and, what's more, he looked great. The sound of collective sighs of relief from the prospective backers of *Peacemaker* and *One Fine Day* was almost audible.

Other directors started to take notice. A month after *From Dusk Till Dawn*'s release, the Batphone rang. Would George be interested in playing the Caped Crusader in the fourth instalment of Warner Bros' series? Do Grizzlies kill in the woods? 'Joel Schumacher called me,' George confirms, recalling the director's first contact. 'I had some pictures of him with a farm animal and he offered me the role, which I thought was only fair,' he adds flippantly. 'Val Kilmer, who did the last one, had a conflict in his schedule. He was doing *The Saint* then, so it became a problem. And they called me up and asked me if I wanted to do it.'

Picking up the ball after Kilmer had dropped it was not a problem for the *ER* star. He was opportunistic enough to know that you had to grab your moment when it came, regardless of trajectory. 'You get too few windows of opportunity in this business,' he avers. 'You have to take advantage of them.'

He was also mature enough to realise that there are film stars – and there are film stars. 'I'm still unproven, I know that,' he said in 1997. 'I met Tom Cruise recently. I flew back on a plane with Mel Gibson. I was humbled. Those guys are movie stars. With me, I'm still on deck. We don't know how I'm going to do at the plate. I've been up there a couple of times, and I've walked and singled. And we have to see if I'm going to be the guy that can smack one out of the park.'

In 1996, George did not mind how the chance to hit a home run arrived, as long as it did. Before the Fox executive had offered him the part in *One Fine Day*, he had to wait until first Tom Cruise, then Kevin Costner turned it down. That's the way it goes with scripts, he says. 'Four or five people above me have to look at it, say they're too busy, then I get it. It's not bad – I like it that way. The truth is that same handful of stars can't do them all. And then one might take a project just for the pay-day. And then you'll get the good script.'

Without Cruise and Costner, George would never have been offered the role of Jack Taylor. Without John Wells, he would never have been able to take it. With shooting on *One Fine Day* scheduled to commence in March, George once again had to become a peripheral figure towards the end of season two of *ER*. As Wells saw it, it was a price worth paying. *ER* had made George a star and he owed them; but having a major movie actor in their series could only be good for sustained business and there was no chance of George walking out on the show. 'I'm going to honour my contract,' he said at the time. 'I made a contract and I'm going to stay on the show. Remember, this is not like, "Oh, it's too bad he's stuck on this sad show." It's not just a popular show, it's a really great show and most of the episodes we do are as good as any film I could ever do.

'Without this show, I'd have an acting career, but I wouldn't have had the acting career I have now,' he added later. 'It's a great place to be.'

Fans concerned about the thought of Dr Ross being marginalised for a month or so should not worry, George said. After all, there was a precedent – although audiences may not have realised it at the time. 'You know, last year when I did *From Dusk Till Dawn*, I did it the whole time I was doing the show and no one ever knew that I was missing,' he said. 'You work three days on the show and two days on the movie and vice versa. Mix it up and you do that in the beginning or the end of the [*ER*] hiatus.'

By way of example, *One Fine Day* is set in New York but, to accommodate George's last days on season two of *ER*, five weeks' initial filming – including some very convincing scenes inside a yellow cab trawling the streets of LA – was done in Hollywood before transferring for seven weeks to NYC for the authentic outdoor shots. For once, LA's unseasonably bad weather matched with New York's traditional early year downpours, minimising continuity glitches.

Filming threw up its own continuity dilemmas for the *ER* star, though. Having foisted his number three haircut on audiences last September, he had been steadily cultivating another look of foppish dishevelment in preparation for his forthcoming film role. Whatever the length, it was still discernibly darker than the light brown of season one. And with the onset of white specks giving a slightly greying effect, he had gained the air of a maturer figure in the space of a season. The consensus view was that the older image suited him. He had always had the look of a man older than his years, hence the failure to land parts that went to the likes of Brad Pitt or Judd Nelson. Now though, if it was boyish charm within a manly frame that was wanted, there really was only one actor in the field to call. And Michelle Pfeiffer was calling.

One Fine Day started life as a particularly bad 24 hours for *Fisher King* and *Sleepless in Seattle* producer Lynda Obst. 'I was having a spectacularly impossible day logistically,' she says, 'in which I was trying to do my job and deal with the exigencies of a teenage son. My situation, it turned out, was quite similar to that of several of my friends who had their own share of hellacious career/child juggling days. I suddenly realised that the new definition of heroism was simply surviving the day as a working mother.'

Taken with the possibilities of domestic heroism, Obst took the idea to Michelle Pfeiffer who, with business partner Kate Guinzburg, had recently set up production company, Via Rosa. Their corporate credo was 'no victims' and they were specifically looking for films to explore this. They were hooked.

'Lynda came to us with the idea of doing the day in the life of a single mom,' says former 'single mom' Pfeiffer. 'I really loved that idea because there are so many funny things around the day that happen, even at the worst moments.'

Guinzburg contacted her friend, Ellen Simon, writer and daughter of playwright Neil Simon, to develop the idea. 'Ellen came on board and we changed it to a day in the life of these two single parents,' Pfeiffer says, 'and it became a romantic comedy with a really delightful, funny script.'

Coincidentally, Laura Ziskin's Fox 2000 division of the studio giant had been established with a view to tipping the scale in the gender war. 'We've been a testosterone-driven business for a long time,' she says. 'Now I'm looking more at an oestrogen-driven business.' *One Fine Day* would make the perfect female audience-friendly follow-up to its summer 1996 release, *Courage of Fire*.

With the deal in place, *Soapdish* and *Restoration* director Michael Hoffman was brought in to bring the event to fruition. Pfeiffer cast herself as the female lead, successful architect and single-mother Melanie, while George was considered so perfect for the role of *Daily News* scribe Jack Taylor – after Cruise and Costner, that is – that he did not even have to jump through the traditional hoops for the part. One glimpse of the Clooney charm and Pfeiffer was putty in his hands. 'George didn't really audition,' she says. 'He came in and we talked. I felt I liked him. I thought, "This guy is not going to make my life miserable for three months." He's funny – we got each other's jokes – he's charming, he was smart, he could be a little bit devilish and kind of get away with it. So he had all the things I felt the character needed.'

Director Hoffman was equally glowing in his assessment of his lead man. 'He has a roguish charm coupled with a remarkable comic ability,' he says. 'He's like watching Cary Grant. Men will like him because he's a respectable and viable advocate for their position. And women obviously love him.'

Lynda Obst could reasonably be called one of those women. It was she, after all, who labelled him Swooney Clooney on set. 'He has a real visceral masculinity,' she gushes. 'The force of his attractiveness is not just his chiselled, classic good looks. There's something that women call being a real guy. It's hard to describe, but we know it when we see it and he's it. He has a wonderful ability to make a woman weak at her knees.'

If Pfeiffer agreed to this extent, she wasn't admitting. 'He's definitely trouble,' she says knowingly. 'Bad, been there, done that. He was certainly not as narcissistic or self-centred as some I've worked with. He doesn't take himself that seriously. I had to be the responsible one. But for all the bravado, there's something very vulnerable about him.'

Given the buzz surrounding his vampire-slaying antics, Pfeiffer knew she was fortunate to have secured the actor when she did. 'George is hotter than hot and we were lucky to get him,' she admitted at the time. 'In fact, we got him cheap. We're paying him just over $2 million and he's getting a fortune from Warners for doing Batman.'

Money differentials aside – he was getting closer to $3 million – George had leapt at the role with his eyes open. Tarantino first, then Pfeiffer, Spielberg, Batman: he was career building, assembling a résumé beyond his wildest dreams. 'It was another gigantic break,' he admits. 'I can't even explain how big a break. For the first time I was doing a romantic lead in a movie, and I was eye to eye with one of the top five leading women in the country.'

It would be most men's idea of heaven to spend twelve weeks in close company with the former Miss Orange County, but for once George's legendary bravura threatened to let him down. There was even a hint of performance anxiety. It could not have helped that he was largely responsible for the drubbing handed down to her husband David E Kelley's Chicago Hope. 'Talk about a living hell,' George recalls. 'Mandy Patinkin could've been doing this role!' Then there was the fact that he had dated and dumped his co-star's baby sister, Dedee – again, a fruitless worry. 'She still speaks highly of him,' Pfeiffer insisted. Which only leaves the fact that he was in awe of his co-star's abilities, a charge he readily admits. 'The script was really great, but I was intimidated to work with Michelle, due to her great beauty and talent,' he says. 'A chance to act with her actually made me very nervous, because I'm coming in from television, and she's made so many movies. But she made it easy for me.'

Not that easy, though. As soon as shooting got underway, George's qualms were confirmed. 'I remember, early on, I was just trying to remember my lines and get the rhythm of the scene,' he recalls. 'But when we did the first take, Michelle had all these other things going on. I walked over to the director, Michael Hoffman, and said, "Oh man, I just got my hat handed to me." I just realised, on so many levels, how good she is.'

It was not long, of course, before any initial nervousness was displaced by the trademark Clooney flippancy. 'I am quite popular,' he joked with one reporter who suggested he'd fallen on his feet with this job. On the other hand, he said of his co-star and producer, 'She has no talent and she's kind of ugly.'

For its plot, *One Fine Day* concentrated on the classic staples of main leads falling in love from a position of mutual loathing against a backdrop of time pressures and all known odds. Melanie Parker has the prospect of a presentation for a billion-dollar contract ahead of her at work – as soon as she has delivered her son and her friend's daughter on a school field trip, that is. Unfortunately her friend decides to elope with her new boyfriend that day, thrusting child-care duties onto ex-husband Jack Taylor. Columnist Taylor has his own daunting agenda – he has a day to find evidence of corruption at City Hall to back up yesterday's column or the mayor will sue and he'll be out of a job – but with daughter Maggie safely at school, he should have plenty of time to get the information he needs. Except . . . By the time Jack meets up with Melanie, they have missed the boat – literally. The ferry carrying the school trip has left and the adults are stuck with their kids. For the whole day.

When other baby-sitting alternatives draw blanks, they agree to help each other out by sharing minding stints throughout the day. Melanie is uptight and professional and hates the happier-go-lucky Jack. When Maggie says, 'I'm hungry, Daddy,' and he answers, 'Have a Tic-Tac,' their different views on child rearing are starkly exposed. Melanie accuses Jack of having a Peter Pan complex; he accuses her of a Captain Hook complex. Their loathing is mutual but they agree to bury their differences to get through the day.

'It's like a modern Tracy/Hepburn version of two equals battling it out for control when they don't really want control,' Obst says. 'They're just too frightened to share it.'

For George, the film conjures memories of Doris Day and Rock Hudson but more for its technical application. Because the script calls for both pro/an-tagonists to be in separate locations for most of the action, the film draws heavily on mobile phones – 37 conversations in all. Rather than weigh down proceedings with rapid chopped scenes trying to keep up with the rhythm of the dialogue, Hoffman went for the split-screen option so that both stars, and often their children, share the screen for the maximum amount of time. 'The split screens and phone conversations gave a kind of *Pillow Talk* vibe to this story,' George says. Hoffman adds: 'It allowed Melanie and Jack to be together when they're not. One could be on West 9th Street and the other at 42nd and Park.'

George's *ER* schedule meant that a few other tricks had to be employed. During the phone call scenes in particular, he often did not have the luxury of his co-star on set to deliver her lines. 'Michelle would shoot one of her scenes first and I'd film mine later listening to playback in my ear,' he says. 'It came down to timing, memorising exactly when she pauses and when there should be speaking. I began to get the hang of it – after about the thirtieth take!'

As a lot of actors will confess, comedy is a lot harder to do well than drama; romantic comedy even more so. Even when you're professional joker George Clooney and legendary diva Michelle Pfeiffer, there are still nuances that need to be ironed out – or in – to make on-screen actions seem 'real' to an audience. Throughout shooting, Michael Hoffman was concerned that reality and perceived reality matched. To cope in an average day, the human brain has to process data at a phenomenal rate, he realised. But when two people are framed in close-up on a cinema screen and there is nothing else competing for a viewer's attention than the dialogue, then the brain processes the words more quickly with the result that the actors appear to be dragging their heels. Confused? George was.

'We had to keep speeding it up,' he admits. 'We would do a scene, and then we would look at the tape, and Michelle would say, "It's got to be faster." And I would agree. So we would do it again, and it would still need to be faster when we looked at the tape. We just kept speeding it up until it felt very strange while we were doing it, but it looked and sounded right when you viewed it. Strange, huh?

'Of course, that's the way I like to work anyhow,' he says. 'Just throw the lines away, not try to fill the space with anything. On *ER* – whatever I do – I'm always just throwing them away because I'm not good enough to fill the spaces with anything else. That's just what makes me comfortable.'

As a consequence of the interior shots being done first in LA, other logistical problems came to light. If he had any doubts about acting with Pfeiffer, the fact that their first scene together was the film's only love element, performed to the strains of *The Wizard of Oz* (David E Kelley had wooed his wife with the same film in real life), should have cleared them.

As well as both characters' apartments, interiors filmed on Fox's West Coast soundstages included the inside views of the Big Apple's Natural History Museum, municipal buildings in Brooklyn, a Greenwich Village school and a branch of chain eatery Serendipity, all of which hosted scenes in which a comic mishap befalls one of the adults, usually Melanie tripping or spilling something. By the time the production decamped to New York, there was a list of 44 external locations to be filmed, including four-day shoots at the Circle Lane ferry terminus to capture the five-minute boat-missing scene and days more hanging around Central Park.

The business of movie-making is painfully slow at the best of times. It is also all-consuming. Filming real-life buildings and locations can bring an area to a standstill for weeks at a time. Whether it is pop sensation Alicia Keys closing London's Brick Lane for a video shoot, Bruce Willis hogging Harlem's main roads in *Die Hard with a Vengeance* or Doug Ross commandeering the Chicago walkway 'outside' County General for a few background fillers, the short-term impact is usually severe, but local business-es and residents are often more than happy to welcome the interlopers to their town just for the entertainment factor. It is not so straightforward in New York. The mayor's office there has a film liaison officer to cope with the multifarious demands made on the city's skyline, architecture and streets by directors of films, commercials, videos and documentaries. Hardly a week goes by without some film crew collecting second-unit background images for an upcoming movie.

By the time the *One Fine Day* circus arrived in Manhattan's Upper West Side, the locals had just got over the inconvenience of Barbra Streisand's visit to the area. Filming of her *The Mirror*

Has Two Faces had dominated the immediate vicinity for days on end and restless residents were put out by yet another big-money company buying its way into their neighbourhood, restricting locals' movement and generally interfering with day-to-day life. As shooting wore on, emergency service sirens responding to fake calls and wailing car alarms peppered the filming backdrop like a wave of bees. It didn't speed up the filming – on the contrary, it exacerbated the situation – but there was some satisfaction. From the producers' point of view, it was not as bad as the bomb threats they were receiving for daring to film during the Israeli Day parade. From George's point of view, it was nowhere near as scary as suffering an allergic reaction to the pesticides swamping the Central Park grass. Just another fine day in New York City.

Unlike filming of *From Dusk Till Dawn*, where he stayed on location in Mexico, the weeks in LA for *One Fine Day* meant that George could live at home and still get to both jobs in good time – Casa de Clooney is no more than a ten-minute drive from the heart of film-land. Trying to juggle both jobs proved more taxing than he had expected though. While no method actor by any means – 'I just look at the script and see what I've got to do' – George felt, rightly, that he had more ownership of the Doug Ross character than the myriad directors drafted in to helm each episode. Each individual director, it seemed, wanted to stamp their mark on the series, to make their instalment 'special'. For George, that usually meant only one thing, for which he generally had an antidote.

'In television it's not easy to be directed because you have a different director every week,' he reaffirms. 'Each tries to make this the *ER* episode that Dr Ross cries. If you're doing one episode that would be fine, but you're not, you're doing 22. You're the landlord of this character so you have to watch out for it.' Between being directed by Robert Rodriguez and *One Fine Day*, he had slipped back into some bad TV habits. 'It was very difficult for me to work on a feature film and to do what Michael Hoffman asked. He would say, "Do this," and I wouldn't do it. And he would come over and say, "You're not doing it." And he was right. I had to change my ways a little bit, and thank God because he was right on every instinct that he had. He's got great comedic instincts. He's an amazing director.'

As he had done with *From Dusk Till Dawn* and *ER*, every time George was present the set was alive to his inestimable feel-good factor. 'George is not one of those people who come onto a set and suck out all the energy,' Pfeiffer says. For his own personal amusement he arranged for Waldo Sanchez, one of The Boys, to be enlisted as 'Hairstylist for Mr Clooney'. Typical George – if someone was going to be paid by Fox for watching George do his own hair, it might as well be one of his friends (he doesn't use a make-up person either, for the simple reason he has always refused to wear make-up on screen). Waldo's sinecure meant that there was always someone on set for George to goof around with when the crew were running for cover, and more often than not he was included in the press tours that George would have to undergo. He also provided willing opposition on the optimally placed basketball court that George rigged up wherever he was filming. Michael Hoffman was another willing player and many a lunch break was spent with star and director going one-on-one with each other. Great fun and good for morale among the lads. Whether it went down so well with the female members of the cast and crew is another matter.

Hoffman soon had cause to revise his opinion. When the director was back in his canvas chair, George would take on all-comers. During one particularly committed session with a member of the crew, George came off second best against his opponent's elbow. His smashed eye was closed by hideous purple swelling reminiscent of Tommy Lee Jones' Two Face in *Batman Forever* and medics confirmed a ruptured socket. Not exactly the look for a handsome leading man.

There was no choice but for the star to take a week off his film work. But while Hoffman could shoot around him, George's *ER* schedule was not so forgiving and every trick in the book was employed to distract attention from the heavily made-up left eye. 'I had to do things like hold a baby in front of my eye until the swelling went down,' he laughs. 'My eye was swollen shut and I still had to put make-up on it for a long time to cover up the purple bruising.' Apart from the baby trick, the second season ends with lots of profile shots of Dr Ross which feature his 'good' side.

Invalided off the basketball court, George's competitive spirit found other ways to make itself known. He devoted a lot of time to goading his co-star that his film daughter was a better actor than her film son, a challenge Pfeiffer more than rose to. It was hard to call who was correct. Mae Whitman, who plays Jack's daughter Maggie, had already appeared in *Independence Day* and *When a Man Loves a Woman*, as well as having a regular role on rival quack show *Chicago Hope*; Alex D Linz, who plays Melanie's son Sammy, had starred opposite Jim Carrey in *The Cable Guy*, as well as making the part of the 'McDonald's kid' his own. Impressive pedigrees both – altogether more promising than the films George started out on or Michelle Pfeiffer's debut in *Grease II*.

George's rapport with his screen kids was as immediate and real as with any number of juvenile extras on *ER* or with young Lia Savini on the set of *From Dusk Till Dawn*. He has a real affinity with children and they connect with him, like everybody's favourite uncle, so scenes in the film where he pretends to be dragged into a fish tank for his daughter's amusement were second nature. The relationship works both ways. George was full of faux paternal pride watching Whitman turn on the tears at Michael Hoffman's command and instinctively stepped between the young actress and the film crew's gaze until she was ready. 'The kids in this movie were great,' he declares. 'They were more adult than I was. Mae Whitman, who plays my daughter, is one of the best actors I've ever worked with. The director would say, "I need you to cry," and she'd go, "OK, hang on." Then he'd say, "Now I need about 30 per cent less," and she would cry 30 per cent less! I hate her.'

Great thespian or not, at the end of the day Whitman returned to her parents and George could step away for a few beers with his pals. 'He was like the uncle who comes over and gets them all riled up and teaches them bad words and they don't nap,' Pfeiffer says of her colleague's mischievous brand of parenting. 'And then he leaves and wonders, "Why are those kids so out of control?"' For Pfeiffer, the parenting never ended. Her children were always on set and, between takes looking after Sammy and Maggie, she would disappear 'to be mom' to daughter Claudia Rose and new son John Henry.

For George, it was an eye-opener (sadly not a literal one for his injured optic) witnessing how she, Hoffman and scriptwriter Ellen Simon knew instinctively the pressures of juggling a family with a career. 'They all had a great understanding of these things of which I knew nothing,' he admits. 'Because all I have is a pet pig.' But a 150-pound one.

If anything, the experience of shooting in a child-friendly environment crystallised George's views on having a family. 'After doing *One Fine Day* and playing a paediatrician on *ER*, I will never have children!' he insists. 'I'm going to get a vasectomy. No, I just think children are a huge responsibility, and I am probably not the most responsible guy in the world, so I don't think I want to jump into that.

'Actors are a dangerous group to have kids,' he says, warming to his theme. 'We're toying with the idea that we're still kids ourselves, it's part of the attraction to this industry. It's dangerous because we're a little indulgent and I think you have to find a way to not be so indulgent before you have a child.' Michelle Pfeiffer had the advantage of a successful career behind her before she decided to have children. George is probably referring to people like his own father who unwittingly put their family's mental health on the line to various extents while they chase a dream. It can leave a child confused and hurt, as George found out. 'I remember thinking, "This is stupid," ' he admits. 'I just think it's a great responsibility and I think you're very lucky if you have time to raise a kid and spend time with them. I worry about that.

'It's not something that you can half-ass do,' he adds. 'If you fuck up there, you've fucked up generations. I don't want to be responsible for someone else that I could hurt.' Not a child, anyway.

For all his best-intentioned protestations, few believed him, then or now. Aunt Rosemary was quick to dispute his stance in 1999 when she said, 'I can see him as a father so quickly. He has such ease with children. He kind of herds them along.' Ironically, she is probably typical of the entertainers he believes have had children when perhaps they were too focused on their careers to cope with the emotional requirement.

Worrying about your profession is not a sin, George is quick to make clear. For him, the only crime is doing something not to the best of your abilities. What he passionately believes is that you cannot give your all to raising a family if you are serious about making it in show business. Both require selfish dedication to do well. More than most, he knows that when fame beckons you have to oblige. You can't pick the moment and you'll never get it back. 'I really do believe that there's a period of time when you can actually make your mark,' he says. 'And there's no better time for me than right now. This is my shot. And I understand how unkind and unfair it is not to be available.'

The last word on the subject – for now – goes to Michelle Pfeiffer. Watching him cavort his way around the children on the *One Fine Day* set, she bet him $10,000 that he would have kids of his own by the time he was forty. 'I know he will have children,' she insists. 'There's a saying about protesting too loud. He just talks about it too much for it to be real. He's going to have a gazillion kids and he'll be a good father.' George took the bet despite the fact that he was just 35 and that anything could yet happen. But he was confident that for the next five years, at least, his career would come first. It was what he had been building up to his whole life; it was the chance to do work that mattered; it was his attempt at immortality. 'My dad and I were once talking about longevity,' he says. 'I said that I love the idea of doing movies because they will be around long after I'm gone. I said, "Maybe the movies are my children." '

11. I WAS TOM AND NICOLE'S BODYGUARD

George Clooney takes great pleasure from normal things. Like getting his hands dirty. He spends rare days off tinkering under the bonnet of one of his vintage cars. He buys dilapidated motorbikes and repairs them. He does odd jobs around the house, fixing broken white goods, wiring up chandeliers. He doesn't have to, but he likes to. It's part of who he is and who he wants to be. He wants to remain a regular guy despite everything. Hence surrounding himself with The Boys instead of fawning acolytes. Hence the great attitude with fans and friends alike. Hence the respect for money.

Across the hall from his bedroom in Casa de Clooney is an office. In that office is a desk. On that desk is a typewriter. Like a lot of the things in the house, it is not a new toy for show. It is not even a new model. It's a 1972 IBM Selectric, lovingly restored by its celebrity owner. Over the years, George has banged out fake résumés, invites, film ideas, love letters and rants on that old machine and he sees no reason to replace it. 'Got to get email, I guess,' he says, 'but I love the sound of a typewriter. I'm always typing away on it.' It is another habit George has picked up from his father. 'We're both big letter writers,' he says. 'We like to write letters to the editor.'

George has never been one to let a small thing like international fame prevent him from airing his opinion as shock jock Howard Stern found out when the rising star took offence at the comments of one of the DJ's guests. The show had just started syndication in LA so naturally it was the channel that took the brunt of George's typed wrath. As a man of humour and principle, George was soon won over by the DJ. 'About six months later, I'd be driving along and I'd be listening and kind of laughing and then I started listening to it all the time and then you start to feel like the biggest hypocrite in the world.' By 1998, George had forgiven the jock enough to appear on his show, but his original action was par for the course for the man who risked his livelihood by standing up to industry bully Ed Weinberger and had been on the wrong end of a pasting more than once for standing up against bigots back in Kentucky.

Two years earlier, in 1996, another piece of correspondence left George's trusty Selectric, again intended for a studio's head honcho. The addressee this time was Linda Blue Bell, a producer at Paramount. Her company produced the shows *Entertainment Tonight* and *Hard Copy*. The former is a piece of television fluff, shamelessly plugging new releases, harmless gossip and inane celebrity interviews; the latter presented itself as a 'proper' reporting programme, fronted by former news anchor folk, but essentially offering the same pointless fare as its stable mate, albeit with a harder edge.

What constituted news on *Hard Copy* was paparazzi stills taken with mile-long lenses or video clips won by a cameraman stalking a celebrity until he or she flipped and took action to get some dignity. Depending on the level of reaction provoked, the tapes could fetch hundreds of thousands of dollars. What show wouldn't pay for footage of Sean Penn laying into another journalist? As captivating as it was for the viewing public, the guerrilla tactics were not just limited to innocent film gossip. Tennis player Arthur Ashe was effectively 'outed' by the paparazzi after the press learned that he had AIDS; he was forced to make a televised statement to head off further intrusion. *Psycho* actor Anthony Perkins was informed by a filming cameraman that he, too, was HIV positive – a nurse at the actor's hospital had sold the information. Most sickening of all, the parents of passengers on the fatal TWA Flight 800 had the news of their loved ones' deaths broken to them on the airport concourse by zealous bounty-hunting kids clutching hand-held video cameras and tape recorders.

In the main, though, celebrity tittle-tattle formed the core of *Hard Copy* and similar shows *American Journal* and *Extra*. For more than a year, George Clooney had been a regular sight on *Hard Copy*, sometimes twice a week. Reporters eavesdropped his conversations, photographers tried to break into his house, and the new breed of 'stalkerazzi' was forever trying to goad him into violent action by heckling him and whomever he was with. 'Who's the fat chick, George?' they would enquire after any companion. 'Does she give good head?'

By February 1996, George had grown sick of seeing his own face on the show – every time he was featured meant he had been harassed earlier that day. The final straw came when he was having a restaurant meal with a friend. A couple on a nearby table appeared to be celebrating a birthday, right down to having waiters bring over a cake and sing 'Happy Birthday'. George was aware that the couple's video camera, ostensibly recording the celebration, was actually aimed at his table, red recording light permanently on. He leant over and asked them to desist and waited. Sure enough, the tape was aired on that night's *Hard Copy*. The programme even named his companion as *NewsRadio* actress Maura Tierney – it was not her. George had had enough. He sent a letter to sister-show *ET*'s Linda Bell Blue.

'I said, "Look, you guys have always been nice to me," ' he recalls. ' "I do an interview with you once every two weeks. But I'm not going to help you make money so you can use it to buy a paparazzi video of me." '

The response was instant. Frank Kelly, President of Creative Affairs for Paramount Domestic Television, called George to broker a deal. 'He said, "What if we say you're never going to be on *Hard Copy* again?" ' George explains. 'I said, "If you put that in writing, we've got a deal." ' For a 'news magazine' show to make this kind of promise was 'insane', according to George, and he waited for a cop-out excuse to follow. It didn't. 'He sent me the letter which said, "We agree that you will never be on *Hard Copy* again, and we're going to look into this practice of buying paparazzi footage. Other people may do it, but we will not." I framed the letter and hung it on my wall.' Job done. Just a small indicator of George's growing power within Hollywood at that time.

Another note to go up on the Clooney wall was the one he received from Steven Spielberg during Thanksgiving 1995 asking him to star in DreamWorks' inaugural film. For all the scrutiny that the debut feature from the first new studio in Hollywood since 20th Century Fox's formation in 1935 would be under, the bosses did not seem particularly concerned to start with all guns blazing. Obviously they hoped to, but 'it's not like we had a choice of twenty things and picked *The Peacemaker* because it's some kind of statement,' Jeffrey Katzenburg says. 'It went the way movie developing typically does: first one in, first one out.'

The first-one-in started life as a piece of investigative journalism for *Vanity Fair*. Family team Leslie and Andrew Cockburn had unearthed chilling facts about the former Soviet Union's supposed disarmament programme for the majority of its nuclear capability. In particular, the black marketeering of armed nuclear warheads and ICBMs stolen by corrupt army officials for sale to the highest bidder. The prospect of such weapons falling into the wrong hands is too horrific to bear, as the film's script portrays.

Crimson Tide writer Michael Schiffer was entrusted with transferring the facts to the screen. In so doing, he concocted a political action thriller with a post-Cold War twist. Dusan Gavrich, masterfully underplayed by Marcel Iures, is a politician in the former Yugoslavian republic of Bosnia who has seen his country torn apart by in-fighting and terrorism and, worst of all, the supposed peacekeeping forces despatched by the UN and the USA. When he witnesses his daughter shot down by an anonymous sniper, in a scene not too dissimilar from the pedestrian terror which ravaged Washington DC in October 2002, he is pushed over the edge. Gavrich plans to set off a nuclear warhead at the UN building in Manhattan to punish those he sees as responsible for the rape of his country; he has no demands because his daughter is dead and his homeland is dying.

In 1996, for a film villain to be driven by no other motive than vengeance was unheard of. That Gavrich intends to detonate the bomb personally, at the expense of his own life, is a shocking realisation: could a terrorist ever think like that? George Clooney's character, battle-weary Lt Colonel Thomas Devoe thinks not. No villain in the history of villainy has ever been beyond a price, beyond a single demand, not even political terrorists. Not in James Bond, not in Jack Ryan.

That flaw in Devoe's all-American logic is his one error in the entire film. George plays his gung-ho army man with a straight bat, but Devoe betrays a shallowness in failing to comprehend what is staring him in the face. It does not take too much imagination to extrapolate the character's total uncomprehension and replace it with the disbelief that affected the world after 11 September 2001. As far as the US was concerned, Osama Bin Laden's attack on the World Trade Center was unprovoked; to followers of Al-Qaeda it was the first blow in an agenda of revenge as a result of a domineering, aggressive West. What is clear is that Bin Laden had no demands. The collapse of the Twin Towers was a show of strength, not a bartering tool. Just like the attack on the UN in *The Peacemaker* five years earlier.

Charged with bringing this political doomsday scenario to fruition was a new face. By the time of the film's release, Mimi Leder had picked up her second Emmy for *ER*; but she had never helmed a movie before, certainly not an action romp, and definitely not one with a $50-million budget for a brand-new Hollywood studio. After more seasoned hands such as *Goldeneye*'s Martin Campbell, *Outbreak*'s Wolfgang Petersen and *The Saint*'s Philip Noyce had all passed, Steven Spielberg put his foot down with his original choice. Just as he'd taken a punt with George to carry the film onscreen, Spielberg looked at Leder's award-winning way behind a television camera and recognised a transferable skill. Cue another one of his daunting messages.

'Steven called me one day and said something like, "I've got a big action movie that spans several countries and many different languages, and I'd like you to direct it," ' Leder recalls. 'I said, "What makes you think I can direct this big action movie?" And he said, "You do it every day on *ER*." '

Leder, the first female cinematographer to be accepted into the American Film Institute, was no stranger to pioneering work. Apprenticeships on *LA Law*, *China Beach* and *Crime Story* earned her her stripes. Even so, the commendations flying her way from the boss of DreamWorks were pretty special. 'Her camera had wings,' Spielberg says of her work on *ER*. 'I would spend ten minutes watching a rough cut and say, "This one belongs to Mimi." She would always have a signature moment. There was always more emotional intensity inside the drama.'

No sooner had Leder become one of the few women in Hollywood history to be given her chance to mix it with the action boys than tragedy struck. To compound various glitches caused by DreamWorks steamrollering the project through before its cast had set, Leder had to cope with her father's gradual succumbing to the ravages of lung cancer. The finished film is dedicated to his memory. As could be predicted, George was there for his director friend with his own brand of seize-the-day comfort. Yes, she should continue. Of course she should. Her father was a film-maker: it is what he would have wanted. 'She would say, "I don't know what to do," ' George recalls. 'But he would have killed her if she hadn't jumped all over this opportunity.'

On 17 May 1996, filming for *One Fine Day* wrapped in New York. Four days later George Clooney, his hair shorn once again, started work on *The Peacemaker* in the same city. The film was played out across two continents and five countries, with its spectacular dénouement taking place outside the UN building on the Big Apple's East 44th Street. George was getting good at doing things backwards by now. For the same reason that *One Fine Day* began its shooting programme in LA, *The Peacemaker* dutifully filmed its final half-hour first: it was the only way for George to keep the tail-end of his *ER* commitments.

'Because of George's schedule I couldn't start in Europe, go to New York, then go back to Europe again,' Leder explains. 'So I had to start with the third act. It was extremely difficult to start with your emotions so high and geared in fast motion. We were constantly questioning ourselves: have we gone too far?

'There were moments when I thought, "What am I doing here," ' she admits. 'But if I had thought about the fact that I was shooting a huge movie, the first DreamWorks movie, I would have become paralysed emotionally. I didn't approach it that way. I took it scene by scene.'

Apart from external forces, there were other pressures. In the film's closing set-piece, shot first, Devoe and Kidman's nuclear scientist, Dr Julia Kelly, have just disarmed a warhead inside a church but have to escape through the arched window before the standard trip-mechanism explosive detonates. For once George had been talked out of doing his own stunts (he did a lot of them on *From Dusk Till Dawn*). The explosion was triggered a fraction too early and the actors' stunt doubles were caught in a shower of stained glass. Kidman, her hair a ridiculous shade of purple-brown for the film, cried as she comforted her wounded doppelganger and George was shocked. Fortunately, both stunt-men were OK and able to continue. After nearly losing an eye on the set of *One Fine Day*, George had probably pushed his insurers' pulse-rates as far as he could.

That was not the only problem to beset the New York shoot. For the movie's climactic chase scene, George and his FBI crew are seen swarming over a dozen East Side streets at a time. Cue further gridlock. 'New Yorkers hated me,' Leder admits. 'I was blocking streets, I was hustling and working around mass transit. But that's how you do it. Just try to stay focused, to tell the story the way you want and try not to compromise.'

Even before the actors arrived, there had been nineteen days of principal photography. Sections of Fifth Avenue were closed for hours at a time as Leder and her cinematographer Dietrich

Lohmann gathered exterior shots. The Peninsula Hotel, which features heavily, was filmed inside and out with the production team occupying an entire floor. General background flavouring, courtesy of the famous library lions, the UN building itself and other landmarks, were duly added. A hundred-year-old high school was also requisitioned for part of the epic chase sequence and a fake church interior was erected within a vast downtown warehouse.

Considering the film's next locations would be Macedonia and Slovakia, Leder found the Manhattan sequences the most taxing. 'It was harder shooting there than in Europe,' she says. 'You have people screaming at you all the time. My television background helped in many ways because you have to do things quickly.'

Sharing the same background, George was equally unfazed, despite problems beyond his control. 'It was another big break,' he says. 'But it was the first film I'd done where the script was in serious trouble from the very beginning. The story was compelling, and Mimi Leder did a really good job telling it, but the dialogue had problems. Still, it was me as an action star, something I'd never done.'

The script problems meant that there was concern over the type of movie *The Peacemaker* was trying to become. George and others favoured a lighter touch; Spielberg was known to desire something closer to the vérité style of Costa-Gavras's *Z*; Leder wanted an A-to-B action approach. 'There was no real way of telling what kind of movie we were making,' George says. In the absence of any conclusive direction from the script, its actors began to contribute lines and, in George's case, jokes. 'Everyone kind of started adding things in,' he reveals. It was up to Leder to leave them in or smile benignly before cutting them. More often than not, it was the shake of the head. 'Mimi's very good at that passive-aggressive thing,' he explains. 'She is the kind of director that I've always adored and that's the kind who doesn't try and make you do what they want,' he says. 'If you don't get it right, she points you in the other direction but she lets you do your own thing first.' Despite the rumour mill in Hollywood insinuating that DreamWorks' first production was a kettle about to boil over, this was still her shoot. 'I never thought we were out of shape,' she insists.

The LA whispering campaign did not end with her abilities. There was talk that George Clooney's name, even supported by

Nicole Kidman, was not strong enough to carry a film of this magnitude. Some even said he was cast out of type. Leder is vehement in her repudiation. 'The role of Devoe was tailor-made for George,' she insists. 'He brings strength, confidence and intelligence to the character. If I wanted somebody to save the world, it would be George.'

In fact, the level of George's personal fame became one of the movie's saving graces. The net result of the myriad script doctoring is that very little becomes known about Devoe or Kelly's personal lives once the action kicks off. It is fortuitous, then, that George's first scenes in the picture involve Devoe answering charges in a military court of spending $5,200 on a single night out that ended with his being arrested in the company of a prostitute. For the first and last time, George is afforded space to let his natural charisma flood out, encouraging the audience to assimilate his playboy background with that of his character. Even on the subject of four-wheel vehicles, he reveals a personal preference: 'I like the Bronco myself,' says the proud owner of said vehicle. Whatever happens hereafter, Devoe seems to be saying, I'm still a good-time guy outside work. Just like George.

While he drew the line at jumping over another car – 'I think that's what they make stunt people for' – George lapped up the opportunity to wreak havoc through the streets of Vienna during the film's chase scene. 'I got to go to stunt-driving school,' he says, 'and I had to do all the 360s in the car and I got to smash about six of the BMWs up, which I highly recommend. Take a $100,000 Mercedes and just smash up a bunch of BMWs – you don't need therapy.'

In order to keep up with a fast-moving plot that skips from the Urals to Vienna to the Iranian border and finally NYC, the majority of *The Peacemaker* was shot on location in Macedonia and Slovakia. Leder, producer Branko Lustic and production designer Leslie Dilley had spent four months scouting locations and building sets and it was money wisely spent. Without the comfort of an LA soundstage to work with, Dilley worked wonders to transform an unfinished trade and conference centre near Bratislava into a convincing full-size Boeing 727 interior and a state-of-the-art two-storey Pentagon war room. He also brought a 200-foot White House corridor to life within an ice-hockey arena.

For the East European shoot, the 27-strong American contingent was outnumbered by the 100-plus Slovakian and Croatian unit. For its stars, this shoot was a chore. The fact that there was only one golf course in Slovakia was the least of George's troubles. 'It was a tedious shoot, away from the controls of the United States,' George admits. But, he adds, 'Having seen it now, you go, "Great, it was worth it." '

Fortunately, he had a few familiar faces around him for company. Reprising his role as key stylist from *One Fine Day*, Waldo Sanchez was an essential part of the company's retinue to tend to George's hair and partying needs. Other Boys had also made the trip. In only his third film, George had flexed a little muscle to get auditions for occasional house-mates Matt Adler and Thom Mathews. Adler took the part of Kidman's assistant, Alan, while Mathews added Major Rich Numbers to his résumé. Another familiar face, *ER*'s John Wells, was credited as executive producer on the movie, causing him to visit every so often.

Unusually for an action film, there is no obvious détente between the bickering heroes and not one shared kiss (excepting a paternal hair nuzzle when the relieved Devoe comforts Kelly after an attack). Devoe invites Kelly to lunch at the end of the film, but on a platonic footing. It is not an oversight. *The Peacemaker* was a bona fide attempt to create an action film that had at least one foot in reality. 'Nicole and I are really proud of the fact that there isn't any sex in this movie,' George says.

That's the official line, anyway. As usual, the leading man strung along more than one interviewer with his feigned disappointment. 'There was no sex,' he told Rosie O'Donnell, 'and that was kind of a rip-off. I really lobbied for the sex. I wanted it to be a full sex movie with Nicole and I, just sex.'

Joking aside, both George's director and co-star seem disappointed that the actor's sex appeal was not exploited. 'It's very hard to look into those eyes and not be completely intoxicated,' Leder says. 'It's in his eyes,' Kidman confirms. 'He can say so much without saying a word. You can't stop looking at him.'

During the filming of *One Fine Day*, tabloid coverage in the USA and Britain carried stories of George cuddling up with co-star Michelle Pfeiffer over cozy dinners. It was total fabrication, as Pfeiffer explains. 'I loved working with George,' she says. 'He was charming and funny and he humanised the character.

But we never even had lunch together. He'd go off and play sport with his pals and I'd go and be a mom.'

Similar rumours were soon abounding about George's relationship with Kidman. It was equally baseless, both parties claimed but, as George had learned with his racism accusation, since when has being right ever been a good enough defence? Considering the fact that Mr Kidman, Tom Cruise, accompanied the shoot to Eastern Europe, there was no opportunity even if there was the inclination.

'Tom was in Slovakia all the time,' George says. 'He's a nice guy. We're good friends; we spent a lot of time together. I think Tom was bored but Nicole would always say, "You boys go have fun," so we would play ball. Nicole is great, she's a lot of fun but she is also the consummate professional.'

Everything in Hollywood is relative and standing next to Tom Cruise makes you feel very relative indeed. George was summarily ignored by the entire population of Slovakia while Cruise was around. 'They thought I was Tom and Nicole's bodyguard,' he laughs. 'They'd come up and go, "Is it OK to go and ask for an autograph?" It was good, I charged them $3 a time.'

Apart from providing a welcome basketball opponent, Cruise also helped wangle George and Nicole a mini-holiday during filming. His own action spectacular, the impenetrable *Mission: Impossible*, was having its European launch on 4 July in London's Leicester Square and obviously he wanted his wife to be there. Clutching onto the couple's A-list coat-tails, George was handed a 48-hour pass by the DreamWorks bosses. When Tom Cruise asks a favour, you don't say no, regardless of how far behind production is slipping.

It was fortunate that George did go to *Mission: Impossible* and the after-show party held at Harrods. Otherwise what would the Friday tabloids have written about? As it was, accounts of his night of romance with powder-puff TV presenter Dani Behr jostled with the actual film in the battle for prime newspaper coverage. If he read the papers on his morning flight back to work, George did not seem overly concerned. It was par for the course and a small price to pay for being able to work on a $50-million film with people like Nicole Kidman. He would survive.

12. THAT'S WHY SUPERMAN WORKS ALONE

Nicole Kidman ended the *Peacemaker* shoot by putting her money where Michelle Pfeiffer's mouth was. After three months spent in close proximity to George Clooney, she was prepared to match Pfeiffer's bet of $10,000 that he would become a father by the time he reached forty. As before, George was adamant in his denials. In fact, he even devised a money-making opportunity. 'It costs $2,000 for a vasectomy,' he deduced, 'so I figure I'm eighteen grand up, right? I don't think that I'm going to be rushing in to have children. I'm barely good at keeping a pig.'

Relationships and him were not good bedfellows, he advised. Work, work, work was the most important thing in George's life. There was room for fun – there was always room for fun – but romance? That was another matter. That was a little more time-consuming and, in all honestly, George's time was spoken for at least for the next six months. Seven-day working weeks juggling *The Peacemaker* and *ER* and soon *Batman & Robin* left him drained. The last thing he wanted was a great romance to sweep him off his feet.

If one is not in the mood for love, it's normally advisable to avoid places like Paris. But when another break in filming of *The Peacemaker* meant George had a couple of days to sneak off, that is where he headed. In his defence, he was not looking for anything as he moped his way around Europe's most romantic city. 'I would go into a café and drink until it closed,' he recounts. 'Then I would sit in another one and drink coffee until I sobered up.'

Céline Balitran was working as a waitress in the trendy Barfly when George and a Paris newspaper columnist stopped by for drinks. A 23-year-old law student and former nursery teacher, she was working shifts during her summer holidays. Smitten at first sight, George returned to the café again and again until he found the nerve to ask the waitress out. It was an old habit. 'In high school – and even in college – I was the kind of kid who'd be sitting at a bar and staring at some girl and she'd be staring back at me and I'd never go over and talk to her,' he says. 'And then I'd go home and beat my head against the wall and think, "Why didn't I talk to her?" So, in my old age, I've finally gotten a little bit braver.'

It seems his procrastination was unnecessary. 'As soon as I saw him I cracked,' Céline admits. 'He smiled at me and I smiled at him. We looked at each other and couldn't take our eyes away.' It is not difficult to imagine why. George was tanned, his hair was cropped and neat, the deep brown eyes that so bewitched Nicole Kidman and Mimi Leder were fixed on perma-twinkle, his head was almost certainly doing its 'Diana' tilt and his regulation struggling actor outfit of jeans and black T-shirt was cut to show off his athlete's physique. And he was smiling. Beaming back at him was a fresh-faced, sparkling-eyed, slim, tall, gorgeous blonde – what the papers would soon be calling a 'stunner'.

A date was imperative. A stranger in town, George consulted his writer friend for tips. 'The next day he calls and says, "How can I get to know this beautiful girl?" ' the journalist recalls. 'So I suggested he take her for a moonlight walk by the Château de Versailles because it's very romantic. He said, "Great idea." Then, after months of not one word, a few weeks ago I got a call from Céline saying, "Thank you, I'm in love with George in Los Angeles." '

The local advice had obviously paid off. 'We went for a walk and suddenly he seized me in his arms and kissed me,' Céline says. 'I realised he was the man of my life. We realised we couldn't live without each other.' There were the small matters, however, of George's film schedule and the fact that the new lovers lived on different sides of the Atlantic. Not to worry, George's obligations in Eastern Europe were very nearly over and he was wanted back in Los Angeles immediately afterwards to be measured up for his Batsuit. He wanted Céline to be there with him. She did not need to be asked twice.

'Within a day I packed up and left,' she says. 'I gave my furniture to my best friend, paid off my bills, put my papers in order and told everyone I was going to live in the US.' And so, in summer 1996, Céline Balitran became the first woman to move into Casa de Clooney.

After a string of affairs with actresses and wannabes, it was refreshing for George to finally meet someone who liked him for who he was. Strange as it sounds, Slovakia was not the only country where his face was not instantly recognised. When he first encountered Céline, she had no idea who he was. 'When I met her, she was working part-time as a waitress in a restaurant in Paris and I was just another guy coming on to her,' he says. 'We went out without me telling her what I did for a living. The TV series wasn't on in France and the films *One Fine Day* and *Peacemaker* weren't playing so no one gave me a second glance. She was so natural. We talked about her work as a law student and how she was paying her way by working part-time. In fact, we talked about everything but me, which was great. She admitted that she must be one of the few people in Paris who didn't go to the movies. She actually said, "Actors always seem so big-headed," and I thought, "Is she having me on?" '

It was only when the couple stepped out together in LA that she began to twig that he was more than a rich American. 'We went out and some people started calling, "Hey, George." She turned around to me and said, "How do they know your name?" '

Apart from not being an actress (yet), Céline fitted George's other preferences. 'I am turned on by a woman with a strong mind and a will of her own,' he says. 'Someone who answers me back, who keeps me on my toes and makes me laugh. I don't care about age, shape, colour or background.'

Introductions were swiftly made to The Boys as each one swung by to check out the girl who could so turn their mate's head. Some didn't have far to travel. Quite whether Céline expected to be sharing the Hollywood Hills house with Matt Adler and other occasional guests is unclear, but she never complained. When the regular Sunday taco-fests were reinstated now that George was back in the US, she willingly played the hostess, waving the menfolk off for their morning cycle ride then entertaining the various wives and girlfriends who turned up for the afternoon barbecue. While George was at work, she surreptitiously set about turning the oversized frat house into a home, adding rugs and paintings and various twentieth-century accoutrements. The kitchen was finished, the half-finished screening room given attention. There was certainly room for improvement, as Adler points out. 'I wouldn't say Céline redecorated,' he jokes. 'She decorated.'

Of course, there was another resident at Casa de Clooney to whom Céline had to be introduced: Max. When George had rescued Max from the set of *Roseanne*, George was assured that he was a miniature breed – the pig was doubling for a rat on the show, after all. Kelly Preston, for all her other charms, had not warmed to Max as George had hoped – 'she wasn't really an animal lover,' Grant Heslov explains – and she didn't exactly put up a fight to keep him after the separation. George, on the other hand, has been through a lot with Max. 'It's the longest relationship of my life,' he deadpans, 'although we don't have sex anymore.' Max nominally lives in a shed built by George next to the tennis court but has free rein of the sprawling house and can often be found wandering around the downstairs rooms with 'Wash Me' etched on his dusty hide. George also admits that Max is allowed to sleep at the foot of his bed, depending on who else is sharing the room.

When The Boys are not around as a target for his humour, Max quickly becomes the butt of George's jokes. He isn't above feeding the pig honey-baked ham just to watch a cannibal at work and refers to him as 'my earthquake survival kit – the big one hits, I'll mash an apple in his mouth'. On one occasion, he thought he might have to put this theory to the test when a large quake shook LA. George had a six o'clock alarm call that morning so was furious to be woken by Max two hours earlier and spent a few minutes kicking at the pig to leave him alone. In reality, Max had sensed the tremors before his owner – maybe it was something to do with the house falling apart. As soon as he realised what was going on, George leapt out of bed and dashed out of the house, followed closely by Max. If ever *Hard Copy* should have had a tape rolling, it was then.

'It was a beauty,' he laughs, 'and it scared the shit out of me. I came running out of the house with Max – he was naked too – which was quite a sight at four-thirty in the morning, a naked man being chased by a pig. My buddy Ben, who was in the guest house down below, came running out naked with a gun, because he thought someone was breaking in. And we were hiding in the lattice-work at the front of the house.

'The idea of hiding in an archway of a door – which is what they say you should do – is horseshit. I mean, how many archways of doors do you see standing after an earthquake?

'And I'm trying to write a note to explain to my folks: it's not what it looks like, you know – two naked men, a gun and a pig! It would have been the end of my career even if I'd survived, because it would have been one of those entertainment cable channels – *True Hollywood Stories!* or something. Horrifying!'

No matter how many times George tells the story, he cannot help laughing. And it's real laughter, too, with the eyes not just the mouth. No wonder the ER bigwigs pushed him forward as their spokesman in the early days. But it is not just humour that he is straight with. There is genuine fondness when he talks about Max.

An all-smelling, all-grunting dust ball is not every girl's idea of a pet and more than one date had refused to go near the 150-pound half-deaf behemoth. Céline had no such fears. From the moment that George made formal introductions between her and Max – as though the pig were human – she fell in love with the animal. And watching George show such obvious devotion to his porcine pet, she fell just a little bit more in love with the owner. If that was possible.

For a short period, all was bliss. It did not even seem to matter that they had different life goals. 'We are madly in love and for me, a love story means marriage and babies, which may not be the wisest thing to say to a man who once vowed, "I'll never marry again and never have kids," ' Céline admitted to *Paris-Match* magazine early on in their courtship. If there was any pressure on him, George did not notice. He had a few days off in LA, and he intended to be attentive and fun. He took Céline out on his motorcycle for the grand tour of Beverly Hills, invited her to the 'office' to see him filming and escorted her to a number of A-list parties just to show her off. 'This is my girl,' he would say proudly as inquisitive acquaintances approached. And she was. But she was no wallflower, no inert piece of eye candy. Maybe her dazzling looks had first got George's attention, but Céline possessed a quick, subtle wit and an effervescent outlook which George never tired of. 'The crazy thing is, it's very difficult for me to meet anyone but actresses,' he said. 'Most of us have partners who are in the same kind of job. I've broken out and am enjoying the experience. Céline doesn't need constant reassurance. She spends her days working with children rather than buying clothes. And she doesn't talk constantly about her image and box-office figures.'

Even The Boys noticed. 'George likes a woman who has a personality, who gets the joke, who is funny and likes to do stuff,' Ben Weiss says. 'Not just an arm-piece. Céline totally gets the joke.'

She got the joke in two languages which is more than can be said for George. Fortunately for the relationship, Céline speaks fluent English, a bonus considering the state of his French. 'I took four years of French in high school,' he says in mitigation, 'but that was in Kentucky. That's where English is the foreign language. I took four years and I literally can't speak a word of it!'

Before Céline, George claims, he had never asked a girl out: that early fear of having his ego pummelled had stayed with him into stardom. But maybe the rules didn't count overseas. Dates, he says, had sort of just evolved with people he already knew. Maybe friends of friends, co-stars on a show or fellow celebrities. Famous people get thrown together with dozens of like-minded people on a daily basis. There is also the small consideration that he has never been short of women willing to make the first move, for all manner of motives. 'When I was nineteen years old, women wanted to sleep with me because I was a funny kid, or because I was an athlete or even because I was Nick Clooney's son,' he says. 'There are always reasons you're attractive to someone and they're all make-ups of your personality. It's not that I lead this oblivious life where I think I've got such a great personality that people want to spend time with me. If someone has a poster of you or asks for your autograph, clearly you can't take them out on a date. It's not that interesting if someone is just interested in you.'

Apart from phantom relationships with Nicole Kidman and Michelle Pfeiffer, George had recently been linked with models Elle Macpherson and Naomi Campbell (he was alleged to have had a threesome with the former, a claim he forlornly denies; and with the latter, he reportedly gave her a present at dinner – his hotel-room key). In reality, he had spent the last couple of years, on and off, with actresses Kimberly Russell and Denise Crosby, daughter of Bing. He also had a dalliance with model and former MTV jock Karen 'Duff' Duffy, although he denies this, citing the 'just-good-friends' mantra that has become his stock response. Whatever their status, when they were regularly seen together in 1995, George was the perfect gent, especially in the face of her occasionally debilitating immune disorder, sarcoidosis. 'George made me feel beautiful when I was really going through a rough time,' she says. When Duff briefly lost some ability to move her arms while sharing Thanksgiving dinner with the Clooneys, George immediately stepped in to help with a bedside manner that Dr Ross could not have topped. 'I was kind of embarrassed but he was incredibly gentle. He held my hands and cut my meat with me. And he did it with such panache. He is incredibly smooth.'

George's powers to please were in great demand in summer 1996. Almost immediately he finished in Europe on *The Peacemaker* he was wanted back in LA for his most high-profile role to date, that of the Caped Crusader. Not only would the film propel him into the consciousness of just about every sentient being in the universe but it would also make him rich. Very rich. After a couple of films earning $3 million, his fee for *Batman & Robin* represented the first instalment of a three-picture deal he had signed with Warner Bros, not including the option on a fifth Batfilm. $28 million and a guaranteed three, maybe four, films to be made by one of the biggest studios in the world? To purloin the George Best anecdote, 'George, where did it all go wrong?'

Having made a decent fist of resurrecting the Bat franchise with the lightweight *Batman Forever*, Joel Schumacher was retained to direct episode four. Chris O'Donnell would return as Robin, Arnold Schwarzenneger would play Mr Freeze and Uma Thurman would appear as Poison Ivy. But Schumacher had his eye out for a new Batman. Inspiration came at thirty-thousand feet. 'I was on a plane and I saw an ad for *From Dusk Till Dawn*, a movie that George made with Quentin Tarantino and Rob Rodriguez,' he reveals. 'And for some reason, I took a black Magic Marker and I drew the Bat cowl on him, and he looked good. Then I went to see the movie, and he is a movie star.'

There was only one problem: Warner Bros already had a Batman contracted to the film. But when Val Kilmer decided to swap cowl for halo and run after *The Saint*, Schumacher was glad to see him go. As far as he was concerned, Kilmer had been unpleasant to work with and it would be no skin off the director's ample nose if he did not appear for phase four. 'I had been told he was very difficult,' Schumacher reveals. 'He wasn't, until one day he started going ballistic.

'He was screaming at the cinematographer and the first assistant and we had a fight in his trailer because I had to discipline him about his shocking behaviour. Val got carried away and grabbed me and threw me into the wall of the trailer. Much to my surprise, I grabbed him and pushed him right back. So Val ordered me out of his trailer and I said, "Excuse me, I'm paying for this trailer. You're my guest, you cannot order me out." He said, "If you don't leave, I'll leave." So I threw open the door and said, "Be my guest." Then he stormed out and didn't speak to me for two weeks, which was bliss. People are always saying he's a difficult actor. The truth is, he's the most troubled.'

One man's failure is another's opportunity, and a relieved Schumacher started casting round for a new hero. *The X-Files'* David Duchovny was one of the first to try on the famous cowl. 'I looked great in the suit,' he recalls, 'but my nose was too big.' The same could be said of George Clooney. While a feature of his good looks has always been his pronounced, cartoon-like features, at last he had found a role that not only welcomed them, but required them. Joel Schumacher saw it the instant George put the head-gear on. 'George does have an extraordinary nose,' he gushes. 'When I look at the comics, he looks more like Batman than Michael [Keaton] and Val. They were both great as Batman but George is the best, and not just because he was my choice. There is something very manly about him.'

Producer Peter Macgregor-Scott agrees. 'George's chin is a little squarer than the previous Bats,' he assesses. 'But he has strong lips and looks great in the new suit.'

Ah, the suit. Where would playing a superhero be without gripes about the costume? Christopher Reeve was famous for bitching about the support wire that facilitated the Man of Steel's aerial agility and Keaton and Kilmer had no fondness for their Batsuits. George, at least, is realistic about it. 'Let me tell you,' he says, 'the suit is reason enough not to do the part. But you know, you're finished after five months, and you get to be Batman. So that's the trade off.'

Adam West's 60s hero merely had to put up with sniggers as he paraded around Gotham City in his grey, lycra-style snug-suit. The modern-era hero has slightly more to contend with. George's garb is a human-shaped carapace, physiologically accurate body armour that he does not so much wear as carry. 'It's made of hard rubber and weighs about fifty pounds,' George reveals. 'But the hardest part is that your eyes and ears are covered and your nose is plugged up. I think the most I can keep it on for is fifteen minutes, and then I'm out of it and just soaking wet. If you really had to wear this thing, everybody would kick the hell out of you. I mean, the most elaborate stunt I've been able to do is walk to my trailer. Some superhero.' Excessive perspiration is not the only fluid problem. When he asked Michelle Pfeiffer for any tips based on her role as Catwoman, she advised getting a trapdoor installed. It wasn't to be. 'I just pee in the costume,' he jokes.

For all George's whingeing, Robin actor Chris O'Donnell is convinced his co-star got off lightly with the costumes. 'He got to the wardrobe people before I did,' he reveals, 'and had looser costumes and half costumes made so that he didn't always have to put on the whole suit.'

Getting the chance to play Batman was a childhood dream for George. 'When I grew up, the TV show was a big hit,' he recalls, 'so I grew up putting the little cape on. I stopped a couple of weeks ago,' he jokes. Cousin Miguel was also a fan so he was the first to hear George's news. 'Guess what I'm going to be doing in September?' he teased. 'I'm going to be in *Batman*.' 'Oh that's nice. What are you going to do, be a helper or something?' 'No, I'm going to be Batman.' Miguel's response is unfit to be printed in a family book.

With his Buzz Lightyear jawline and toy-soldier swivel-action eyes, George does as much as can be expected inside the cowl. Although he apparently had to lose eighteen pounds just to get into it, the suit has little need of a human wearer. It is sniggeringly authentic, from the protruding nipples to the prominent six-pack. Only in one area did George's own physique have any bearing. According to interviews Joel Schumacher gave at the time, George required a slightly more capacious codpiece than his predecessor. George, of course, would never make such boasts. True to form, he actually turned the accusation on its head and said that co-star O'Donnell must have been very good to the costume department. 'George was kidding me about tipping the costume person,' he laughs. 'But some of us have bigger codpieces than other members of the cast, and there's a little jealousy there.'

George backed this up live on the *Oprah* show. 'He's got a package on him that I've never seen before,' he said in front of a squirming O'Donnell. 'I couldn't believe it.'

Comparisons between the 'Camp' Crusader and his sidekick were to be an integral part of Schumacher's lighter view of the franchise. His film opens with *Baywatch*-style close-ups of Bruce Wayne and Dick Grayson pouring into their skin-tight costumes. The sequence wears its homoeroticism on its rubber sleeve as first Batman's, then Robin's backside are slowly focused on, before the camera runs seductively up and down muscle-defined torsos, rippling legs and bulging crotches. Quite a different kind of Batpole to the one Adam West used to have.

Shooting of *Batman & Robin* ran from September 1996 through to the end of January 1997, in other words parallel with the third season of *ER*. Just as he had been on *One Fine Day*, George was back on seven-day, one-hundred-hour weeks. Monday to Thursday he would tend Chicago's needy as Dr Ross; Friday to Sunday he would cross the Burbank Warner lot (occasionally via Howard Hughes' cavernous Spruce Goose hangar at Long Beach), don rubber and kick frozen ass. Hard work, but it wouldn't be forever, he told himself. 'You get too few windows of opportunity in this business,' he says. 'You have to take advantage of them. I talked to Joel Schumacher before I started *Batman*, and he said, "All right, we're talking about seven days a week. Can you do it?" And I said, "Physically, can I do it? Yes, I think so." But a couple of weeks ago I was sitting in the middle of the Batsuit, in hell, which is the most miserable thing. There's fake snow all over me, I'm covered in water, I'm sitting in this chair trying to wait for them to call me onto the set, and I said to Amy [Cohen], my assistant, "I don't think I'll make it." But you do.'

George's partial presence over five months meant he rarely had down-time on set as Schumacher attempted to squeeze a week's shooting into three days with his leading man. The schedule was not helped by the restricted availability of Arnold Schwarzenneger. Despite paying him a reputed $20 million to recreate Otto Preminger's pun-spouting Mr Freeze, Warner Bros had only secured the Austrian Oak's services for a six-week period (it clashed with his pre-booked heart surgery). Logistically, it was *One Fine Day* all over again, but worse, as director of photography Stephen Goldblatt points out. 'We had to work completely out of continuity because we almost never had the two of them on the same set,' he says. 'Normally you go onto the same set once or twice, but our first unit – never mind our second unit – went onto some sets as many as eleven times, using doubles to shoot over-the-shoulders and stuff.'

The inconvenience factor associated with him aside, George's addition to the Batcast meant that there was a greater levity to the project, not least in Akiva Goldsman's script. After three films spent dwelling on his parents' murder, Bruce Wayne George-style is looser and more at peace with his billion-dollar empire.

'It's fun to be Batman,' George insists. 'Bruce Wayne sits around, going, "It's so hard to live because my parents were killed when I was little." We as an audience, go, "OK, you're rich, you're schtupping the most beautiful babes in Gotham City, you've got a mansion and the coolest gadgets. Get over it." He's got a great life and he knows it, he has a sense of humour about it.' During a group interview with the *LA Times* in 1997, O'Donnell jokes that George could be talking about himself. 'It just dawned on you, didn't it?' he shoots back, seriously.

There are further similarities between actor and character. Perhaps his most heart-felt delivery goes to a line in a conversation with screen girlfriend of a year Elle Macpherson (they were a couple at last!). When she says she wants to settle down, Bruce says pointedly, 'I'm not the marrying kind.' Are you listening, Céline?

As well as investing Bruce Wayne with a sense of proportion, George also turned Batman into something more than a brooding action figure. As parents the world over know, having someone else to look out for puts everything else into perspective. His relationship with Robin/Dick is the source of a lot of bickering and some of the film's best jokes. Arguing with his young ward about the Batmobile, George looks to the camera and says, 'That's why Superman works alone.' During the first set-piece fight scene at the Gotham museum with Arnie's Mr Freeze, he warns, 'You break it, you buy it.' Most cheesy of all, he childishly tries to outbid Robin to 'buy' Uma Thurman's bewitching Poison Ivy at a charity event. When the auction price soars into millions, he produces his own Bat-logo'd plastic friend: 'I never leave the cave without it.' Priceless. And can anyone imagine Michael Keaton jockeying with O'Donnell over Poison Ivy's 'nice stems' and 'nice buds' and Alicia Silverstone's shapely Batgirl? This was *Batman*, Boys-style.

Off-screen, when he wasn't feeling sorry for himself being trapped in a rubber prison, George was his usual man-of-the-people charming self. 'He treats the crew real well,' Chris O'Donnell says. 'George is one of the funniest actors I've every worked with and the guy's got more stories than anybody I've ever talked to. I don't know if he makes some of them up, but they get pretty ridiculous!'

Jeep Swenson, who plays walking steroid mountain Bane (who in the original comics breaks the dark knight's back) backs this up. 'George is just gold,' he says, amazed at the superstar's easy charm. 'He is unbelievable. Here is a guy who would rather talk about selling clothes at a "big and tall" store in Cincinnati than talk about how well his career is going. He remembers where he came from.'

Just as he shielded Mae Whitman from the spotlight on *One Fine Day*, George found himself stepping in to help out someone a bit older on *Batman*. Octogenerian Michael Gough, who plays Alfred, can't thank him enough. 'George is a real mate,' he says. 'A lovely thing about him is that because I'm old and stupid I'll sometimes say, "Joel, I don't know what I say in this scene," and Joel will say, "Cut." Before I can apologise, George says, "I'm sorry, Joel, I put him off. I was coughing. I caught his eye. My fault." '

Even Arnie, not traditionally the most generous analyst of those sharing his screen, has only good words to say about the new Bat, although characteristically they're couched in marketing terms. 'I felt that George would be a great addition to the film, not only in this country but internationally,' he admits. 'He has this great appeal overseas and also in this country for men and women, so I thought he would be terrific for the thing. And he did a really did a great job.'

The backslapping was mutual. When he was not telling interviewers that Arnie was scared of him because he had been his stunt double in *Conan the Barbarian*, George was extremely proud to have worked with him. 'Arnold Schwarzenegger is so great. Not just funny, a very giving, nice man,' he insists. 'I worried about being a guy and going on with a big matinee idol like Arnold, because, quite frankly, people as famous as him can be very tough on the guy the next rung down. But Arnold has been nothing but great to me. Overly great, out-of-his-way great, to the point where I'm actually moved by it. That's a real rare thing.'

They had met before, although it only made an impression on one of them. 'Years ago, the girl I was living with was in the film *Twins* with him,' he says, referring to Kelly Preston. 'I was on a TV series at the time, but of course he had no idea who I was. He's one of those people like Clint Eastwood. You can walk into a room full of stars, but people like Arnold and Clint have great presence.' Fortunately, they also have a great sense of humour. While George was kicking around Europe filming *The Peace-*

maker, he took the liberty of goading his super-rival. 'I was in Europe working at the same time as Arnold was doing a publicity tour for his film *Eraser*,' George says. 'I would go to all the Planet Hollywoods and leave a cigar for him with a note saying things like, "Hey, Freeze, Batman is looking for you." He completely jumped into it and it became the most fun I've ever had before I even started filming.'

Of course it would not have been a proper 'George' set without the obligatory basketball games during breaks. Since everyone knew him on the Warner Bros lot anyway, there was never a shortage of players. For a while, a regular opponent was *The New Adventures of Superman*'s Dean Cain, who was shooting on a nearby soundstage. While George is adamant that Batman always whipped Superman's butt, he confesses there were occasionally other victors. 'Dean Cain, Chris and I took on these three guys at Warner Bros, and they beat the hell out of us,' he chuckles. 'They got to go home and say they beat Batman, Robin and Superman.'

Sadly, for him, the ball games came to an end. It was bad enough when he broke a finger halfway through the shoot, but when a twisted ankle towards the end meant that he was hobbling round the set on crutches Schumacher called time on the rough-house antics.

Another decision of Schumacher's that George objected to was the one to 'loop' every scene. It is standard movie practice to overdub lines during busy set-pieces, when the microphones would struggle to pick up any words during actual filming. But Schumacher and his assistants opted to record voice-over parts for every scene, even those conducted in a quiet room between George and Michael Gough. 'The entire film was completely looped – even when Bruce Wayne is sitting there talking to Alfred,' George says. 'I am the most hated man on the looping stage. As likeable as I like to be everywhere else, on the looping stage I'm the devil. After the first season of *ER* I never looped. Every time I see a loop on screen I notice the dead air and see how it takes away from the performance. I'd rather hear scratching noises in the background and get the real performance. It's part of where the studio system went wrong, trying to gloss over everything.'

For his part, the 35-year-old George was happy with his contribution to *Batman & Robin*. 'It's much easier to be the third

Batman than to be the second,' he admitted as shooting drew to a close. 'Val Kilmer had it a lot tougher than I did, because now we've established that I can be replaced. I'm just hoping not to be the first guy to mess it up.'

13. THE SEXIEST MAN ALIVE

Filming of *Batman & Robin* meant that George's blossoming relationship with Céline was under pressure from the start. Not only was he working a seven-day week but he was also too drained to do much more in his short evenings than hang out in Casa de Clooney with the following day's scripts. The bright lights of Hollywood would have to be explored by Céline on her own – not that much fun when you do not know a single person in town. The best palliative the pair could come up with was to have Céline spend as much time on-set with George as possible. She would often swing by in one of George's fleet of cars to see how her superhero was getting on, doing her best not to giggle too much as she watched him sweat his way through take after take in the rubber Batsauna.

Even a year before the film's projected release, before a single reel had been shot, interest in it was huge. For a start, Joel Schumacher had managed to persuade Warner Bros to give him a new Batman for the second film running so all of Hollywood wanted to know how Dr Ross would cope. Then there was the fact that the paparazzi were all scrambling to get pictures of imminent heart-op star Arnold Schwarzenneger in his bald ice cap and 70-pound Freeze armour. Most of all, though, there were rumours that George Clooney had a new love in his life.

As the clamour for daily scoops increased, three people were arrested on the *Batman* set for trying to get pictures of its stars. One of the three had previously claimed to be an ex-lover of George's. Her story achieved notoriety because she asserted that they had never consummated the relationship as George had always been too drunk to 'close the deal', as he dismissed it. She was allegedly found to be carrying five fake IDs when caught. As George points out in despair, 'That's the "reliable source" they use to run the big story.'

Some illicit footage did make it out of the secure sets. Secret video of the film's stars appeared on the gossip magazine programme *Inside Edition* a few days before the arrests. George was disappointed, but there was little he could do. TV programmes were paying such good prices for any images, however they were obtained, that people were willing to risk their liberty for the chance of a quick buck.

Then, on 23 September, *Hard Copy* ran exclusive footage of George and Céline backstage on the *Batman* set. Nothing incriminating – just the young lovers strolling and talking – but totally against the spirit of the agreement George had reached with Frank Kelly earlier in the year. The content of the paparazzi film was academic. The point was that George had reached an agreement with Paramount and they had reneged. For a Kentucky boy, there is no better cause than a fight of principle. He would not let this one go.

The restored Selectric was soon burning hot. On 24 October 1996 George wrote a coruscating response to *Hard Copy*'s shameless double-cross and sent it not only to the producers of sister show *Entertainment Tonight* but also to the press. It made great reading: 'Well, we gave it a shot,' it began. 'And for a six-month period Frank Kelly kept his word. My name wasn't on *Hard Copy* and I did several interviews for you. I guess the statute of limitations for keeping your word is about six months for Mr Kelly, or maybe it was a landmark and I should feel honoured. Last month *Hard Copy* did an undercover story about my girlfriend and me. A probing in-depth report that will have great significance in the world. The story doesn't matter. The point is that he broke our deal. A deal that he proposed.'

Still baffling George was the fact that Kelly had put the deal in writing: 'What an idiot.' But what could be done about it? George had no hesitation.

'So now we begin. Officially. No interviews from this date on. Nothing on *ER*, nothing from *One Fine Day*, nothing from *Batman & Robin*, and nothing from DreamWorks' first film, *The Peacemaker*. These interviews will be reserved for all press but you. *Access Hollywood*, *E!*, whoever. It won't affect you much. Maybe other actors will join me. Maybe not. That doesn't matter. It's about doing what's right.

'Again, I am sorry. You're a nice bunch of people and you have always treated me fairly. But your company and Mr Kelly have to be responsible for what they say and who they say it to. And so do I.'

Wow. Living outside the microcosm of LA it is difficult to surmise just how brave this action was. Hollywood is a small world, cocooned from reality by wealth, fame and privilege. A major player in this miniature republic is the media; they can make and they can break. And George Clooney was going up against them. If the various outlets joined forces, the effect on his career could be fatal. His brush with the Anti-Defamation League and other spurious stories had taught him how pernicious and all-pervading the press could be in certain circumstances. But it was a gamble worth taking, a stand worth making. It was about doing what's right.

As *Entertainment Tonight*, *Hard Copy* and Paramount consider- ed their options, they were soon appraised of the limited reality. George was not the only celebrity to feel invaded by *Hard Copy*'s implicit encouragement of bounty-hunting paparazzi to go to extreme lengths to get their shots. New mother Madonna, a victim the previous week of *Hard Copy*'s desire to show the first shots of her new baby Lourdes, joined in the fight. She issued a statement saying that she, too, would be off-limits to *Entertain- ment Tonight*. She was not alone. Whoopi Goldberg, Dean Cain, Rosie O'Donnell, the entire cast of *ER*, Mr and Mrs Tom Cruise, Jim Carrey, Ellen DeGeneres and Lauren Holly all came forward with similar messages of support. There was more. 'I got a call from Steven Spielberg,' George discloses, 'who said, "I have a little project called *The Lost World: Jurassic Park II*, and *Entertain- ment Tonight* won't get any of it if we don't get some of this changed." ' As the director said, 'It beats litigation.'

Game over. Kerry McCluggage, Paramount TV Group Chair- man, issued a statement saying that the company as a whole would no longer buy videos or pictures of the insides of people's homes or the children of celebrities. The company also pledged not to purchase footage where the cameraman has attempted to 'create' news by goading a star. For his part, George said that since he had heard it all before, he would have to be forgiven for not jumping too high in the air. He would monitor *Hard Copy*'s behaviour and they could take it from there. But in private he was delighted. What had started out as a one-man boycott had escalated into an intimidating campaign supported by the biggest names in show business. If the media had not worked it out already, he was not a man to be messed with. He was a player. A very powerful player.

He was also very smart. When he despatched his October missive, George had been careful not to get into the debate of censorship. Freedom of the press is enshrined in the First

Amendment of the American Constitution and, as a devotée of journalistic values, there was no greater supporter of it than Clooney. On the contrary, his point had been about facts, about real stories and about keeping your word. It was against guerrilla-tactic gossip mongering masquerading as news and about TV giants encouraging kids to break the law to obtain footage for them. As a result, the industry's real newsmen were fully supportive of the boycott. 'I'm really happy that I chose this particular fight because it was an innocuous story,' he says by way of explanation. 'It wasn't some story about me screwing a sheep.'

Ironically, because of George's fight, the clamour for inside information about the forthcoming Batfilm was greater than ever. As production continued throughout the winter of 1996, everyone associated with *Batman & Robin* knew that it would take an incredible turkey of a film not to capitalise on the public fervour.

Speaking of turkeys, Christmas was looming and Fox had just the film for the holiday market – just not this holiday. *One Fine Day*, a perfect Valentine's Day film if ever there was one, was released in the USA on 20 December. Forget the fact that it was actually shot in spring and that it is an out-and-out love story, the powers that be thought that it could fill the public's seasonal need for escapism and blockbusting thrills. Over the same period, Wes Craven's *Scream*, *Beavis and Butt-Head Do America*, Chris O'Donnell's *In Love and War*, Tom Cruise's *Jerry Maguire*, Arnie's *Jingle All the Way* and John Travolta's angelic *Michael* would all enter the box-office fray.

Fox's scheduling decision seemed to be vindicated when the first reviews were filed. The *New York Times* was pleasantly surprised, although for all its claims as an international news organ it dwelt with unnaturally parochial glee on how various NYC landmarks had been treated in the film. Ooh look, there's the Radio City Music Hall! The film, it said, was 'sunny, pleasant fluff' which confirmed Michelle Pfeiffer's status as a great actor ('she shows a flair for physical comedy') and announced George's arrival as a romantic lead: 'The film goes to needless lengths to let some of its minor characters coo admiringly about Mr Clooney. But he's such a natural as a movie star that he hardly needs false flattery.'

Variety agreed and predicted 'strong box office with good legs lies ahead' for the film. 'A pretty ideal baby-boomer romantic comedy made with the right breezy insouciance and performed with consummate sexy allure by Michelle Pfeiffer and George Clooney,' it opined. George was particularly strong. 'He's the rare major actor who, like Clark Gable, holds equal appeal for men and women, and here shows a light touch that offers further evidence of considerable range and ability to dominate the big screen.' Like Clark Gable? Hadn't Michael Hoffman said the same thing? It would not be the last time George heard that.

Village Voice, the *Washington Post*, the *LA Times*: the story was the same. Enjoyable, lightweight stuff featuring gilt-edged movie star George Clooney. What could go wrong?

Every so often, events happen which remind you that the media's original role was in reporting behaviour rather than instigating it. Despite glowing press references, *One Fine Day* did not break box-office records. It opened at number one, taking $14.6 million in its debut week, but fell swiftly as audiences realised they had better things to do over Christmas. Looking back, Fox now agree that the movie should have been protected from the highly competitive seasonal scrum. George thought that all along.

'*One Fine Day* was a disappointment,' he reflects. 'It was a nice, sweet, little romantic comedy that should have been released over Valentine's Day, not in December with all the Oscar heavyweights.

'Working with Michelle Pfeiffer was an unbelievable experience. *One Fine Day* is a film that will remind people of the kind of movies that were made in the 30s and 40s when there was still some romance in the world.'

While George reflected humbly on his good fortune rather than the fact that his name was co-opening a film, others seemed eager to rub his nose in the movie's relatively poor performance. He was exactly not the type of person to rise to the bait. 'Someone said, "Hey, *Jerry Maguire* and *Michael* are kicking your butt,"' he recalls. 'And I went, "Oh, you mean, Tom Cruise and John Travolta are bigger stars than me? Whoa, you've got to be kidding."'

Like a lot of his down-to-earth characteristics, George's modesty can be infectious. Although immensely proud of *One Fine Day*, he was soon vying with *Batman* co-star Chris O'Donnell about who had had the bigger turkey that holiday season. O'Donnell's *In Love and War* had been similarly overlooked by a holiday audience. 'Chris and I were on the set at the time going,

"How'd yours tank? Mine tanked pretty bad! Hey, there's always dinner theatre!"' George laughs. 'We're going to be doing *The King and I* next.'

For all his bravado in dismissing *One Fine Day*'s critics, George was acutely aware that these were crucial times for his movie career. *ER* had overtaken *Seinfeld* as the number-one show and he had proved his diversity in *From Dusk Till Dawn* and *One Fine Day*. He was the undisputed king of TV drama, a feature in most magazines' polls for hunkiest actor and the sole reason, it sometimes seemed to him, for the *National Enquirer*'s very existence. But ever since he had risked his life in the Danger Car just to get to Hollywood, George had had one dream: to be a movie star. A major one. Someone who could open a big-budget picture. Even when he was making a living from sitcoms he knew there was more to him. 'I used to call myself a movie actor,' he admits, 'who just happened to be doing TV.'

By the end of January 1997 George had shot four movies. In each instance he had accepted the part before seeing a script – they each presented their own unmissable opportunities: his first film, his first romantic lead, his first action thriller, his first dollar-haemorrhaging blockbuster. But if he were honest, they all would have happened without him. For his next step, he needed to show a touch more discernment.

One way of ensuring higher quality control in Hollywood is to become a producer. It is common practice for stars to set up their own production companies as soon as they have achieved a little success. Ghost companies are often bestowed upon a studio's favourite stars as a vanity project, something to boost their perceived power in Tinseltown. In reality there are few celebrity companies which achieve any success. Michelle Pfeiffer had her Via Rosa; Arnold Schwarzenneger had his Oak Productions; Danny DeVito fronted Jersey Films; Ron Howard had Imagine, all of which had done good work. Among actor-driven ventures, though, they are in the minority.

But if anyone's conduct in Hollywood had proved them suited for such a career step, it was George's. His career to date had comprised a series of carefully plotted steps. It may have occasionally appeared sporadic, but he was rarely out of work and, television-wise, each job moved him steadily up the career ladder. Not only that, but he had been on long-term contracts with major studios and knew it was just a matter of time before his chance arrived. To outsiders he may have looked like just an actor, but to insiders he was something more. He was a 'player'. Look how he had secured Julianna Margulies' job on ER – even before the series had started and before he became the most in-demand face in town. Look how he was on first-name terms with every studio head in town. And look how he is the fulcrum of everything The Boys seem to do. Not only is George seemingly obsessed with how things work – from the machinations of a motorcycle engine to the inner movements of the film business – but he is also a control freak. And what could give him greater control than being a producer? It passes control of his destiny back to him, in a way Rosemary and Nick Clooney never achieved. 'The reason why you produce is because there will be a period of time in the not-too-distant future when people will be sick of seeing you,' he says. 'But then you have something else to do and you are still involved in the industry.' It would be the 'fall back' that his father had wished for him back in 1982.

After a series of potential-scoping meetings with Warners, he took the plunge with Maysville Pictures, named after his father's home town. 'I wanted to pay tribute to the old man,' he says by way of explanation. The company was set up as a partnership between him, Robert Lawrence and Pam Williams. Lawrence would run the feature side and Williams the television component. Conveniently for George, the company's office was set up on the Warners lot, approximately fifty feet from the ER soundstage. Thanks to George's tireless production-line of ideas and the endless stream of people wanting to work with him, Maysville hit the ground running. Over the next few years the company would become one of the largest actor-driven production concerns in town, with eleven employees and as many as thirty projects with major network deals pending at any one time. It would also produce big-budget films and make a number of pilots based on George's own script ideas. A decade after he first earned his reputation as the pilot king of American television, he was treading the same water again, only this time as a producer. But the feeling of helplessness as he waited for the studios' interminable focus groups to report back still remained.

In January 1997, though, George was still very much in demand as an actor and scripts were being passed to him on an almost daily basis. A few caught his eye but none lived up to its billing.

'You think you'll reach a point in this business and you'll only be getting better-than-average stuff sent to you,' he says. 'Well, wrong. At one point I was getting five scripts a week for months, and with script after script it was like, "God, this is awful." Then you hear of the stars who wind up doing it, and you think, "Man, were they stoned?" It's a test of your will, reading all those scripts. You hope you find something that's good to do before they stop sending you stuff.

'I was just finishing the shooting of *Batman* and I knew I had to find a script that was a little more on the ball,' he recalls. 'I read a bunch of scripts, I passed on a bunch, I didn't get a few, and this was the one that – well, luckily I think Travolta was busy,' he grins.

The 'one' in question was called *Out of Sight* to be made by Danny DeVito's Jersey Films. It was based on a novel by crime writer Elmore 'Dutch' Leonard whose complex character-conscious plots had previously proved notoriously difficult to film. DeVito, however, had broken that tradition with his company's *Get Shorty*, the Travolta comedy vehicle, which successfully retained the book's original characterisation, comedy and plot and was still a good film. Quentin Tarantino (whose Dutch-influenced *Pulp Fiction* was produced by Jersey Films) was also about to bring Leonard's *Rum Punch* into cinemas as the blaxploitation homage *Jackie Brown*.

George was sold on the film before he had finished the first scene.

'I read the first four pages of the script and I set it down and I said, "This is the one I want to do," ' he says. He knew it was for him and let it be known he was interested. 'I actively sought it out because after *Batman*, which was not the most fun to do, I wanted to do something that I felt was great character stuff and great fun to do.'

The *Out of Sight* screenplay was written by Scott Frank, who had also adapted *Get Shorty* to such acclaim. With *Shorty* director Barry Sonnenfeld on the project as executive producer, there was enough of the earlier film's team in place to ensure that this project would be as well delivered. All that was missing was a director to bring Frank's script to life.

The first time Steven Soderbergh heard about the project was when Universal asked him to meet with Jersey Films' Danny DeVito, Michael Shamberg and Stacey Sher. 'We had always admired Steven's work,' Shamberg says. 'He's a director who can combine storytelling and humour and action, which is exactly what the film required.'

It was a bold choice. Having made his name with *sex, lies and videotape* in 1989 – the film which is credited with putting Miramax on the distributing map (something to do with a $100-million return on a $1-million film) – Soderbergh collected a Palme d'Or in Cannes then pretty much disappeared off the commercial radar. He followed the lower-case oddity with the cerebral (that is to say, impenetrable) faux biopic *Kafka*, starring Alec Guinness and Jeremy Irons, the Depression-set *King of the Hill*, an unwelcoming film-noir thriller called *The Underneath* and the Spaulding Gray monologue piece *Gray's Anatomy*. He had just finished the most audience-challenging of them all, *Schizopolis*, when Universal made contact. Quite how they thought the man who had just delivered a non-linear, barely filmable, quasi-autobiographical portrait of himself was the best guy to helm Elmore Leonard's thriller was questionable.

Unusually for a major $49-million project, at the stage Soderbergh came on board, it was to be met by a finished script and a contracted actor. 'I inherited George Clooney and I couldn't be happier,' he admits. 'The role of Jack Foley allows him to do all the wonderful things he's capable of doing and I felt that it was a showcase for him, that he would sit like a gem at the centre of the film.'

It helped that the director was aware of the star's work, on TV at least. 'When I first saw George on *ER*, my reaction was, "That's a movie star," ' Soderbergh says. 'In other films I felt he hadn't been allowed to show what he can do. He has an undercurrent of anger – he can do light comedy, but he also has that edge that Steve McQueen had.'

With George established as the film's 'gem', Soderbergh saw no option but to cast the rest of the film specifically in relation to him. For the role of George's nemesis, federal marshal Karen Sisco, they were looking for someone who could spark off George. The whole plot of *Out of Sight* hinges on his character, a bank robber, falling for her, and vice versa – and the audience believing it. After a series of high-profile candidates had been seen, the winner was chosen: Jennifer Lopez. Despite some credible performances alongside Jack Nicholson, Michael Caine, Robin Williams, Sean Penn and a giant snake (in *Anaconda*), it was not necessarily experience which won her the part.

'George had this noisy leather couch in his study,' Soderbergh recalls. 'We had a lot of actresses audition, all the good ones. Jennifer Lopez was great, but what convinced me was that George was better with Jennifer than with anyone else. He was different, and that's what I needed.'

George saw it, too. Apart from supplying the couch, he takes little credit for what happened. 'We knew she was the one the second we did the first scene together,' he says. 'The thing is you know you're doing your job when the scenes are working. You know the scene works when you're shooting it. But you don't know, whether or not there's any chemistry, and you can only find that out when you see it. It's pot luck.'

The rest of the casting would be done by the director. He would also work with Scott Frank on the final shooting script while the actors went about their lives for six months. Filming would run for three months from 1 October, beginning in California's Mojave Desert and taking in Louisiana, Florida and Detroit – perfectly coinciding with George's fourth season on *ER*. As soon as the third season was out of the way, George could devote more time to being with Céline. This would be their first summer break together and his first for three years. After their tumultuous experiences in the glare of the media spotlight over the last six months, they had earned it.

Of course, there's resting and there's resting. Working seven-day weeks for so long is a hard habit to get out of and the idea of doing nothing, physically nothing, for any amount of time was anathema to George. His mind is always buzzing, thinking of ideas, opportunities, pranks or ways round problems. Even when he is not busy on his day job, then there are plenty of other things to occupy his time. Apart from his increasing obligations to Maysville Pictures and its TV arm Mirador Entertainment, he was continually on the lookout for work of his own. Shortly after he signed up for *Out of Sight*, he heard a rumour that Terrence Malick was preparing to make a new film. Now that would be a project to be involved with. This would be Malick's first film for twenty years after making the seminal *Bad Lands* and *Days of Heaven*. The likes of Sean Penn, Nick Nolte, Woody Harrelson, John Cusack, Ben Chaplin and even John Travolta were already on the team and George was desperate to get involved.

For all his status as a Hollywood player, there was no getting away from the fact that a little politicking was needed. Just as he

's very easy to sit in a room at 23 and have everyone
, "You're the greatest," and believe it. Which I think I
d for a minute, to be honest. I thought I was pretty
appening because I had good TV hair' – and good
ovie hair. George Clooney, 38, sporting the Billy Tyne
ok at the Hollywood premiere of *Three Kings*, October
999. (© Galella Ron/Corbis Sygma)

'It's the longest relationship of my life, although we don't have sex any more' George talking about Max the Vietnamese pot-bellied pig (right) rather than partner-at-the-time Kelly Preston. Pictured in December 1988 at the trio's new million-dollar house (© Neal Preston/Corbis)

'Atropine! Dopamine! Three hundred CCs saline!' Just another day in the life of everyone's favourite maverick paediatrician, *ER*'s Dr Doug Ross. (© MO/Corbis KIPA)

When George met Barfly waitress and law student Céline Balitran in Paris, she had no idea who he was. 'She actually said, "Actors always seem so big-headed," and I thought, "Is she having me on?"' Pictured at the 55th Venice Film Festival, September 1998. (© Arici Graziano/Corbis Sygma)

Batman, Robin and Batgirl and those rubber suits. 'If you really had to wear this thing, everybody would kick the hell out of you. The most elaborate stunt I've been able to do is walk to my trailer.' (© Corbis Sygma)

'As soon as they got in the room, it was as if there wasn't enough air' – Section Eight partner Steven Soderbergh on the electric rapport between George and *Out Of Sight* co-star Jennifer Lopez. Pictured at the film's Chelsea West cinema premiere on 24 June 1998.
(© Azzara Steve/Corbis Sygma)

As Captain Charles Bosche in Terrence Malick's *The Thin Red Line*. 'They might have cut my lines to almost nothing so that if you blink you miss me, but I feel it is my most important film experience yet.'
(© Corbis Sygma)

With co-star Holly Hunter at the press conference for *O Brother, Where Art Thou?*, Cannes, 13 May 2000. The film only got made because he took a cut in salary. 'If the movie makes money, I make money; if it doesn't, then we got to make the movie.'
(© Cardinale Stephane/ Corbis Sygma)

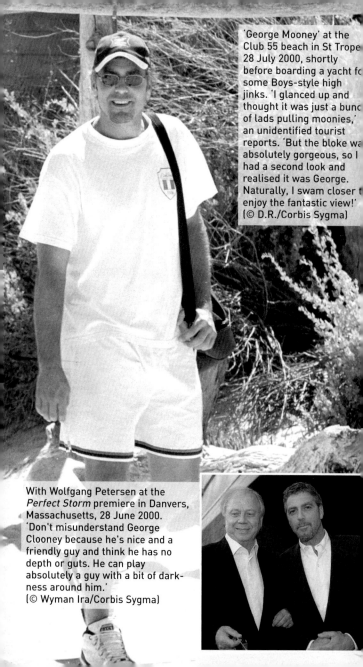

'George Mooney' at the Club 55 beach in St Tropez 28 July 2000, shortly before boarding a yacht for some Boys-style high jinks. 'I glanced up and thought it was just a bunch of lads pulling moonies,' an unidentified tourist reports. 'But the bloke was absolutely gorgeous, so I had a second look and realised it was George. Naturally, I swam closer to enjoy the fantastic view!' (© D.R./Corbis Sygma)

With Wolfgang Petersen at the *Perfect Storm* premiere in Danvers, Massachusetts, 28 June 2000. 'Don't misunderstand George Clooney because he's nice and a friendly guy and think he has no depth or guts. He can play absolutely a guy with a bit of darkness around him.' (© Wyman Ira/Corbis Sygma)

ABOVE: 'If you want to talk about heroes, parents are heroes.' George with his own 'heroes', Nick and Nina Clooney, at the New York premiere of *The Peacemaker*, 22 September 1997. (© Pace Gregory/Corbis Sygma)

BELOW: With *Ocean's 11* and *Confessions Of A Dangerous Mind* co-star Julia Roberts. 'George is this great, wonderful kind of goof of a guy. And the fact that he can make it go away when the camera's rolling is a pretty funny trick that he does. He becomes very charming and suave when that's just not the way he is at all.' (The Kobal Collection/Warner Bros/Marshak, Bob)

'I think when you list the names of the actors in this category – Jim Carrey, Robert De Niro, John Cusack and Mel Gibson – that you've got to figure I'm going to win this. What have they done?' Best Actor In A Comedy Or Musical winner George Clooney at the 58th Golden Globes, 21 January 2001.
(© Trapper Frank/Corbis Sygma)

had for *ER*, he picked up the phone and campaigned for a part. 'I called up Terrence Malick when I heard he was doing it and I said, "I'll carry your camera case, I'll do anything you want," ' he reveals. 'He said, "OK," and found me two scenes in the movie.'

The movie in question was *The Thin Red Line*, an account of the United States' attempt to liberate the Pacific island of Guadalcanal from Japanese control in 1942, based on the anti-war novel by James Jones. It was to be shot in Australia and Guadalcanal over five months although George's contribution as Charles Bosche wasn't expected to take more than a week.

'I have a cameo as a military captain who comes in after this terrible battle and says that from now on everything will be different,' George explains. 'From this point on, all the crap stops. He's a man who knows that war has the power to poison the soul, but he's a military man so he has to keep the troops going.'

And so he and Céline found themselves flying to Australia for a working holiday. With only two days' actual shooting, the flight was almost longer than George's time on set, but at least it gave the lovers some time together away from the cauldron of LA, and gave George the opportunity to work on his golf swing. It also meant he got to ask his hero Malick about his 'lost weekend' – all twenty years of it. 'I wanted to get the big secret about what's going on? "Where were you for the last twenty years?" ' George says. ' "Well," he said, "I went to Paris and just kind of hung out." There's no story. That was it. But he is one of the best film-makers I've ever seen.'

What the shoot lacked in length, it made up for in fear factor. 'It was a little intimidating,' he admits. 'Not only Malick and all the tanks, but great actors whom I've never worked with. I happen to think that Sean Penn is the most talented actor of my generation – we're around the same age – so it was a little intimidating working with Sean for the first time.'

Another problem of the tiny role, like that of Travolta's, was billing. George was willing to work for free just to be involved. 'I just wanted to work with Terrence Malick,' he says, 'because before you get hit by the bus, you want to be able to say, "Hey, I worked with Terrence Malick, by the way." ' What he didn't want, was to be exploited by the film's marketing team and put his more worthy co-stars' noses out of joint. 'They offered us all "favoured nations" pay, which is where you make a big chunk of money and then everybody gets the same billing,' he explains. 'I wouldn't take that because they said then they would be able to advertise the film using my name. And they'd have the right because they paid me for it.

'What happens is that you see an entertainment report, and it will say, "*The Thin Red Line* starring George Clooney", and it insults those guys who worked for five months on the film. I just show up, stay in a nice hotel room in Australia and play golf and then put on some fatigues and do the last scene of the movie. I really try and downplay it.'

As for the film's title, George found comparisons between its message and his own life. 'The thin red line is the line between the sane and the mad,' he explains. 'It's rather like walking the thin red line of success and failure in showbiz.' And he should know. Fittingly, as the third season of *ER* came to an end, George found himself picking up an award that honoured his years of unswerving commitment to the industry, his impressive development work with Maysville and his selfless stand against paparazzi journalism: *People* magazine voted him 1997's 'Sexiest Man Alive'. Wherever you were when the announcement was made, you probably heard the howls of derision emanating from Casa de Clooney as The Boys mocked their celebrity pal. And laughing loudest of all was George himself.

14. I THINK I BURIED THAT FRANCHISE

For decades, beauty pageants have been won by Identikit *Stepford Wives*-type women professing a need to travel the world and help children. It seems to go with the gig, along with the sashes and fake smiles. Fortunately the title of Sexiest Man Alive comes with no such responsibilities. It's just as well. George has always had more than enough pet causes of his own to campaign for. In 1997, the topic was racial equality in Hollywood. Again.

As he had said back in 1994 when the Anti-Defamation League had victimised him, without evidence, Tinseltown is rife with racism and bigotry. Three years later he felt he could prove it. After three seasons, during which the show had risen to number one in the ratings, *ER* had provided cover stars and stories for every entertainment magazine in America. George's lantern-jawed features alone had looked demurely up from hundreds of titles, not least the respected weekly *TV Guide*. The same magazine had also run front-page stories on Noah Wyle, Julianna Margulies – all of the show's main cast, in fact, apart from one. Eriq La Salle – the ensemble's only black actor – had never been featured on the cover of *TV Guide* despite posing for three photo shoots for the magazine. Something was not right.

George takes up the story: 'Eriq wanted to go after *TV Guide* and rightly so,' he explains. 'He'd done three photo shoots for them, and they never put him on the cover. Maybe you do one and they don't put you on the cover, but not three. The problem was, his complaining made it look like he was an actor who was upset about not getting on the cover of a magazine as opposed to the bigger issue of racism.'

Yet again, George saw a fight worth instigating. And yet again, he had everything to lose. He was the most sought-after actor on American television and about to open in a $100-million blockbuster. Warner Bros almost certainly did not want his name associated in any way at that stage with racism, just in case it reflected on the film. As George had learned in his earlier fight, just the implication of bigotry is enough to get the presses rolling, whatever the rights and wrongs. But he would not be stopped. His attitude towards race issues was beyond reproach but, he reasoned, what was the point of being a hero on the screen if you lived a coward's life off it? He persuaded La Salle against his action and took over the fight.

'I said, let this cast, all of us, take this up,' he explains. 'First thing we had to do was research. Then I called the editor and asked, "Why?" He said, "You can't tell us what to do." I said, "Absolutely not, but I can point it out when you don't do it." ' Once again George was campaigning using his journalist's instinct. This was not about censorship; on the contrary, it was about freedom of speech and equal opportunities.

In the case against the country's biggest-selling listings magazine, George had stepped up as a man. He did interviews on the subject because he wanted to, not because it was in any deal. It says a lot about him that he felt so compelled, especially considering how important it was at that time that America like him. *TV Guide* vigorously denied any wrongdoing and, in the end, the matter disappeared off George's radar after the death of Princess Diana.

Less than six months after filming had finished, *Batman & Robin* was gearing up for its world premiere. The publicity trail had started early – George and his fellow Gothamites were speaking to magazines in early spring, with newspaper, radio and TV spots closer to the big day: 20 June. The campaign culminated with a special *Oprah* show featuring Batman, Robin, Mr Freeze and Joel Schumacher. Whatever his film billing, when it came to the chat-show schtick, George was the big draw. He sat down first to be joined by Chris O'Donnell, then Schwarzenneger and finally Joel Schumacher. Despite Oprah's inane questioning and continuous interruptions (standard for most US talk-show hosts; Letterman and O'Donnell are the worst culprits), George had the studio audience mesmerised with his self-deprecating put-downs and good-natured banter with his co-stars, in particular O'Donnell.

The US premiere was everything that Warner Bros could hope for, with all the cast and seemingly every cameraman in America in attendance. George escorted Céline along the red carpet and into the theatre, stopping to give one-line interviews to the encircled press. Céline's radiant face and amazing figure appeared on dozens of front pages the next day. By the time the couple got to bed that night, they were already a recurring item on most cities' rolling news services. This was a far cry from working in the Barfly and, for the time being, it went some way to making the constant paparazzi intrusion less painful.

After more than a year's feverish expectation, fans rushed to see the film in their millions. On its opening weekend, *Batman & Robin* grossed $43 million, just $8 million down on *Batman Forever* and more than double Julia Roberts' *My Best Friend's Wedding*. And then the reviews kicked in. 'My Best Friend's Wedding kicked Batman & Robin's butt,' George winces. It was not the only film to do so, but at least it was a different market. Unfortunately *Batman* did not perform well against the other big-budget fantasy releases. A few weeks before, *The Lost World* had run off with $90 million in its first four days and was still packing them in; Barry Sonnenfeld's *Men in Black* was also a big summer hit. *Batman*, on the other hand, saw audiences drop by more than fifty per cent after the first week. The message going round was clear: if you want over-the-top escapism, then there were at least two films to see before you checked this one out.

The movie was not just a big deal for Warner Bros in the States, it was the focal point of their summer release strategy the world over, with simultaneous release in most territories. And where there was the film, there was an event. In a twenty-day burst, George and various others touched down in no fewer than seventeen cities. On 23 June, just a few days after the US launch, he was joined in London by Arnie and Uma Thurman – the film's deliciously camp Poison Ivy – for the UK premiere at the Warner Village multiplex in Leicester Square. Despite the word trickling through from America, an estimated five-thousand fans packed the tourist precinct to catch a glimpse of the stars. As George arrived with Céline, crushed fans had to be rescued by police as the crowd surged forward. Arnie, accompanied by his pregnant wife Marie Shriver, may have had his name over the film, he may have earned six times more than George for a fraction of the work, but there was only one reason why that crowd had turned out. The Sexiest Man Alive was in town.

If George was fazed by the cacophonous screaming that greeted his every step along the red carpet, he did not let on. With one hand hovering proprietorially behind Céline's black-suited back, he waved to the crowd, laughed as girls declared their love for him and posed for photographs like it was the most natural thing in the world to have five-thousand people squealing his name. The truth was, of course, that it was becoming more natural than most people could appreciate.

Just as in America, Warner publicity in the UK was on overdrive. Before the charity screening began, the stars took part in an interview broadcast live to twenty cinemas around the country, the same twenty that would carry the real film on its 27 June release. Added to another nine in London, it amounted to one of the largest distribution pushes in British history. By giving as many people as possible the chance to see it in the first week, while the massive hype was still fresh in audience minds, a canny studio could minimise the effects of bad reviews and disappointing word of mouth. Was this Warner Bros' plan? Well, given that exactly the same sales pattern occurred in the UK as in the US – box office was down by more than half in the second week – they could well have been right.

The publicity buzz did not end with the premiere, however, giving further fuel to gossips who said that Warner Bros knew they had a stillborn product on their hands. The studio had spent a fortune overhauling one of the River Thames' most famous landmarks, the disused Battersea Power Station, for the aftershow party, transforming part of it into Wayne Manor. As the Batsignal seared brightly into the night sky, the stars swept into the magnificent building amidst the furious popping of flashbulbs and camera spotlights. If the film itself did not qualify for coverage in the following day's newspapers, this garish extravagance surely would.

And it did. Clooneymania had arrived in England and that was what the papers wanted to talk about: this man who plays a disreputable medic on an overbusy TV drama was causing the sort of storm normally reserved for pop stars, and young boy bands at that – not 36-year-old men with salt-and-pepper-flecked hair and a live-in lover. How did it happen? Why did it happen? What was his story?

From a personal point of view, as he had forecast all along, it did not really matter to George if *Batman & Robin* won less than adulatory notices. Just being associated with something on this scale had moved his career into a new echelon. He was on the international map, walking among those stars considered 'fire proof' by critics. It was just as well. *Kapow!* 'Holy steaming batjunk' said the *Observer*. *Blam!* 'A pile of batcrap' mocked the

Sunday Times. Krack! 'Clooney aside, you know a film is in deep trouble when the best performance is given by Arnold Schwarzenegger' muttered the *Sunday Telegraph*. Still, in most people's minds, George was an improvement on Val Kilmer in terms of bringing humanity to Bruce Wayne, and he was streets ahead of Michael Keaton as far as filling the Batsuit went. And really, hype aside, *Batman & Robin* was slicker than the first film, funnier than the third and more pacy than the second. It just needed a plot.

For all the hype, positive and negative, *Batman & Robin* would go on to make $250 million at the box office, even without the fast-food chain tie-ins and income from Poison Ivy dolls and other merchandise. Not a total failure, then, for a film with a $100-million budget. 'The movie made money,' George confirms, 'but not as much as the studio expected and it was considered a big disappointment.' A lot of the credit for the massive international interest has to be lain at George's door. As the press carnival roared round the globe, he became the film's roving ambassador, whipping up each market's interest in the film long after Arnie had returned to his presidential retreat. It won him a lot of fans, even among critics who hated the film, as he popped up on every major network and in every mainstream publication, flirting and joking his way through increasingly repetitive interviews. The overlying message was clear: see *Batman*, it's not brain surgery but it's great fun. The underlying message was different: my name is George Clooney; remember me. Media-savvy player that he is, George realised that *Batman* had to work for him and there was no better way of breaking his name in far-off territories. If he did his best now, people would be more amenable when he wanted to sell something he cared about. As he says, '*Batman*, as bad a movie as it became, was the biggest break of my life. I don't regret a moment of it. I don't know how anyone would have turned it down.'

If George had proved himself a canny operator by using the film to give his personal standing a leg-up, it was small beer compared to the spin he invented for himself a short while later once the dust had settled. Having worked harder than anyone else to promote the film, he was conscious that the public perception of his judgement would be questioned by the movie's poor reviews. No problem, he would just let fans into a secret: he thought it was a bad film as well. Look back at the *Oprah* show, he could point out, did I say it was a good film then? 'When you have to go and sell a movie you know isn't very good, it's a trick,' he reveals. 'You get paid pretty well to do these things and it's your job to sell them, but it's difficult when you don't like the movie. You learn to say things that might help but that aren't lies: "It's the biggest movie I've ever seen . . . It's got great effects . . . Arnold's a blast to work with."

'You have to look guys in the eye and dance around the subject when all you really want to say is that there is no script and that I wasn't any good in it.'

Some interviewers picked up on the film's inadequacies. When George appeared on *The Tonight Show*, Jay Leno struggled to find compliments. In the end, he liked the backdrops. 'You have to worry when people start talking about how good the colours are in a movie,' George laughs.

Before the year was out, George was questioning the film in public. 'I thought *Batman* fell short,' he admitted a few months later. 'I think that in a couple of months I'll have to take another look and see where my responsibility lies in that, because you can't point at everyone. I can't point at Joel Schumacher, who's my friend, or the writer, and say, "Well, this fell short" or "This didn't work". I need to take another look at what I could have done to make it better first.' Within a year, in a knowing lift of JFK's *mea culpa* response to the Bay of Pigs debacle, he was demanding all blame be directed at himself and cracking jokes about his own liability. 'I think I buried that franchise,' he laughed. 'I think that one's done.' He refused even to credit Joel Schumacher with any of the blame as BBC interviewer Jonathan Ross insisted. 'I don't know. I'd love to blame somebody else. I wasn't very good.'

Today he is a little more candid. 'I don't take the full heat for that personally,' he reveals. 'I do publicly. I go, "Hey, it bombed, I'll take the heat." But I don't know what I could have done. I saw part of it on cable the other day and cringed through it. It's a tough one, because the script isn't there at all.'

A fortnight after *Batman & Robin* had premiered in Europe and seven months after it was released in America, *One Fine Day* was finally given a European run out. Were Fox thinking they would capitalise on the free publicity that the Warners circus would provide for their star? As one UK reviewer observed, 'Films are like buses: whatever time they leave they end up nose to tail somewhere along the road.'

As with the Batflop, George was quick to draw the positives from the film. 'The movie was what it was,' he says. 'It wasn't groundbreaking stuff, but it makes you smile. And it made a lot of money. Was it a great film? Absolutely not. Was I proud to be in it and was it a lucky break for me? Absolutely.'

Unfortunately, for UK reviewers the fresh memory of the actor doing the media rounds with such a straight face on behalf of *Batman & Robin* still rankled and comments on *One Fine Day* took the brunt. 'The movie so falls over itself to make sure we find him adorable – he clowns at restaurant windows, plays with kids and kittens, splashes in puddles and other fun things – that it provokes precisely the opposite reaction, namely the heartfelt desire that he'd fall under the nearest bus,' thundered the *Sunday Times*. 'Clooney is one of those people who look like Identikit composites of a man you might suspect of being a star,' sniped the *Evening Standard*. 'But I can't warm to him. He's all surface, which is characteristic of TV performers who suddenly get enlarged to cinema-screen size.' The *Daily Telegraph* was more blunt: 'I once thought that Clooney might be a new [Cary] Grant. But here he's more a poor man's Mel Gibson.' Ouch.

There was some comfort from the *Independent* ('Clooney is effortlessly appealing') and *The Times* ('he displays an easy charm and light touch') but, without doubt, his best personal press came from the *Financial Times*. It was still obsessing about the fact that he had two films out within as many weeks: 'But who can complain when this man's charcoal eyebrows, rag-doll limberness of body language and basso jocoso voice make a mediocre romantic comedy watchable?'

And who says there is no consistency with critics?

With his head still spinning from the UK press's unanimous declarations of his other-worldly brilliance/smug incompetence (delete where applicable), George managed to find the time for a bit of R&R in sunnier climes. What was the point of having your first summer break in years if you did not take a vacation with your nearest and dearest, he thought? As he left Casa de Clooney for a seventeen-day golfing trip with The Boys, pig-sitting Céline might have asked the same question. But hey, at least she'd been on the Bat-tour.

It was just as well that the trip was a good one (good being defined by the amount of drinking knocked back rather than the quality of the golf) because no sooner had George returned than he became embroiled in yet another press fight. The targets were the same: the paparazzi and the parasitic tabloid media which encouraged their lawless ways. But this fight was sparked neither by a colleague's feeling of discrimination nor by a programme breaking its word. It came about as the result of the death of a woman. A princess.

As mother of the future heir to the British throne, the life – and loves – of Diana, Princess of Wales was still of massive news interest on 30 August 1997. When she left the Paris Ritz with current beau Dodi Fayed, son of the hotel's owner Mohamed al Fayed, she was under closer photographer scrutiny than ever. Shortly after midnight, and with the press pack camped outside the hotel, the couple opted for a three-car decoy strategy to reach Fayed's Champs-Elysée apartment. His Range Rover, driven by his regular chauffeur, and a Mercedes, were stationed outside the main entrance. A third car, a hired black Mercedes 280SL, waited at the back entrance of the hotel. Its driver, Henri Paul, was not one of the hotel's retinue of official drivers.

As Diana, Fayed and bodyguard Trevor Rees-Jones stepped into the Mercedes, it was clear that the decoy ruse had not worked. Men in cars and on scooters flanked the car as it made its way down the Rue de Rivoli on the way to the river, going to extreme lengths to capture a photograph of the backseat couple. At the wheel, Henri Paul went to further lengths to keep them at bay. Travelling at four times the speed limit in places, the Mercedes wove in and out of traffic and made late turning decisions, trying to shake off its gnat-like pursuers. Along the Cours de la Reine the bizarre motocade went, then on to the Cours Albert 1er. As the Mercedes approached the winding entrance of the Pont de l'Alma tunnel, it was speeding at close to 120 m.p.h.

To this day the exact details of what happened next remain the subject of animated dispute. Witnesses have spoken of a paparazzi vehicle trying to force its way in front of the Mercedes, others have said that a car travelling from the opposite direction became involved in the chase. What is known is that seconds after the Mercedes entered the tunnel, it span out of control, striking the thirteenth concrete pillar dividing the tunnel, rolling over and bouncing off the right wall. When the car stopped spinning, it was facing the direction it had come from, its horn eerily activated by the driver's slumped body.

The impact of the crash was so great that Henri Paul's torso became mangled with parts of the car radiator. Dodi's death was also instant; Diana's came some hours afterwards, in hospital. Only Rees-Jones, the one traveller wearing a safety belt, survived.

The first photographs of the tragic accident were taken while the Mercedes' engine was still running and while the Princess was still breathing, 'unconscious but moaning and gesturing in every direction'. Stunned paparazzi dumped their scooters and swarmed around the car, but not all of them were checking for survivors. They were clicking and clicking and clicking some more, screaming about the carnage they were witnessing but doing nothing more than recording it on film. When Diana was officially declared dead at 4 a.m. at the Hospital La Pitie Salpetriere, photos of her unconscious body in the car had already been hawked around the world's media agencies for several hours. They had chased her that night hoping for a story and they had got one. The biggest story of their lives.

In preparation for the fourth season of *ER*, George Clooney was asleep at Casa de Clooney when the tragedy struck. Like most Americans, he spent the morning tuned into CNN and other news channels watching developments. Like many, he blamed the tabloids for the death. Everything he had ever said about the culture of inciting criminal behaviour in order to gain exclusive footage had been proved by this event. Look at his own experience, look at the fact that the three trespassers on the *Batman* set had been willing to risk their liberty for the sake of a few seconds of film. And look how *Inside Edition*, the tabloid programme that was buying their tape, was able to piously wash its hands of the situation and deny any wrongdoing. 'If the show had sent their own reporters to go undercover on the set, steal walkie-talkies, forge identification and do all the things that are illegal to get to that point, and got caught, then *Inside Edition* would be responsible for what they did,' George says. 'Instead, they're "buying" something that's already been done illegally.'

Fearing for their commercial lives after an anti-paparazzi backlash, many of the world's tabloid magazines rushed out statements of mourning and sorrow. The *National Enquirer* was no more or less contrite than anyone else, but it had the unhappy coincidence of carrying a Princess Diana cover story on its latest issue. While editor Steven Coz gave statements about the tragic accident, copies of his magazine with the headline about Diana's amazing sex life were still on sale around the US.

Given his earlier run-ins with the press, George was the obvious person to approach for the 'voice-of-Hollywood' view. It was not a position he wanted to accept. This was not about his fight, it was about two boys who had lost a mother, and others who had lost children. However, when he received word that a group of other actors was planning to make a stand against the media intrusion in their own lives, he felt he should act. 'When Princess Diana died, I wasn't going to get involved at all until a bunch of actors, who shall remain nameless, started calling me and said they were going to hold a press conference and talk about how unfair and how miserable their lives are,' he recalls. 'I said to them all, "Three months from now this will be an old story and what will be remembered is a bunch of you making $20 million a year complaining about your lives."'

No, he resolved. If a statement had to be made it would not be for personal gain. The media had blood on its hands and he would say so. On 3 September 1997, George called a press conference. Beginning by explaining how 'this is not about me', he pulled no punches when it came to pointing fingers: 'Princess Di is dead, and who should we see about that? The driver of the car? The paparazzi? Or the magazines and papers who purchase these pictures and make bounty hunters out of photographers? The same magazines, television shows and papers that use their pages, creating the news, causing altercations and then filming them. Well, you must feel exhilarated! You bought and paid for one of the greatest news stories of the year! And for your success, you must be accountable.'

Because of his high media visibility on news channels after the accident, Steven Coz, editor of *National Enquirer*, suffered the brunt of George's speech. 'I watch as you scramble for high ground, saying that you won't purchase these pictures. Pictures of a dying Princess trapped in her car. Well, I'm impressed. What ethics! Your cover of your magazine this week is: "Di can't get enough sex". It's on the stands still! I also watch as you take your position on CNN saying as long as there is a market for this, then you're just supplying the goods. It's because of the public's insatiable appetite for celebrities, they're to blame. The public is.

All right. So let's use your argument. There are also thousands of people with an insatiable appetite for crack. The person who supplies that is a dealer and if he gets caught, he goes to jail. A photographer will commit a crime to get compromising pictures and later, you merely buy those pictures – absolving yourself of any responsibilities. If you weren't hiding behind the profession of journalism you would be an accomplice to a crime and you would go to jail.'

The words 'malicious intent', which seemed to protect most tabloid actions in law, would have to be examined, George said, and he swore not to rest until they were. He ended with a direct comment to Coz and his contemporaries: 'I wonder how you sleep at night? You should be ashamed.'

Strong stuff. The harsh words and the calm manner in which they were delivered earned George coverage on every news channel and in every paper that night. Editorials were devoted to applauding or lambasting him, depending on whether the journal in question was in the spotlight or not. True to his word, George stepped up a gear in his search for legislative change. Lunches with the Los Angeles mayor and meetings with law-makers and real journalists became part of his daily routine. It would not happen overnight, but he felt that change would come. It had to.

From sticking up for black kids at school to introducing a more democratic dining policy at the ER studios, George had never been afraid to stick his head above the parapet. His bust-up with Ed Weinberger on the set of Baby Talk could have got him blacklisted in Hollywood, but he would not let a co-star be publicly humiliated by anyone. His outspoken campaign against Hard Copy could have backfired totally, but he thought it had to be said. And now he had gone on live television and accused vast swathes of the world's media of complicity (to varying extents) in the death of the Princess of Wales. He could not begin to imagine what the industry's revenge would be.

He should not have worried. A few snooty editorials about 'dumb actors' here, the odd sarcastic remark from photographers there but, all in all, nothing he could not handle. The most enterprising show of defiance from the camera-wielding industry came at the New York premiere of his latest film, The Peacemaker. While the likes of Steven Spielberg and Nicole Kidman fought their way through the photo-snapping throng, George was subjected to ... absolutely nothing. On cue, as George stepped from his limo, every single press photographer, paparazzo and film cameraman in attendance put his camera on the ground. This Clooney guy was not the only one who could do a peaceful protest. His Gandhi-of-Hollywood shtick was wearing a little thin and so they would deprive him of the oxygen of publicity that people like him need to survive. That would learn 'im.

On a list of celebrities who would be worried about not being photographed, George's name would be very low, if it appeared at all. As a man, he appreciated the civilised and pointed demonstration. As a thinking man, he knew he had already won. And he told them so.

'I actually issued a challenge to them,' he says. 'I said, "OK, from now on, you're boycotting me because of my stance against tabloid television. I'm never going to change that stance, ever. So here's the challenge: you never take my picture again. Not ever. I'm the only one taking risks here. My guess is it will have no effect on my career at all. None. I'll take that bet, and if I'm wrong, then I'll be the one who loses." It was a big win that night, on all counts.'

The point that the protesting photographers missed was that he was not advocating censorship. 'The only thing worse than an out-of-control press acting with no regard for decency would be restricting that very same press,' he had said. What's more, he fully accepted the public's right to be kept up to date about misbehaving stars.

'Look, if I'm walking out of a cathouse with some hooker on my arm, and they get a picture of it, I deserve it,' he says. 'I'm a celebrity, a public figure, that's fair.

'But come with me through an airport one day and watch what they do to the people I'm with. When seventeen-year-old kids with video cameras go "Who's the fat chick?" and so you go "Fuck you," and then they sell that – that's creating news. And that to me is the problem.

'If you say to somebody, I'll give you $250,000 for a shot of Madonna's baby, you've created bounty hunters. What's to say for $250,000 somebody doesn't just kick the fucking door in and take the picture. I would.'

While American newspapers obsessed about the great paparazzi stand-off, they mostly overlooked the fact that George was in town that night to promote his new film, *The Peacemaker*.

Some people were interested, though. Very interested. Forget Clooney: this was the first picture from DreamWorks.

If Jay Leno's desperate talk of the *Batman* colour scheme was interpreted as the only nice thing he could find to say about a dire movie, what are we to make of a film which provoked so many to talk about its producer's logo? The saccharine image of a boy fishing into clouds from the moon seemed to interest just about everybody. Which is more than can be said of the film. With its European release following swiftly on from its US debut, DreamWorks were treated to a double whammy of sighs from disappointed audiences from both sides of the Atlantic. Unlike *Batman*, where there appeared to be industry resentment at the way the film was being beaten into the planet's consciousness, *The Peacemaker* appeared to inspire genuine disappointment. People expected so much more.

'A dull debut,' said *Time* magazine; 'clean out of your head before the end credits have played out,' said *Screen International*. 'By no means a triumph, by no means a disaster' – *Empire*; 'for all the huff and puff of Steven Spielberg and associates, what emerges is last year's model of a global-crisis melodrama' – the *Evening Standard*. For most reviewers, Mimi Leder's wham-bam-thankyou-mam linear approach to moving plot lines along betrayed her *ER* apprenticeship but, to be fair, the fact that the film concluded with yet another race-against-time bomb-defusing scene meant that the script was not exactly alive with originality. *Village Voice* best summed up the general feeling: 'If the first film to be released by DreamWorks SKG is any omen of the studio's fortunes, expect things to start slow, pick up steam and then plateau at a level where money and high technology tend to mask a general lack of ideas.'

After weeks spent talking about the Princess Diana affair, George had a conspiracy theory of his own. 'DreamWorks was being reviewed rather than *The Peacemaker*,' he claims. 'It was the first time I'd gotten bad reviews ever in my life. Actually, *Batman* came out first, so it was like a one-two punch.' He obviously hadn't seen the UK press for *One Fine Day* . . .

Actually, George's own contribution scored the most favourable remarks. So he didn't exactly spark against Nicole Kidman's Julia Kelly, but that was more to do with the fast-moving plot. The majority of reviewers kindly overlooked the fact that his natural John Wayne-like lopsided swagger was the worst attempt at a military gait ever and focused on his charm. And his looks. And the fact that he was the new Clark Gable. 'Much credit to Clooney, who has perfected his head-down, eyes-up look of longing to a lucrative art,' said the *FT*. The weekend broadsheets vied to come up with the most original compliments: 'With his cropped hair, great dry-cleaning and purring bedside manner, he seems to be an actor made up of almost entirely velvet textures, the mere sight of him is enough to put the camera in a spin,' suggested the *Sunday Times*. Not to be outdone, 'he has the body of Action Man and the eyes of a ferociously attractive cow', said the *Independent on Sunday*. The only dissenting voice, in fact, was to be found in the *Guardian*. 'Clooney must be the most wooden action hero since George Lazenby,' it railed. 'His control of his facial muscles, however, is absolute: the head remains tilted, as if in thought; the chin is tucked, as if in resolution; the mouth occasionally widens, as if in mirth. "As if" being the operative phrase.'

After three years of almost endless unbridled flattery for his role as Dr Doug Ross, George was finding the step-up to carrying a $50-million film a lot more demanding than he could ever have imagined, and it had nothing to do with the physical demands of acting. He was the one in the shop window, he was the guy being shot at for things that were not necessarily his fault. Putting his neck on the line for a cause he believed in was one thing, but to be slaughtered in print for just doing his job was a brand-new experience for him. How he handled it would go a long way to defining the length and quality of the rest of his career.

At least there was one place where he could still do no wrong. In September 1997, George met up with the rest of the *ER* cast to begin work on the fourth season. With four films under his belt, interviews to promote the new episodes concentrated on one area, just like they did every September. Was he going to jump ship or at the very least demand a massive salary increase to stay with the show?

No, was the short answer. 'I'm perfectly willing to do things that I'm supposed to do,' he says. 'People have made a big deal about my renegotiating the *ER* contract, but the truth of the matter is that wasn't something spectacular at all. It's a scary profession we're in when just doing what you're supposed to do is some kind of distinction.' He said it.

15. WOOF WOOF WOOF

In December 1995, college friends Trey Parker and Matt Stone put together a short cartoon for a Fox executive to give out as a Christmas gift. Despite being called 'The Spirit of Christmas', the show was extraordinarily foul-mouthed and blasphemous, featuring not only an ill-tempered fight between Santa Claus and Jesus Christ but also the death of a child. Like most recipients, George Clooney, could not believe his eyes – or ears – as he put the tape into his VCR. It was the funniest and filthiest piece of TV he had ever seen and he could not wait to share it with his friends. 'I made about two-hundred copies and sent it to everybody because I thought it was hysterical,' he says. And from there it snowballed. Of those two-hundred copies, several found their way into the hands of George's friends at the major studios and deals were struck. *South Park* the series was born.

Naturally he downplays his involvement today – 'sometimes they give me too much credit,' he shrugs. 'I didn't start it, but I sent it' – but Parker and Stone were in no doubts. When the series got green-lighted, they wanted him to appear in the show, and they had the perfect character.

'They called me up and said, "We're going to do a TV show and do you want to play Sparky the gay dog?"' George laughs. 'They brought a mike to my trailer while I was shooting *ER* and they said, "Just bark." So I barked several different ways, woof, woof, woof, and I saw Noah Wyle walking by with a what-the-hell's-goin'-on look on his face. I go, "I'm Sparky the gay dog." And he walks away.'

As payment for his ongoing contribution, George is still sent unsanitised versions of each show. 'I have all the episodes of *South Park* unedited,' he says proudly. 'They do them first unedited – unbleeped – and it's hysterical. Horrifying but hysterical.'

His debut appearance, in the episode 'Big Gay Al's Big Gay Boat Ride', was aired on 3 September 1997 – the same day as his 'Diana' press conference. Moral crusader by day, victimised canine by night. Not your average Hollywood lifestyle.

* * *

George's campaigning approach to life manifests itself in a variety of ways. When he is not trying to green-light a cartoon series or enforce legislative change for the media, his mind is forever bubbling with new interests, new causes, new ways of doing things. A restless workaholic by instinct as well as opportunity, it is only the lack of hours in the day that keeps a lot of his ideas from being given a public airing. In conversation – real conversation, not interviews – he flits from one topic to another. He thrives on new environments and loves bouncing thoughts off whomever he is talking to. He cracks jokes endlessly. In his day-to-day life he attempts to multi-task as much as possible, often with chaotic results. And he is a born fidget. Watch him on chat shows as he picks bits of fluff from his clothes or taps his fingers on the host's desk. His mind is constantly on the go, 24/7.

As a result, watching George get bored can strike trepidation into the hearts of friends, family and colleagues. He doesn't handle ennui well and it normally means bad news for those around him. They know he is only moments away from distracting everyone with a new prank. Or, even worse, more work.

Obviously George's summer programme of film launches, interviews and political rallying, squeezed between precious moments with Céline, had not been enough to occupy his mind. With ER comfortably installed as the number-one show at the end of its third season, George could have been forgiven for resting on his laurels and just looking forward to easing himself back into Dr Ross's scrubs that September. But no. He had been thinking, and he had an idea that would test everyone on the show.

For the new season, George wanted to do an episode of ER live. On TV, with ad breaks just like normal, but totally unrecorded. Why? Well, why not? He discussed it with Anthony Edwards who thought it could work. When he took the suggestion to John Wells there was bemused panic. And then he realised that George was serious. 'Let me think about it,' Wells said, privately wishing someone would find the star a film to keep him busy. But he knew George too well to think the idea would pass.

The fourth season of ER premiered in America on 25 September 1997. It was the usual hurly-burly affair with Carter restarting his residency, this time in the Emergency Room,

Morganstern suffering a heart attack and a new character, British trauma specialist Elizabeth Corday, joining the fray. Dominating the show, though, was a TV crew's obstructive attempts to capture a 'typical' day in the ER by shadowing Dr Greene, hence the title of the episode: 'Ambush'.

The first day in a new job can be daunting for anyone, so pity *Moll Flanders* star Alex Kingston. Her debut as Dr Corday just happened to be on the same day that the most successful drama in American TV history was to be broadcast live. Welcome to George's world.

To his credit, John Wells had tried to minimise the risk as much as possible. Having the season kick off with the experiment gave everyone longer to prepare than they would normally have had. And then there was the fake TV crew taking up the corridors of County General. Writer Carol Flint had come up with a plot device that meant if the actors occasionally looked a little at odds with themselves, it was because their characters were nervous about being filmed. And if you saw the odd cable or microphone in the operating room, that must belong to the TV crew, too. Perfect.

In the event, the precautions seemed unnecessary, even a little obvious. With director Tommy Schlamme keeping the action tight and fluid, the show went off without a hitch – not once, but twice, as it was performed live for both East Coast and West Coast regular time slots. (A special composite edition featuring the first half of the East Coast version and the second half of the later showing was put together for syndication airing.) Unless you count the fact that Dr Weaver appeared to be walking without her cane in the last scene, there was only reason to praise the whole endeavour. Who could not have smiled watching Doug Ross catch a few minutes of the Cubs-Astros game – being broadcast live that night on rival channel WGN?

As it transpired, no one. 'Ambush' was a huge success. NBC's market share shot healthily in the forties and the reviews were unanimous: they had pulled it off. The episode was Emmy-nominated for Lighting Direction and Directing and won for Technical Direction/Camera/Video. Another landmark in the show's history; another feather in the cap for that man on the inside, George Clooney. Was he becoming one of the most powerful men in the Warner empire or was it people's imaginations? Time would tell. Perhaps.

The challenge of the live broadcast had reinvigorated George as far as his day job went. But it was not enough to hold his attention completely. Within a month of arriving back at Stage 11 at the Warner Bros lot, he had to switch back to the seven-day-a-week work load that had dominated his last eighteen months. The extra work was great for his career, of course, but it played havoc with his domestic set-up.

'I am committed to my work and that is a problem for my personal life,' he admitted at the time. 'It is very tough on Céline because her identity is very much associated with me. Yet she has none of the advantages because I am hardly ever there. A television series is a full-time job, fourteen hours a day, five days a week, nine months of the year with no time off. I also do a film in my spare time and vacations, which means working weekends and nights and all that stuff.'

Five days a week Céline busied herself with a part-time job at a kindergarten, but it only kept her occupied until two in the afternoon. That still meant a lot of George-free time in a strange land. 'She has friends in Los Angeles, and people she likes being with, but I cannot pretend it is easy,' he confessed. 'We don't have vacations and I would imagine that bothers her. It would bother me. It is just that, for the moment, I am unable to do a thing about it.'

Keeping George away from her this time was *Out of Sight*, which started shooting on 1 October. When he had signed up for the film in spring it was with a sense of foreboding about his as yet unseen summer releases. Now, with the less-than-bowled-over reviews still fresh in his mind, he felt vindicated in his decision. 'I wasn't the greatest Bat,' he says. 'Rubber and me just didn't get along too well. After *Batman*, I just said to myself, "Right, here's the deal. I'm going to do movies I would go to see myself."'

He was not the only one in need of a professional shot in the arm. Director Steven Soderbergh's previous film, the shoestring-budget *Schizopolis*, had marked the latest nadir in his plummeting commerciality. 'Steven and I were both kind of at creative low points,' George admits. 'Things weren't working so well for either of us.'

Out of Sight was the tonic they were both searching for. Elmore Leonard's quirky crime caper about record-breaking bank robber Jack Foley and his relationship with Karen Sisco, the federal marshal charged with bringing him to justice, had everything the pair was searching for. Great characters, a plot that for once had fewer holes than an average golf course and a fantastic script, courtesy of Scott Frank. 'When I read *Out of Sight*,' George says, 'I knew it was a movie that I would like to see.' Which is exactly what he was looking for.

Somewhere between the talents of Leonard and Frank was the perfect film-writer. Until Frank's own screenplay for *Get Shorty*, none of the many Leonard novels realised on the big screen – including *The Ambassador*, *Glitz* and *Touch* – had come close to doing the writer justice. Even the three he scripted himself, 1985's *Stick*, the following year's *52 Pick-Up* and 1989's *Cat Chaser*, were like bad impressions of the original. Scott Frank was the only screenwriter who seemed comfortable with having people, rather than the plot, centre-stage.

Leonard's way of writing is emphatically character-driven. 'I don't begin with a plot, I begin with characters,' he says. 'I get to know them – what they have for breakfast, what kind of shoes they wear – and they tell me what the story is about. The plot just comes along.'

The idea for *Out of Sight* was inspired by a newspaper picture of a pretty law officer and the possibilities her life could offer. 'A few years ago, I saw a picture in the *Detroit News* of an attractive young woman who was a federal marshal standing in front of the Federal Courthouse in Miami,' the writer recalls. 'She held a shotgun which was resting on her cocked hip. As soon as I saw that picture, I knew it was a book.'

The rest of the novel, and the film, followed from there. 'So I invented a guy who, unarmed, has robbed maybe two-hundred banks in his career and a female law enforcement officer who must hunt him down, and I put them together in a situation in which they find they are attracted to one another.'

When one character has just escaped from prison, holing up in the boot of a car with the other character at gunpoint, the scope for a nerve-testing action film is enormous. But neither Leonard nor Frank was interested in that route. *Out of Sight* is a love story, a sad story in many ways, with the concept of 'what might have been' at its core. Sure, it has gun fights, murders, attempted rape, blackmail, bullying and robbery, but almost by accident. 'It's about the road not taken,' says Scott Frank, 'which is the saddest thing.'

During interviews for *One Fine Day*, Michelle Pfeiffer had let slip how there was more to George than his laddish playfulness. 'For all the bravado, there's something very vulnerable about him,' she revealed. Tommy Hinkley, one of The Boys, has gone on record with a similar insight. 'If you hang out with George for even ten minutes,' Hinkley said, 'you would sense a sadness to him. He believes you have a choice. You either have a career or you have love.' (During an interview with *Vogue* in 2000, George called out mockingly to the reporter who was in close conversation with Tommy and Grant Heslov, 'Are we on "There's a sadness in George?"' ' One imagines how well that level of analysis usually goes down at Sunday afternoon taco-fests at Casa de Clooney.) If Pfeiffer and Hinkley are even half right, then George was the perfect choice for fatalistic, romantic Jack Foley.

Scott Frank is convinced they got their man. 'What's so great about George Clooney's performance is that he conveys that sadness,' he says. 'If I hadn't robbed all those banks, I could have been with this girl.' It is the key characteristic of Foley's character. Yes, he is a charmer, and a handsome one; he's smart enough to know that if he gets sent back to prison, it will be for good; he's a natural leader and hates bullies; but overriding all this, he is just a guy who falls in love. He is prepared to follow his heart, even when it leads him into the arms of the law. Literally.

In the film's defining scene, Foley bundles Karen Sisco and himself into the boot of her car as she tries to prevent his escape from Glades Correctional Institution in Florida. With the mighty Ving Rhames as Foley's confession-obsessed accomplice Buddy driving the vehicle, they undertake a twenty-minute ride, spooned up together like lovers and lit only by the car's brake lights and Foley's torch. He is instantly more taken with his captive than his own impending freedom; she is coquettish and calm in response as she attempts to talk him into giving himself up. They talk, almost in lovers' hushed tones, about their favourite films and their favourite movie law-breakers – *Bonnie and Clyde*, *The Flight of the Condor*, *Network* – and the idea of dying by gunfire. Their close proximity means she cannot reach her handgun – but would she use it anyway?

The crux of the scene comes when Foley asks Karen if she thinks they would have a chance if circumstances were different. She demurs to his face – as far as she can see it – but it is an idea that haunts both characters throughout the film, pushing each to take risks to discover what might have been.

'It's the most important scene in the film because if that doesn't work, the rest of the film doesn't work,' George elucidates. 'We're always asked to accept the unusual on film – that a comet will hit the earth, that a giant lizard will roam the streets of New York. In this, we ask the audience to accept that a female federal marshal being held hostage in a car boot could be open to meeting a nice guy who just happens to be a bank robber.'

It is no surprise to learn that the trunk scene was the one chosen as the audition piece back in George's office that spring. His big leather couch creaked and cracked as the various combinations snuggled up on it, but Jennifer Lopez got the part. As far as George and Steven Soderbergh were concerned, she combined the traffic-stopping sultriness they wanted with a forcefulness that came across on camera. Which was just as well, considering the demands of the role. 'You have to believe she'll pick up the gun and shoot you, and you have to still want to chase her around the couch,' George says. 'That's a tough thing to play.'

Lopez – or J-Lo as she would later call herself – was no stranger to being forceful. Born in the Bronx to Puerto Rican parents, she had recently earned a reputation in the artificially saccharine world of Tinseltown as a bit of firebrand following a Movieline interview in which she slagged off every name actor in town. Cameron Diaz? 'A lucky model.' Winona Ryder: 'I was never a big fan.' Gwyneth Paltrow: 'I heard more about her and Brad Pitt than I ever heard about her work.' Madonna: 'Do I think she's a great actress? No.' Even Jack Nicholson does not escape: 'A legend in his own time and in his own mind.' If she could channel some of this Latina fire into her on-screen relationship with George Clooney's character, then there was definite potential – and Soderbergh thought she could. 'Both those actors have a lot of energy,' he says. 'As soon as they got in the room, it was as if there wasn't enough air.'

If that was the effect in a spacious office, imagine the asphyxiation with the pair locked in a claustrophobic trunk. Even allowing for the special Hollywood version – ie, with one side cut out to allow for full camera access – J-Lo and J-Fo looked cramped throughout as gimbals – versatile ball-and-socket lifting mechanisms – rocked the tomb-like set, throwing the pair into each other and the metal casing. What made the situation worse was the fact that Soderbergh was not happy with the first take. Or the 41st. It took 44 attempts before he finally got his shot, which George was less than impressed with.

'Around take thirty I was like, "I'm never gonna get it," ' he recalls. 'I went home after the first night so defeated. Our bodies are sliding around in the trunk and I'm covered in mud. And I'm doing some of the lighting with a flashlight, so it was about not shining it on her breasts too long, or anywhere else that would be wrong.'

George has never been the kind to kick up about hard work. He was more concerned about his own limitations as an actor. Whatever magic he mustered in the early takes he was pretty sure would be lost to him by the end. 'I can't give you one-hundred-and-fifty takes,' he admits with refreshing candour. 'I can't even give you thirty different ways of doing it! I don't have the talent or the range for it. Kevin Spacey can do that.'

Soderbergh is not convinced by this blanket dismissal of his talents. 'George is a better actor than he thinks,' he muses. 'I encouraged him to strip everything away and simplify – it's the hardest thing in the world for an actor to believe he can do nothing and still be compelling. It took a while just to get him to sit still.'

'He is a unique star in the States now,' Soderbergh adds. 'There's nobody else his age and nobody has his vibe. There's the generation older than him and then there's all these boys. George is a man. And he's a real throwback to classical movie stars like Cary Grant and Steve McQueen.'

Although it provoked wistful reminiscences of Clark Gable (him again) and Claudette Colbert's embryonic love-forming in *It Happened One Night*, the scene was not mould-breaking in itself – unlike the next time the couple spend any time together. Soderbergh took one look at the narrative script and ripped it up. The king of budget art-house flicks was not going to shoot a bedroom sequence that could be found in any old movie. Why would he?

'Steven is a really smart film-maker,' George enthuses. 'Read the script and it's just a love scene. Basically it's, you know, we make out. But the way he made that scene, it's actually a really unique love scene, a very special love scene.'

Actually, something similar had been done before, but not in a mainstream action picture. Scott Frank had described how

Marshal Karen Sisco is joined in her Detroit hotel bar, unannounced, by the man she is hunting. They flirt, they get verbally intimate, and continue their conversation in the lift and finally in her room. There was nothing wrong with the sequence per se, but it did nothing for the director. Reaching back to Nic Roeg's *Don't Look Now*, which featured a fragmented love scene between Donald Sutherland and Julie Christie, Soderbergh rewrote the scene so that all the talking takes place in the bar and all the action happens in the hotel suite. By cutting between the two, he was able to give the impression of continuing conversations; closer inspection reveals that not a word leaves either's lips as the lovers reach the room, undress and make love. 'We did not talk from the moment we entered the bedroom, which was sexy,' Lopez says. 'We communicated with our eyes and there are no words, just a soundtrack.'

If she had been confused by the actual shoot, she does not let on. George, of course, is honesty itself. 'I didn't understand what Steven was doing when we did it,' he admits, 'because the way it was originally written, it was two different scenes – down in the bar and up in the bedroom. He said, "We're going to do all the dialogue down in the bar and then we'll just shoot the stuff upstairs without any dialogue." The whole time I was like, "You're high, I don't know what you're talking about." Then when you see it you go, "Wow, that's really cool!" '

The actual sex scene itself achieves that rare feat of being erotic without being explicit. Lopez strips to her underwear, George to his immaculate white boxers (the navy suit he first discards is actually from his own wardrobe), and they make out but with only their heads in shot. 'The thing that's great is you don't see completely naked bodies,' George says. 'It's done in a more subtle way. It was fun to do but it's not your standard love scene, that's for sure. In the book it's much more linear.'

'It is all about anticipation,' Lopez adds. Having experienced a full nude scene filming *Money Train* with Wesley Snipes (she insisted on 'love pillows' to cover groin and breasts), she was as relieved as George that *Out of Sight* played more on suggestion than sensation. Any lingering insecurities were alleviated by her leading man's refusal to take the situation seriously. 'We did the sexy scenes early on in the shoot, but I hit it off with George right from the start,' she says. 'The whole piece is driven by the fact that these two are after each other. George and I had to get along and we did, just great. Filming those scenes is weird and can be difficult, but with George it's a lot easier. That man is fun. He loves to keep the whole crew laughing.'

If George was put out by the demands of delivering his lines over and over while being battered by the earlier scene's rocking trunk, he feared a whole lot worse on one of the film's location shoots. For the flashback scenes set in the maximum security Glades Correctional Institution in Florida, where he plots the diamond heist, the production took over real-life Louisiana State Penitentiary in Angola, an hour's drive from Soderbergh's hometown of Baton Rouge. For authenticity's sake, the film used five-hundred of the five-thousand inmates as extras in the exercise yard. For the first time in his movie career, George was required to play basketball for a part, something he had always dreamed of. Somehow, he never expected to be going one-on-one with convicted murderers though. 'What's wrong, Batman?' the cons would yell. 'Can't fly to the top of the hoop?'

'Most of the people playing close to me were stunt guys but the real inmates were all around and that was intimidating,' George is the first to admit. 'I can hold my own on a basketball court but there are five-thousand capital offenders in that prison and they're there for rape and murder, not embezzlement. They'd be saying, "Yeah, I was just a victim of circumstance – I went to the house to rob it and the family was there so I killed them." '

If ever a shoot required the actor's renowned sense of humour, it was this one. He could have been forgiven for hiding back in his trailer as soon as Soderbergh yelled 'cut', but that would have been hypocritical. While the crew was there, he was there. Autographs, hand-shakes, shared stories – the full Clooney charm repertoire was on show for this one. 'George in prison was great,' the grateful director says. 'He made that situation easier on all of us by being gracious and patient and staying on the yard all day.'

Apart from Angola, the movie also used the Mira Loma Detention Center in Lancaster, California to stand in for Lompoc Prison. Filming there followed work at Universal's LA soundstage where they captured all the film's internal shots, from the final shoot-out inside Richard (Albert Brooks) Ripley's mansion to the hotel suite where Foley and Sisco get down and dirty. After Lancaster came Angola and then the entire production headed east for ten days in sun-blessed Miami. With location shots of the

South Beach area, the airport and Fort Lauderdale all bagged, it was time for the final leg of the troupe's American tour.

Detroit in December can be an unforgiving place. With Foley and Buddy spending a lot of time in the night air, it was hard on everyone. But spirits remained high with that man Clooney leading the laugh lines. 'You come on set with me and there will be a lot of joking and kidding around,' he promises earnestly. 'Life's too short for us not to enjoy it and not to make fun of how ridiculous it can be at times and how ridiculous I can be at times. I love this business but it can be silly in lots of ways.'

The silliness was put on hold for a short while when Elmore Leonard checked in on proceedings in Detroit, but George won him over. 'The first time I met him was on the set in Detroit,' he says. 'He comes over, and I go, "Mr Leonard," and he goes, "Call me Dutch." Dutch. Right. He's really something.' The feeling was mutual. Before filming was out, Dutch told George that he would be perfect for the lead role in the film of his latest – his 34th – novel, Cuba Libre. It is not every day that George Clooney's head swells, but that meant a lot to him. Suddenly Detroit was a warmer place.

His confidence was also boosted by the fact that a couple of bigger movie stars than him were willing to take uncredited cameos in the film, just to be involved. Maybe his desperation to get in on The Thin Red Line wasn't so unusual.

In a fabulous movie in-joke, Michael Keaton plays Sisco's pathetic, adulterous FBI boyfriend Ray Nicolet, re-creating the exact same part he played in that other Elmore Leonard film, Jackie Brown. Both times Keaton excels as the kind of nerd you would hate your daughter to bring home – Sisco's dad openly loathes him. 'As far as Tarantino and I could determine, that's a first,' the smiling Soderbergh says. 'I don't think that's ever been done before where two unrelated movies share a character that is played by the same actor in both. We giggled at that.'

If the first cameo is a bit of fun, the second is absolutely integral to the movie's success. The movie climaxes with Jack Foley begging Karen Sisco to kill him so he does not have to return to prison. She shoots him in the leg. The film's final scene sees him joined in the police van that will take him back to Glades by Samuel L Jackson's laconic multiple escapee. It is a virtuoso turn that dictates the entire ending. Sisco has paired the two villains for the nine-hour journey in the hope that her lover will pick up a few tips. 'It's a short scene,' Soderbergh says, 'so we needed someone that, when they implied that they were the pre-eminent escape artist in the country, you believed them right away. It had to be somebody with that kind of impact. Sam Jackson gets on screen and says something and you go, "Whatever you say." ' As it dawns on Foley that Sisco is trying to help him, the small van becomes alive with the sexual energy that had crackled in the trunk earlier. The smouldering smile that creeps from Lopez's lips as the camera pans to her from George conveys more sensuality in two seconds than most films manage in ninety minutes. Soderbergh had been spot on with the chemistry of the pairing. There's definitely a career for this girl in movies if the music career goes downhill.

Out of Sight wrapped at the end of 1997. Steven Soderbergh's last film *Schizopolis* had cost $350,000; this one came in at a shade under $50 million. While the cast and most of the crew disbanded to the four corners of Los Angeles, Soderbergh started the process of putting his film together. After almost a decade of anti-commercial films he had taken on a major studio project featuring two of the most photogenic actors around. The question was, could he deliver? Audiences would not find out for almost a year.

16. HOW MUCH MONEY DO YOU ACTUALLY NEED?

Most celebrities have two ways of handling fame, both of them unhealthy. One is to bemoan the fact that their lives are no longer their own, that they cannot leave the forest-obscured mansion without being pestered for photographs or quotes. The other way is to be totally put out when they are not recognised at all. Often these emotions can occur on the same day.

The cleverer ones – like George Clooney – accept that such trials are part and parcel of the industry he worked so hard to join. The more successful you are, the worse it gets, but that's the price. Autograph requests, posing with strangers, giving interviews? All in a day's work for the guy who hounded Raymond Burr around the Augusta set of *Centennial*.

George puts this unusual technique down to the fact that he and fame collided late in his life. 'If I was 23 and got famous, I would have been in the top of a bell-tower with a high-powered rifle,' he is fond of saying. 'I would have screwed it up really badly.' But really, is the fact that he became a household name at 33 the sole reason for his general magnanimity? No doubt it accounts partly for his near obsession with keeping the crew happy on set, on looking out for the little guy at all times – he has been that little guy. But Nick and Nina Clooney have to take a lot of credit for this, too: that is how he was raised. The key is in the oft-cited phrase that 'fame hasn't changed him' – which means he was a pretty good bloke to start with. How many actors can you say that about?

His other stock defence against charges of him being unprofessionally normal (an ironic proof if ever there was one) is that he has witnessed the fickleness of fame. Rosemary was a goddess, then she was in a nuthouse; Nick took his family from mansion to trailer park. So the phrase 'be nice to the people on the way up' probably has a lot of resonance in the Clooney household for that reason. There is a lot of substance to this theory but, still, it is one thing to notice faults in others, it is something else to pattern one's own life on such observations. That takes character.

There is a third aspect to his make-up: The Boys. Founding member Richard Kind is only too aware of their role in their superstar friend's life. 'We are what makes him George,' he says. 'Everything else makes him George Clooney.'

It says more about Hollywood than George that he seems to stand on the verge of canonisation just for being a 'normal' person in a crazy town. Look at the fuss made just because he – sharp intake of breath – decided to honour his ER contract. He refused to 'do a Caruso' despite the obvious pressures. Why should that make him an exception? In Tinseltown it does. George, though, is not a saint and he has never claimed to be. In fact the criticisms against him make compelling reading. He is dedicated to his career, almost to the point of self-delusion, and claims he has no choice but to put his film work ahead of a holiday with Céline; he is not the first to excuse selfishness that way. And his perennial bonhomie with everyone on the Warners lot? Interpreted by some as a (successful) ruse to ingratiate himself with the suits upstairs. As for all the macho sports on every film set – could that just be a way of stamping his authority on the shoot, making sure everyone knows, in the nicest way possible of course, that there is only one star at work today? You wanna be in George's gang, then you better play some ball. Of course he never stays in his trailer, they say: why would he when he has colonised the entire production? How many sports-indifferent co-workers have felt alienated or threatened by such chest-beating testosterone demonstrations?

And there is the rub. The fact that even attempts at niceness can be distorted in Hollywood gives some indication of the back-stabbing environment George works in. (For the record, Julianna Margulies says he was a breath of non-male air during ER shoots. 'It can be a pretty high-testosterone set when all the guys are on,' she says, 'and probably the most sensitive person there is George.')

Ironically, it is because he registers lower on the 'impressed-with' scale that George is pestered by fans more than other stars. At least that's his theory. 'I'm famous from television and it's a whole different kind of thing, much more intrusive,' he explains. 'You pay eight bucks to see a movie star, they're sixty feet tall and it's a big deal. I was in your house every day. You watched me in your underwear. We were this focal point in people's homes every day.' And the result? 'People think they know you personally. I have gotten off a plane with Mel Gibson and people just stare at him. They speak about him in whispers and keep their distance. I'm standing right next to him and the same people scream out, "Hey, George!" Then they come over, grab my arm and rub my head.'

Some fans are more circumspect, nonchalant even. In May 1997 George attended a correspondents' dinner to which a certain Mr Clinton was also invited. It still amuses him today. 'A bunch of us were standing in this room,' George says, 'and the President, who was on crutches at the time, comes in. He walks into the room, kind of looks around and he goes, "Hi George," and I say, "Mr President." It just cracked me up that, you know, you do an acknowledgement wave to the President!'

Outside of the rarefied cotton-wool protection of star-heavy Hollywood, one finds a different kind of fan. Normally a drunk one. It is a sign of George's normalcy that he likes to visit local bars when he is on location shoots; it is a sign of other people's normalcy that he is always pestered. 'Once people have a few drinks, they get brave,' he sighs. 'All of a sudden there is a crowd of guys going, "Dude!" and hanging on to me. They want to buy me a drink and sit down and talk.' Admittedly, he could swat each fan away. He could even demand a private booth from the barkeep. Instead, his reaction is textbook George. 'The funny part is what I end up doing: I'm polite and I sit and talk to them. I wind up doing the things a girl would do in the same sort of situation at a bar.' Coming from a self-confessed, largely unreconstructed 'guy', this must hurt. The things people do for a vodka and soda . . .

Still, being an international icon is not all guys planting themselves in George's driveway until he agrees to be the best man at their wedding and women writing fake magazine reminiscences of dates that never happened. There are upsides to movie superstardom, big ones. Money and power come pretty close to the top, as The Boys can testify. George normally picks up the tab for their annual holidays although no one mistakes it as any claim of ownership; they're not that kind of people. 'They're not my posse,' he insists. 'But we all enjoy the fact that I can get us a jet and we can go somewhere. Because we all know that may not be the case in a couple of years. So we celebrate that. We go, "We have a jet!" and we enjoy it. You know, nothing's taken for granted. We all guard this friendship really carefully.'

As for power, that comes with the territory in Hollywood, a community founded and run on the principles of 'who you know' and 'what can you do for me?' The trappings of celebrity are widely available (in direct proportion to one's fame) – free meals, the best seats, jewellery loans, women, drugs, no queueing – but, for a player, there is real opportunity to influence. And by 1998 George was definitely a player.

Apart from *The Thin Red Line*, Waldo Sanchez had been 'hairstylist to Mr Clooney' on all of George's films; Thom and Matt had got parts in *The Peacemaker*. In 1998 it was Grant Heslov's turn for his pal's industry know-how in an all-Boy affair.

Waiting for Woody was a documentary-style idea that Heslov had been trying to put together for some time. Its premise was that of an actor trying to win an audition in a Woody Allen film. Along the way various stars, all playing themselves, are interwoven with scripted character parts. Josh, played by Heslov, is awkward and arrogant by turns with the talent around him, despite having last worked as the candlestick in the Disneyland electric light parade. George comes off worst, mockingly called 'Batman' throughout. Richard Kind lends his weight as a doorman and Thom Mathews appears as a bike messenger (and co-produces). Tommy Hinkley was a driver on the set, George's assistant Amy Cohen associate produces and Sanchez is thanked in the credits. But The Boys aside, there was also the small matter of people like Jennifer Aniston, owner of the most famous hair in Hollywood at the time, taking time out to appear in the film, too. It's just possible she heard about it from a guy who played a doctor in the first series of *Friends* . . . Now, that's a player.

In the Hollywood plutocracy, everyone is in a pecking order of some description. George was a bigger star than The Boys and could get friends' films green-lighted, but others were above him. He was well aware of his place in the great casting scheme of things, so it was no shock to be offered roles only after others turned them down. Occasionally, though, he was not offered them at all, which was a cue for another session on the Selectric. Even players have to beg sometimes.

A happy by-product of George's personal standing at Warner Bros was that every now and again he would be leaked scripts that were being considered. As the head of TV and film development companies, he was always looking for new material and it was in the studio's interest to keep him informed of new ideas. They, after all, had first-look rights on any of Maysville's projects. Sometimes, however, he was just kept in the loop because people in higher places valued his opinion. In spring 1998, as he divided his time between hospital duties and running his company, he was shown a script which Lorenzo Di Bonaventura, the international head of Warner Bros production, had commissioned. There was nothing that Maysville could contribute because the deal was being done directly with WB; but George could offer something, he was sure of it.

David O Russell shot to fame with two quirky and headline-provoking independent films. Although *Spanking the Monkey* was an $80,000-study of incest and masturbation, his real notoriety arrived with *Flirting with Disaster* in which he persuaded American institution Mary Tyler Moore to show her bra. Is nothing sacred? In 1997, he had taken a trip to Warner Bros' script library – an archive of screenplays which the studio has bought rights to – and was won over by a one-line description of a piece called *Spoils of War* by John Ridley. Over the next eighteen months he developed his own screenplay based on Ridley's original concept. The studio would back it if an A-list name came on board. They wanted Clint Eastwood, Tom Cruise or Mel Gibson; Russell wanted Jack Nicholson or Nicolas Cage. George Clooney had other ideas.

After *Batman & Robin* had earned him $3 million, George had a meeting with his accountant. 'I said, "Where do I stand?" and he said, "You never have to work again unless you're an idiot". I mean, how much money do you actually need?' he says. 'My house is paid off and it's beautiful – I've made it Shangri-la. I drive up my driveway and I laugh. I'm in a position now where I can live off the interest for the rest of my life and live ridiculously well. So then it comes down to "What is your legacy going to be? What are you going to stand for when you get hit by a bus?"' The answer, he realised, was films that made him proud.

Out of Sight was the first example of his new creative and financial freedom; that would be out in a couple of months. *The Thin Red Line*, if he survived the director's cut, would also stand him well. *Three Kings*, by David O Russell, was in the same category. George fired off a letter to Russell, staking a claim and offering to show him an early cut of *Out of Sight*. He signed the letter 'George Clooney, TV Actor'.

'When I read the script, there wasn't a part for me,' he explains. 'It was written for Clint Eastwood, so the character was sixty. Then I heard they were lowering the age and that's when I started chasing it. So I had to take Mel Gibson and tie him up at my house, so they couldn't find him. They wanted Nic Cage pretty badly, and Nic was really interested, but I just kept lobbying. I sent David a letter and then I followed him to this hotel in New York and showed up and said, "Come on, don't be a jerk. Give me a job." '

Having set up the meeting with the director and producer Charles Roven at the Manhattan Ritz, George assumed it would be a straightforward interview. Wrong. David O Russell would never be so predictable; that is not the way he works. Wearing his off-duty mufti – black T-shirt and combat slacks – and carrying a half-empty sports bag, George is visibly taken aback to be met at Russell's hotel door by a video camera. He breaks into the deep, throaty I'll-get-you-for-this-laugh normally reserved for when he has been stitched up by a practical joke. Of course, in many ways, he has been. The view from the other side of the lens is telling. George recovers instantly, and makes his way warily into the room, dispensing pleasantries en route. He sinks into a deep couch while simultaneously thanking Russell for seeing him. If he is put out by the video intrusion he doesn't show it, not with so much at stake.

'He opened the door with this video camera,' George recalls, 'and said, "Does this bother you?" I said, "It will only if I don't get the job." If I end up in *The Making of Three Kings* and I'm not in the movie, then I'll look like an asshole.'

Ever the diplomat, George was too keen to nail the part to kick up about the director's antics at that first meeting. With hindsight, it was definitely a taste of behaviour to come. But at the time, George bit his tongue and sold himself. When Cage opted out of the running and took Scorsese's *Bringing Out the Dead* instead, he was bought. Now to get the project green-lighted and assemble the team.

Watching the first meetings of the rest of the film's main cast is revelatory. Mark Wahlberg, most recently seen acting with a prosthetic penis in *Boogie Nights*, is taciturn to the point of surliness until the camera is switched off; rapper Ice Cube sits menacingly still and refuses any eye contact while the recording button is on. Only George has the mental wherewithal to operate around the cheap stunt. And that's why he's a player.

Back in LA, others on the Warner lot were beginning to notice George's power. Working full-time on *ER* again since the turn of the year had been almost like a holiday for him and it gave him time to analyse the show. It was lacking freshness, he thought, and there were certain aspects that could be tighter. The opportunities for developing Doug, for example, were growing increasingly limited; where once George paced the outward showings of his character's grief over every eight or nine episodes, a decline in writing standards meant that there was often little else to do to hold interest. It was not real, he felt, to be emotionally entangled every week. He had done his research and real doctors have a healthy detachment for most patients, almost a gallows humour. Without it no sane person could get through a single day. It was typewriter time.

'In the first season we had a guy walk into the show with an arrow stuck into his head, and he said, "Can you tell me where Admitting is?" And we'd point, and he walks off, and that's all,' George said at the time. 'You never see him again. If it were this season, we'd all take him into the Emergency Room and talk about how amazing it is that he's still alive, and then Noah Wyle would start to cry because his parents died from an Indian attack.'

The answer, he said, was to externalise the plots. 'The trick is not making the scenes about you,' he explains. 'And it doesn't win you any awards, and it doesn't get any attention, but I was always most proud from walking away from scenes. We'd sit there and watch it on Thursdays and Eriq La Salle would kind of tap you on the leg when he knew you could've ham-boned one up and you didn't.'

For all his overall concerns, there were still some good moments for George during season four. 'Fathers and Sons', broadcast on 13 November 1997, showed Doug and Mark leave Chicago for a road trip. The buddy bonding session is revelatory and touching, punctured by bawdy and unstoppable laughter although Seth and Richard Gecko it ain't. They are meant to be investigating a death in Ross's family, but Greene's parents end up dominating the show. For a lot of fans, the episode is integral to understanding the way the characters currently behave.

In 'My Brother's Keeper' (5 March 1998), Dr Ross is back in the hospital with a case of poisoning, possibly caused by the six-year-old victim's family. It comes at a time when the doctor is preparing to present a paper on paediatrics, but the child has to come before his career advancement. In the season's penultimate episode, 'Suffer the Little Children', his patient is even younger, a six-month-old baby recovering from methadone withdrawal. George's former *Sisters* co-star Swoozie Kurtz guest stars.

However, the most significant moments of Dr Ross's year come in the series finale, 'A Hole in the Heart', shown on 14 May. He and Hathaway have been trying to help a seven-month-old born addicted to heroin, using any means possible. Pursuing a controversial and unauthorised course of treatment, the pair are brought closer together than ever before. The last season had ended with them kissing, but this was more emotional somehow as they put their careers in each other's hands.

At least there was some kissing in George's real life that month. He had his 37th birthday during the recording of the last show and celebrated with Céline (she supplied flowers, presents and cake). Two days later, however, and he was off with The Boys to Florida for a week's R&R and, if George's good friends at the *National Enquirer* are to be believed, more kissing.

Miami Beach's Delano Hotel was the lucky destination, chosen for its sports facilities. Throughout the week George and Co. took over the local golf course and had daily run-ins on the basketball court, often unplanned. Dressed in a white shirt with white shorts, trainers and socks, George was concentration itself as one impromptu game took place. Looking small but powerful, with a low centre of gravity, he tore past his markers for a perfect lay up. This is a sport he takes seriously. His tennis matches seemed less serious but equally spontaneous if his dress is anything to go by. A pair of Nikes, shorts and a cap seemed manageable, but somehow he had misplaced his shirt. Sadly the same could not be said for his exploits on the baseball field. Swamped by an ugly local baseball shirt but wearing a backwards cap and lycra-style cycle shorts, he looked like a sartorial disaster. Not at all the image the *Enquirer* wanted him to create.

The gossips stood a greater chance back at the hotel when the again shirtless George mingled with scantily clad (that is to say, topless) admirers. As usual, it was The Boys who kept his attention. Autograph hunters came and went throughout the day and even at night, when the lads descended on the town's Red Square night-club. There was even a suggestion from one girl that

George might be gay because he hadn't responded to her overtures. How disappointing if you happen to be a tabloid magazine with offices just up the road from the hotel. But the next night made everything worthwhile and the *Enquirer* published a typically lurid account of an alleged liaison between George and a scantily-clad blonde. Was this payback from the magazine's Steve Coz after the Diana statement?

Whatever his holiday exploits, he certainly needed to recharge his batteries before taking on the next wave of commitments. June was a nervous time for him, make or break in some ways, as he waited for crucial developments on two projects close to his heart.

There was good news at the start of the month as Warner Bros finally green-lighted *Three Kings*. Now that George was the confirmed star, he wasn't dragged over to the East Coast to hear the news: the news came to him. Armed as ever with his travelling camera, David O Russell found the bearded actor playing football in the Warner yard, obviously between stints behind the desk in his Maysville office. Throwing then receiving thirty-yard passes, George looks tanned and relaxed in shorts and T-shirt as he greets Russell. Even the ever-present camcorder and a friend's secondary unit fail to break his smile. The relief is almost tangible as George takes in the news that he will be working that winter after all and a round of hugging ensues. Now only one problem to fret about.

After the critical pummelling George had taken for *Batman* and, to a lesser extent, *The Peacemaker*, he had everything crossed that yet another big-budget picture carrying his name would fare better. Although all of his films had made money there was a distinct mood that he had not yet lived up to billing. On 26 June *Out of Sight* would be released in the US and then he would find out.

The usual bells-and-whistles launch a few days earlier was a welcome confidence boost but, he counselled himself, look at the razzmatazz of the *Batman* opening. It is never wise to judge a film on its post-screening canape budget. He should not have worried. When the first editions came in, there was cause for back-slapping all round. Steven Soderbergh had pulled it off. George was a genuine movie star. And Jennifer Lopez – she had a great career behind her. Sad but true; her full Latina figure won as much citation as her acting, if not more. The *LA Weekly* was priapic: 'Lopez, whose spectacular ass juts out as expressively as her swollen mouth, is terrific.' 'The movie confirms Jennifer Lopez's status as a qualified voluptuary,' the *New Yorker* dribbled. *FHM* manfully struggled to tackle the plot before giving in: 'A dizzying part-thriller, part-love story, played by a perfect cast. Lopez is the sexiest cop ever.'

Fortunately the contributions of others were picked up elsewhere. 'One of the most erotic, electric encounters since Bogart met Bacall,' raved the *New York Daily News*. 'Sharp, funny, dangerously sexy,' summed up NBS News Channel. 'Clooney and Lopez have never been better or hotter,' said *Rolling Stone*. 'The first movie that has truly gotten an Elmore Leonard novel on screen,' judged *Entertainment Weekly*. 'Mr Clooney, like Ms Lopez, makes the most of a splendid opportunity here,' said the *New York Times*. And so it went on, with kind words pouring in from every source. And, for once, barely a mention of Clark Gable. Was George finally getting away from olde worlde comparisons? Not quite. 'Clooney is the suavest-looking thief since Cary Grant played cat burglar on the Riviera,' added the *New York Times*.

All fine and dandy, then. There was only one problem. Although *Out of Sight*'s first week's box office was a fairly healthy $12 million, by the end of its run it had only added another $25 million. All the great plaudits, the fantastic talent and the best scripts counted for very little as the Universal accountants got to work. It was the first (and remains the only) film of George's not to make money. Go figure.

17. I WAS GOING TO KILL HIM

As broadcast live and round-the-clock by CNN and other news
agencies, the Gulf War of January 1991 was a highly successful
made-for-TV movie even while it was happening. Never before
had an international combat situation so merged in the international consciousness with its own representation. Generals Colin
Powell and Norman Schwarzkopf were familiar faces before a
single Scud had been fired. 'Surgical strikes' and 'smart bombs'
entered the vocabulary of the day. Reporters and full camera
crews were valued additions to every military base. The action
was sporadic but the coverage was blanket. Audiences heard over
their breakfast what the day's targets were going to be; they were
shown satellite stills of the offending buildings and given a virtual
demonstration of the arsenal of weapons to be deployed. By
lunchtime they watched as on-missile cameras stalked their prey
through the night sky, with transmission ending with the
satisfying explosion of another enemy stronghold. 'We're going
for a commercial break now,' we were told by our news
providers, 'but don't worry, you won't miss a thing.' If it was not
shown on CNN, it did not happen.

After two months of both blanket and clinical bombing,
Saddam Hussein waved the flag of surrender. Kuwait was
liberated but its oil fires, started by departing troops, would burn
for months to come. Inside Iraq, locals listened as the President
of the United States of America implored them to rise up and
overthrow their despotic leader while the tyrant's military
resources were weakened; America would support them, he said.
In sixteen of the eighteen Iraqi regions, rebellions were mounted.
In all sixteen the insurrections were crushed, the rebels and their
families were tortured and killed. Despite one of the largest troop
movements in modern history, from the day of the cease-fire not
a single American gun was fired in protection of the butchered
Iraqi people. For thousands of professional military men and
part-time reservists stationed on Saudi soil during the conflict,
the only action they saw was as witnesses to the barbaric and
ruthless revenge that Saddam's forces exacted upon his own
people. It gradually dawned on the rebels that the Great Satan

had betrayed them and that its troops were not coming. How did they know? They saw it on CNN.

The action in *Three Kings* commences in the Iraqi desert on 3 March 1991, after the cease-fire was agreed. Four soldiers – three rookie reservists and one almost retired major – set out to steal $23 million of plundered Kuwaiti gold bullion from Saddam's secret bunkers. Just your average action heist movie, in fact. But as they seamlessly go about packing their hoard into dozens of Louis Vuitton bags, the Americans witness the Iraqi army turning its guns on its own civilians to prevent an uprising against Saddam – an uprising that President George Bush called for with the promise of US support. The mercenaries have a simple choice: flee with the gold in the knowledge that the military support is never coming, or stay and prevent a massacre.

When David O Russell left the Warners script library, it was with the agreed intention of reworking John Ridley's straightforward heist thriller. The script he delivered to the studio eighteen months later was anything but straightforward. Part action flick, part comedy, part war thriller, part political statement, it looked to be that most undesirable of beasts: the unmarketable movie. No one at Warner Bros had expected a two hundred-page exposé of the USA's hypocritical foreign policy, but that is essentially what they received. It was the weirdest exposition of the war genre since *M*A*S*H*, with elements of *Kelly's Heroes* and *Catch 22* thrown in. No one denied that it was a very strong script. The only question was: did Warners have the nerve to back it?

The doubts came from two opposing camps. The loudest voice was the pro-American lobby. Did the studio really want to tarnish their country's last great military victory? So what if the US had trained and armed Saddam's elite Republican Guard? So what if they had backed his fight against Iran in the 80s? So what that he was once such a lauded ally that he was the subject of a *Life* profile in the 60s? In 1990 he had invaded another country and it was America's duty to punish him – Kuwait's oil reserves were not a factor. Ironically, the other dissenters were saying the opposite. Could the studio afford to risk protests from religious groups portrayed unfavourably in the movie? At the time, Bruce Willis's *The Siege* was generating controversy through its depiction of Muslim extremists.

There was the added concern that, with just two independent family-based comedies to his credit, David O Russell was probably not the man to pull off such a complex, genre-melding, $50-million movie. Warner Bros, after all, was the only major studio without an independent division. Could the two work together? Fortunately Russell found a champion in Lorenzo Di Bonaventura, who had also backed *The Matrix*.

As soon as Di Bonaventura took a summer holiday, however, the knives came out. The studio's already cold feet had become decidedly icy when a Planet Hollywood was fire-bombed in Cape Town in August 1998 and some executives feared reprisals against them if this political hot potato went into production. 'There was one guy who was pretty high up at the studio who was on the business side and he was trying to cross over to the creative side,' Russell recalls. 'When Lorenzo was out of town on vacation for a week, he tried to convince Clooney to drop out, saying that the controversy, nationally and internationally, would mean trouble. Clooney, to his credit, said, "I don't believe you," so the whole coup attempt failed. Clooney at that point was pay-or-play, so the only way to pull the plug was to get the main pay-or-play guy to pull back.' Eventually the company's outgoing chairman and joint CEO Terry Semel overrode all qualms and took the decision to proceed.

'We had interesting meetings, with the heads of the studio, literally a couple of weeks before shooting started, saying, "We think we should pull the plug on the film because the terrorist temperature has been raised," ' George says, downplaying his own role. 'There was a great fear that we were taking not just the movie company but Time Warner into a dangerous place. I felt that wasn't the case, and the studio should be commended on the fact that they still did it, which is amazing because this isn't a typical studio film at all.'

With its inharmonious origins forgotten, the green light for the project was granted and shooting confirmed for 12 November 1998. Script meetings and rehearsals with the main cast – all recorded, much to the chagrin of the subjects – followed through the summer. George had by now made the role of grizzled major Archie Gates his own – 'it was a script I really fought to get' – despite Russell's reservations. 'Quite frankly, he wasn't the first person who came to mind,' Russell admits. 'I actually had more of a character actor in mind like Nic Cage and not somebody who is classically good-looking like George.

'My perception of him was as a romantic leading man, because he always had a beautiful woman with him in his pictures, whether it was Jennifer Lopez, Michelle Pfeiffer or Nicole Kidman. But I'd seen a little of him in that vampire movie *From Dusk Till Dawn* and there was a little glimmer in there.

'After meeting him, I was persuaded that he really got the whole thing, and had the deadpan sensibility for it. Also he has, I think, a grizzled maturity that Brad Pitt or Tom Cruise or even Cage don't exactly have.'

Co-star Mark Wahlberg, who plays Sergeant Troy Barlow, had been equally unimpressed. 'I had never seen anything that he had done,' he says, 'so when they were talking about him I didn't really know what he could do. It was weird because people normally cringe when they hear I'm up for a part. But then I saw him in *Out of Sight* and I was like, "What's my problem? Where do I get off thinking like that?" '

With Ice Cube as Staff Sergeant Chief Elgin and *Being John Malkovich* director Spike Jonze as redneck Conrad Vig making up the remainder of the gold-stealing quartet, the cast was set for 68 days of desert shooting in Arizona and Mexico. Russell had asked for 80; the Warner Bros accounts dept had beaten him down. It would be tough, especially for George. When filming commenced, he would be into his fifth and final year on *ER*. As with *Out of Sight*, the majority of the shooting would be away from Los Angeles. His relationship with Céline was about to be tested like never before.

Before an inch of film had even rolled, the cast had to get into shape. Military shape. Any actor could wander round with a gun, Russell felt, but he wanted his men to move like soldiers, to react like trained killers. The four leads were put through their paces by a team of military advisers during an intense week-long boot camp in the Arizona desert. Documentary footage shows them taking rooms SAS-style, in full combat gear and with pulses racing. Hard work, but well worth it, they all agreed. Well, nearly all. 'I tried to get out of it,' Wahlberg admits jokingly. 'I thought it would be really hard.'

'They'd take us out into the middle of the desert, where they'd hidden a box which we had to find,' an exhilarated George says. 'They'd give us guns and blank bullets and dress other guys up like Republican Guard to stop us finding the box. That was our training – it was fun!'

'It was cool,' Ice Cube agrees. 'We learned about the army and then we did manoeuvres, we went out and did a mission with firelights, people shooting at you and it got you kind of jacked up. You understood how it would feel if these were real bullets coming at you, which got me ready to do the part. And I think it brought us all together.' Given the conditions they would have to work in, the boys soon needed all the togetherness they could get.

As part of their acclimatisation, the team was also privileged to meet Sergeant Major Jim Parker, who had served in the conflict. Parker attested that American troops had wept openly as they watched Iraqi armies butcher their own civilians. As a condition of the cease-fire, they were forbidden from intervening. Parker is no longer alive, but his testimony lives on in *Three Kings*' forceful depiction of his information. 'The film wasn't written about him,' George explains, 'but as soon as we spent some time with him, it became more of his story.'

In order to re-create the barren plains of Iraq, David O Russell and production designer Catherine Hardwicke transformed an abandoned copper mine in Casa Grande, Arizona, halfway between Phoenix and Tucson. A similar expanse in Mexico was used for other scenes. Entire Iraqi villages as well as giant soundstages were erected on location and the crew settled down to a couple of months in the sun. Given the fight that Russell had had just to get the film that far, he should not have been surprised when even the weather turned against him. For the first time in thirty years, Arizona had snow that winter. Then there was the wind. Entire days' shoots were punctured by the ferocious sandstorms that tore through tents, rendering visibility to zero and making it almost impossible to breathe. 'At 11 a.m. you would get caught in a dust storm or a sandstorm and then in the afternoon it would be so hot you could hardly move,' says Ice Cube. With shooting time already pared back by the studio, there was scant margin for error on what was fast becoming the movie equivalent of the theatrical jinx, *Macbeth*.

George's schedule did nothing to help comparisons with the Scottish play. His final days on *ER* were taking up three days out of seven, restricting the director's flexibility with the scheduling. 'George was great,' Russell says, 'but it was hard because he was working two jobs.' 'I worked until 4.30 in the morning on *ER*,' his star adds, 'got on a jet, went directly to the set and worked for twelve hours.'

'George seems to come and go as he pleases on every movie he does,' Wahlberg laughs. 'He's worth it, though. He's a cool guy and very, very funny.'

Of course he is. Whatever the weather, wherever the location, George is the man for a happy set, everyone says so. It was the same story in Casa Grande. 'It was a boys' club,' he beams proudly. 'We made the film in the middle of nowhere in Arizona, all staying at the Holiday Inn together for almost four-and-a-half months. Cube, Mark and I got to be really good friends. We hung out, played basketball during the day and at night they had a private karaoke bar in the back of the hotel. We must have sung: "Don't Worry, Be Happy", about five-thousand times.' The musical bonding was aided by Mark Wahlberg joining Fat Boy Slim video director Jonze and co-stars Said Taghmaoui and Jay Giannone in Four Of A Kind, a surreal boy band vision for the 1990s, much to the amusement of the Inn's other guests.

Of course, it would not be a Clooney shoot without the rambling stories – 'he'll start jokes that go on for two years,' Nora Dunn, who plays NBS reporter Adriana Cruz says – and the obligatory squirter fights. 'There was an ongoing water war,' Russell laughs. 'He was constantly squirting people in the ass. Not me, Wahlberg or Ice Cube, interestingly!' The director was not totally off limits, however, and became the highest-profile victim of the Clooney 'fake sneeze'. Witnesses say he took a magnificent nostril explosion smack in the kisser, which left him more bemused than amused. Even George's stunt double became a target for George's humour. The actor was spotted tightening his doppelganger's costumes after the guy had been told to lose weight. 'He had him down to eating a grape a day,' Dunn says with mock approbation. She, too, was another victim, this time of George's dead-eye shot. She started it, he says, by initiating a rock fight. 'I go, "You'd better knock it off," ' George recounts, 'and she throws more rocks. So I take the antenna on my Humvee and put an apple on the end of it. It whips and smacks her in the forehead. A one-in-a-million shot – whap! Everyone goes ape shit, I go around getting high fives.' Not from Dunn, though. 'I saw stars for days,' she says.

George was so keen to get the part in *Three Kings* that he offered to forgo a chunk of his salary. As the second movie in his three-picture Warner Bros deal, he was due around $10 million. In the end he offered to take a third of that plus a percentage of any profits ('a healthy back end' deal).

As well as making the shoot possible by keeping his salary affordable, he was also crucial when it came to negotiating with the studio. Russell had extravagant plans that threatened to push the budget into the red, time- and effects-wise. As an interloper at Warners, he had none of the clout of a seasoned player and few of the contacts.

'When George is your ally it helps,' Russell says gratefully. 'He calls them up and says, "Hey, man, let him do his stuff." '

The stuff in question included things like exploding a cow and showing the path of a bullet through a body – from the inside. Nice. 'I was the guy who had to go to the studio and say, "Come on, let him blow up the cow," ' George says. ' "Cost too much money? All right, take it out of my salary." '

The bovine explosion is one of the film's darkly comic moments. When Major Gates instructs his three war-deprived soldiers to practise their manoeuvres on the roadside cattle, the frightened cow steps on a landmine and its bloody remains shower down on the luckless quartet. The bullet-in-the-body, on the other hand, is anything but funny. The sequence is used several times to show the physical damage created by a bullet entering the lung cavity. After decades of action films like *Rambo* and *Die Hard* spraying gunfire around like hose water, Russell was on a mission to 're-sensitise' audience responses, to ram home the reality of violence. 'I felt that bullets had become glib and cartoonish, even in really smart independent movies, so I wanted to render their impact more real,' he explains. 'David is really brilliant at this,' George enthuses. 'He didn't want to just show the effect of the gunshot, he wanted to show it literally. He used to say to us "every bullet counts". He said that every day.' The result is gruesome and accurate. So accurate, in fact, that rumours started flying around that Russell had employed a real cadaver for the 'shot'. Where did the rumours start? Look no further than the director himself.

'I was being interviewed by a guy at *Newsweek*,' he explains. 'He irritated me so I decided to have some fun. And the next day Warner Bros get these calls: "What the hell did he say to *Newsweek*?" The Morticians' Association had called them and said, "This is an unethical use of a corpse, this is unconscionable." Of course we didn't use a real corpse. It was prosthetic, but a damn good one.'

It was so realistic that Warners insisted that test audiences would decide whether the scene stayed or vanished. If the film's stars were anything to go by, it would not survive. 'When I first saw it I got grossed out,' Mark Wahlberg says. 'I don't even want to pick up a gun again.' Fortunately, guinea-pig audiences would prove to be made of sterner stuff and the scene would be voted a hit.

Wahlberg's unease about the gun scene was temporary. Others were afflicted by more serious illnesses following another one of the movie's set pieces. In a shocking depiction of the brutal lengths that Iraqi soldiers would go to to punish traitorous townsfolk, Republican Guardsmen are witnessed destroying a tanker. Its cargo of milk bursts out of the drum carriage and washes Jonze clean off his feet. George, Cube and Wahlberg suffer secondary drenching. For the purposes of getting the right look on camera, the production team invented a milk substitute – with catastrophic results.

'We had to be in this fake milk, which was water and turpentine or something,' George says. 'That took me down.' The normally hardy actor contracted bronchitis and was bed-bound for five days, ripping into the schedules of his film and TV commitments. Even when he was back on his feet he was forced to have artificial air at close hand. 'For about three weeks I had this oxygen mask on set.'

Dairy disasters aside, there was also the suspicion that the locale might not be as healthy as it could be. Russell had chosen the former copper mine because it had absolutely no vegetation whatsoever, just like the terrain in Iraq. But in America, was that not a bit odd? The green mist that occasionally fell was certainly suspicious. 'We were not actually in the desert but on this old copper mine,' Cube shudders. 'What looks like sand is actually residue from the extracted copper that's been on the ground for fifty years. I don't know what they did at this place, because nothing grew. You didn't see a fly, an ant, a bush or anything remotely alive. Breathing that stuff was hell on the lungs.'

Mark Wahlberg was another casualty of ailments unknown. 'I went to the hospital and they stuck this eight-inch needle up my ass,' he says. 'Everybody goes to the hospital to see me, and I've got my pants down and shit. It wasn't fun.'

'We were grateful for the break,' Russell says, trying to put a brave spin on the disasters. 'We were like, "Can somebody get sick every week, please?" because insurance picks up the tab.' George is more serious – only slightly. 'There'll be a day when we all end up growing an arm out of our forehead,' he says, helpfully demonstrating what a wave from such a hand might look like.

With cast and crew dropping like flies (the only flies in the area), it was only a matter of time before Dr Doug Ross was called upon to help. It happened when Mexican extra Rafael Moreno collapsed from apparent heat exhaustion. George rushed to his side and put the patient into the recovery position, checking his pulse, massaging his chest and clearing his vomit-cluttered airway. 'I told you not to have fish for lunch,' he joked with relief as Moreno spluttered proof that he was alive. Only later did paramedics discover that the extra really had suffered an allergic reaction to the lunchtime seafood. If ever George wanted a career in medicine . . .

As well as putting a few insurance dollars into the film kitty, George's hospital break gave him time to think. And what he thought about was the state of the production. David O Russell was an undoubted genius behind the camera, but away from it his people skills left a lot to be desired. 'He's a weirdo and he's hard to talk to,' George summed up, 'but that's what makes his writing unique and interesting.' It was Russell's first big picture so George was prepared to cut him some slack. A lot, actually. But the pressure seemed to be getting to the director and he was taking it out on everyone else. 'There's an element of David that was in way over his head, as brilliant as this film is,' George says. 'He was vulnerable and selfish and it would manifest itself in a lot of yelling.' The actor resolved to double his efforts at keeping a harmonious set, but he would have to speak to Russell.

Being away three days a week and putting in long hours when he arrived left George with precious little time to work on script revisions. Learning his lines had never been a job he enjoyed, and he often used his journey times to prepare himself. The last thing he needed when he arrived at Casa Grande was to be handed entirely fresh material. But it happened. Regularly.

'When you got on the set, you weren't quite sure what you were gonna do that day, so you had to be on your toes the whole time,' George says. 'I had long, long monologues written, and he would rewrite all of it in the morning. That happens on every job, but the hard part was that he was so specific about everything, down to the movement of a finger. He directs by telling you while you're on camera how to say every single line, which is not a way I'm capable of working. David's feeling was:

"What am I supposed to do? Shoot it the way I don't like it written?" And my feeling was: "What am I supposed to do? I don't know my lines!" '

For the first time in his movie career, George had come up against an equal in terms of power and opinion. He had never before been in a position where a director was so vocal in their disagreement with him. How he handled the situation would tell a lot about his growth as a person within the ego-warping Hollywood star system.

The first thing to say is that, while George was undoubtedly the reason the movie got green-lighted, there can be only one boss on a film set and it is the director. Always. Joel Schumacher had made that perfectly clear to wayward star Val Kilmer in the actor's trailer. The difference on *Batman & Robin* was that George and Schumacher got on. George was not tested, his masculinity was not threatened, his acting credentials not questioned. He never said, 'I'm the star,' but he never had to. Hollywood instinctively treats its talent differently; most people don't even realise they do it. But Wahlberg defers to George; George defers to Arnie. That's the way it goes.

On the set of *Three Kings*, George deferred to no one. As usual he introduced his 'boys' club' vibe very early on, quietly exerting his influence more subtly than people like Kilmer and Russell could ever achieve with their tantrums. He ate with the crew, he drank with the hired help; everyone knew that he was 'one of them'. He was the defender of the little man – 'sometimes on a big set, certain people get stepped on,' he says, 'and sometimes your job is to make sure that doesn't happen' – he commanded the respect and friendship of everyone on the set, he was first among equals.

Accustomed to being liked and listened to because of who he was and how he treated people, it came as something of a shock for George to work alongside David O Russell, someone who not only did not seem to care about George's status, but struggled to care about anyone at all. Russell is funny, sharp and intensely knowledgeable in person, but on a film set he cares about one thing only: his movie.

'It's a lot of work with David,' George sighs. 'He has a very specific vision, so it made it difficult for others – not just actors – to in any way participate. David is in many ways a genius, though I learned that he's not a genius when it comes to people skills.' But there were compromises to be worked at. George confronted the director – who also happened to be the writer – with his concerns about the script changes and they agreed that while the amendments would not stop, George would be sent his at least a week in advance. There were also discussions about Russell's man-management skills. Russell had a tendency to shout at just about everyone when things were going badly. Unfortunately, given the time restrictions, the violent weather changes and the random illnesses, things were often going badly. According to George, one day Russell would be screaming at the sound department, the next he would humiliate a set driver. When he made a script supervisor cry with his withering criticisms, George stepped in. He wrote the director a letter and pointed out that anger and passion were fine, great even, but humiliating people in public was just bullying. Even in the wilds of Arizona, the rules of Hollywood apply, he said: no one is going to stand up to you because you're the director and you can make their lives difficult later on. Don't abuse that fact.

To his credit, Russell accepted the comments and relations between the two men steadied. He was always as generous in his contrition as he was explosive in his tirades, and had no problem apologising for earlier incidents. In his defence, he said, he was naturally excitable, he was under unimaginable pressure from Warner Bros and this was his first shot at mainstream directing.

'It wasn't until I got on the set that I realised, "Jesus, what have I gotten myself into?" ' he admits. 'That was when it hit me how big it was. The whole thing was deeply intimidating and I lost a lot of sleep.'

Feathers will always get ruffled, he says, in situations like that. 'Sometimes you chafe,' he admits. 'You're together all day, every day, and you're supposed to be doing what I say. So at some point you're gonna want to tell me to go fuck myself or I don't think it's healthy.'

By the end of the shoot, George was beyond telling him to do anything. He demonstrated with his hands. The situation occurred towards the end of the production, as the company was working on its most complex scene yet. Hundreds of extras, several helicopters and fading light were taking their toll on everyone. The scene had been scheduled to take three days but they were already on day five. An extra had been instructed to hit Ice Cube's character. After three takes, Russell still was not happy. He approached the extra and demonstrated how it should be done, flooring the actor in the process. George watched aghast from the distance. What happened next is the subject of various accounts, but one thing is certain: it was not pretty.

Producer Edward McDonnell takes the expected nothing-to-see approach: 'David was slightly frustrated and showed the extra exactly how he would like Cube to be brought down. George saw it, stood up to him and said, "You can't hit an extra." And David said, "Please George, just mind your own business," and David and George got into this back-and-forth.' George is more explicit in his recollection. He remembers taking Russell to one side and telling him not to humiliate people who are too scared to retaliate. Russell did not take the advice well. 'He turned on me and said, "Why don't you just worry about your fucked-up act? You're being a dick. You want to hit me? You want to hit me? Come on, pussy, hit me." I'm looking at him like he's out of his mind. Then he started banging me on the head with his head. He goes, "Hit me, you pussy. Hit me." Then he got me by the throat and I went nuts. Waldo, my buddy, one of The Boys, grabbed me by the waist to get me to let go of him. I had him by the throat. I was going to kill him. Kill him.'

Russell, of course, disputes this account of the argument. He occasionally passes it off as a misunderstanding, other times he is candid in his recollection. To be fair, George has downplayed the situation as much as he has exaggerated it in the past. It seems to depend on his mood. But Russell holds no grudges against George, nor George against him – other than to be adamant that they will never work together again.

Russell apologised to everyone on the set and work pressed on. For the rest of the cast, it was little more than light entertainment. 'It was kind of funny, to be honest,' Ice Cube says, 'and it kind of kicked the set into a different gear where everybody was focused and we finished strong. I wouldn't mind if the director and the star got into an argument on all my movies.'

18. I BLEW IT

While George was thrashing about in the desert, John Wells and his team were racking their brains. Season five of *ER* was underway, viewing figures were still strong although down on the previous year and the show was still at number one. NBC were prepared to pay a healthy $5 million per episode (more than the programme recouped) just for the kudos of carrying the best show in town and it was still the most respected drama series in the world. But there was trouble brewing and Wells was not sure they could survive it.

With Anthony Edwards and Noah Wyle trousering upwards of a quarter of a million dollars per episode, George Clooney's once-generous $42,000 looked positively measly. His salary was low for one good reason: he had never renegotiated his contract, despite entreaties from the studio to commit to longer. 'He has lost literally millions of dollars by staying on the show,' Wells laughs. Edwards agrees. 'He probably could have – for a lot of good reasons – gotten out of his deal,' he says. 'He's done a very heroic thing by staying on the show.' To George it was not heroic, it was good manners because he had a contract, and also good business sense because the show was a springboard to greater things. But as good as *ER* had been to him, George was following a plan, a five-year one. At the end of the fifth series he would pack up his stethoscope and leave to concentrate on movies.

At least that was the theory, and it was one that NBC were very happy to prepare for. Doug Ross's exit would be the biggest show of the year, without a doubt. When Jimmy Smits had bowed out of *NYPD Blue* in a dramatic dying swan routine, audiences had tuned in in their millions. George was the biggest star in TV – his going would eclipse all before it.

And that was exactly the problem that Warner Bros and John Wells were battling with. On the one hand, they were guaranteed the highest-rating show of the decade if George went out with a bang in the season finale. On the other hand, there was the very real chance that the show would lose untold millions of viewers over the summer as people associated Ross's exit with the end of the show and drifted away. No, Wells decided, they would have to put the show's long-term health first. Clooney would leave mid-term, just as Sherry Stringfield had done, which would give the show a chance to build new momentum to hold audience interest over the summer hiatus.

A high-profile press campaign was launched. Confusingly, it had two messages. With teasing headlines such as 'Gone for good?' being run in magazine adverts, NBC was stoking up the 'will-Dr-Ross-die?' debate to maximum effect. While this was going on, the cast were being wheeled out on a charm offensive to downplay George's role in ER's success – there's gratitude for you – in order to keep viewers. 'People love watching George, and they should, but I don't think that's the only reason they watch the show,' Laura Innes said. 'There are nine of us, and there are lots of story lines. I think people tune in for the writing and the stories.' New girl Alex Kingston agreed with her (staying) colleague: 'In some episodes, he hasn't appeared at all, and I don't think the show has suffered,' she sniffed. 'I don't think the audience has even noticed whether he's been there or not, because the show stands up for itself.' Whatever you say, Alex.

Even John Wells got in on the act. 'We've had many, many episodes where he's not very prevalent,' he admitted. But that did not mean he was not missed, as Wells knew.

A roster of other lost regulars was also trotted out: characters played by such massive names as Stringfield, Maria Bello, William H Macy, Michael Ironside, Ron Eldard, Michael Beach, Rick Rossovich, Christine Elise and CCH Pounder had all loved and left and still the show survived. But did anyone really believe that this list of bit-part players came close to the impact of losing not only the most famous face in television but also one of the world's biggest movie stars? Short of turning County General into a L'Oréal drug-testing laboratory, there could not have been a more seismic shift in the programme's internal structure.

To his credit, George kept an aloof distance, turning down all interview requests prior to the big day. The would-he-survive? debate engendered by the PR campaign even began to annoy the stars – the proper ones. 'I wouldn't take it personally that you're being deceived,' Anthony Edwards told desperate TV critics. 'He will live.' 'He's not going to get hit by a bus, or suddenly develop testicular cancer, which was his great fear,' John Wells added. The viewers were not the only ones to be relieved. Since newspapers had reported a supposed scriptwriter saying that Ross would be slain by a hail of gangland bullets, George's hopes of making return visits had been dashed. 'I wanted an exit that allowed me to return from time to time,' he says. 'It was a great moment when one of the producers said, "We've decided to let you live." '

On 18 February, the waiting came to an end and fans got the chance to see for themselves. The story arc had been raging for some time and Doug's maverick tendencies were growing more out of control with each episode. He had already prescribed illegal drugs, an episode which Greene was doing his best to cover up. Now, in 'Double Blind', he breaks protocol – and the law – and answers a desperate mother's plea to put an end to the suffering of her kid. Hathaway is dragged into helping with the euthanasia and the two watch in tears as the boy's condition deteriorates. In John Wells' 'The Storm Part I', aired on 11 February, matters come to a head when the child dies in the Emergency Room and Ross is punched to the ground by the furious father. A murder enquiry is launched and Ross is investigated although his ignominy does not end there. Mark Greene blackballs him, accusing him of betraying everyone with his behaviour. When a school bus crashes in the falling blizzard, Greene forbids Ross from helping – he has done enough damage. Of course, Ross does not listen. The show ends with his car skidding out of control, and him and passenger Jeanie slumped unconscious. Is this the end for Dr Douglas Ross? Had they lied about him not dying?

Not quite. Death would be a coward's way out of the trouble Ross had got himself into. A week later and the scene is set for a showdown in 'The Storm Part II', again written by Wells. The injured Ross is forced to dial 911 to get help for Jeanie. Meanwhile Hathaway loses her clinic as the penalty for her role in the drugs case and she rightly blames Ross. He apologises and says he has no option but to resign. Will she come to Seattle with him? She is heartbroken. Her family is in Chicago, it's her home, there's no way she can go. Hathaway asks Greene to talk Ross out of leaving but he refuses. He loves the errant paediatrician like a brother, but who wants to work with their brother? It is always worse when family lets you down, and Ross had been doing a lot of that recently. The show ends with Mark Greene and Doug Ross sitting out by the river, talking into the night, just the two of them, like in the very first episode. They had come through so much together; one was yin to the other's yang. They each strove to be more like the other and now – and now, they would have to cope as best as they could on their own. Roll credits. Cue tears.

And so it happened. Dr Douglas Ross vanished into the sunset and at least forty per cent of the TV-watching American public was distraught. What other character could give them affairs with interns, hospital administrators, pharmaceutical sales reps, air stewardesses and even his father's girlfriend? Who else but Doug Ross could make phrases like 'give me six milligrams IV push' or 'it's a tension pneumothorax' sound sexy? As the autopsy on his exit gripped all corners of the media – Would he come back? Was it true he was offered $2 million for every guest spot? Would he be killed off from afar? – George was suddenly grateful that he had several weeks' work still to do on *Three Kings*. It came to something when spending time with David O Russell was the better option, he mused, but all this fuss was a bit too much. A poll on the NBC website said that most fans would like to see him come back as Phoebe's boyfriend in the number-two show *Friends*, others said that Ross should get his own spin-off show like *Frasier*. It did not end there. As each territory around the world caught up with the US schedule, he would have to face the same questions again and again. In the UK there was a double whammy as 'The Storm' went out first on satellite channel Sky One in April then on terrestrial TV the following month. Both times, the press whipped itself into a feeding frenzy.

While flattered by the attention, George had never set out to create such a stir. As far as he was concerned, five years on one show was too much for anyone. 'After that amount of time on the same show you start to run out of things to do,' he admits. 'I would do things just to be different, which would be wrong. I'd watch the show later and go, "What the hell am I doing?" There would be some guy on screen dying and I would be almost laughing.'

His send-off from the *ER* crew had been relatively tame, all things considered, but then they were not losing him forever. His Maysville Pictures office is little more than fifty feet from Soundstage 11, where *ER* is shot, so Noah Wyle can still swing by to shoot hoops and George can drift over to spread the latest gossip. 'There was a lot of sadness when I left because they were my friends,' he says, 'but all of my film deals are at Warners and

I've got an office there so I see them every day. I walk by and go, "How's it going in the doctor's office?" '

Maysville in spring 1999 was finally taking shape. There were almost thirty films in development and one had been green-lighted. *Metal God*, was the true story of an Ohio boy who pretends to be English so he can become the lead singer of metal band Judas Priest. George had already got an actor in place – a young guy called Mark Wahlberg. After watching the *Boogie Nights* star in *Three Kings*, George had no hesitation in offering him a two-picture deal with his company. As usual, the humour masks his seriousness. 'If he fucks up, I'm dead,' George laughs. 'I'm hitching myself to a man with a giant prosthetic.'

George also had hopes for the movie of *Gates of Fire*, based on Steven Pressfield's 1998 novel about the Spartans' battle at Thermopylae. With the likes of Bruce Willis calling every month to check status, that sure had potential, but the real activity was on the TV side of things. Warner and NBC had proved too slow in picking up anything on offer, so George had acquired a first-look deal with CBS, which was paying dividends. A remake of the 1964 Sidney Lumet picture *Fail-Safe* had been sold to the network as a black-and-white live production, and the company had also taken *Murrow and Me*, a TV movie based on CBS newsman Edward R Murrow and his decision to rally against the McCarthy witch-hunts. There was hope too for his bio-pic of Moe Berg, baseball legend and spy. A series, *Blood Brothers*, also looked like being picked up by CBS, along with *Kilroy*, a documentary-style comedy devised and written by George himself that HBO had expressed interest in.

It was the latter which really fired him up. It was a spoof reality TV show about a young actor trying to get work in Hollywood – sound familiar? The way George pitched it, Michael Kilroy was a 23-year-old ingenue who had arrived to make his way in Hollywood. The show would highlight just how ridiculous the life of auditions, acting classes and fake friendships was, and over the series you would see Kilroy become tainted by his environment – was George saying that had happened to him? The twist in the tale would come when the actor won the occasional walk-on part in big shows like *ER* or *VIP*, which you would see him filming with the likes of Alex Kingston and Pamela Anderson, and then talking direct to his own camera crew, Garry Shandling style. It meant that on live TV the character could sit down to watch the televised show – the same show that the public would be watching at that time.

As if the comparisons with George's own career were not obvious enough, he even hoped to have some fun with his old show. 'We wrote one where he does this long monologue on ER and does a great job, and then all of his friends are coming over to watch, and he pushes his answering machine when he comes in the door, and it's the director saying, "I should have called you last week. We had to cut that scene, I'm sorry." And you hear the doorbell ring and all his friends are there. And when you see him on ER, you'll actually see him go, "Uh." And then they'll cut away. He'll be just an extra in the background.'

With George's energies now transferred from Soundstage 11 to Maysville's Room 117 in Warner's Building 81, he was spending as little time at home as he had been when he was working a seven-day week. This was not the plan when he quit the TV show. 'I get to stay at home a little more,' he said at the time. 'I hope Céline will appreciate it.' She never really found out. It did not matter what George was working on, it always seemed to be more important to him than being with her. Even her recent modelling work for Christian Dior could not fill the void created by George's perpetual absence. Why couldn't they spend more time together? Why did he prefer to holiday with The Boys instead of taking her away? And why wouldn't he make an honest woman of her?

There it was, the M-word. Céline had admitted in the press the second she arrived in LA that she dreamed of settling down as Mrs George Clooney, with a string of little Clooneys playing around their feet. After three years of no progress at all, in April 1999 Céline Balitran walked out of Casa de Clooney – and out of George's life.

Despite his reputation as a heart-breaker and a man's man, George was crushed when the relationship fell apart. For all his jokey bluffing, he knew that Tommy Hinkley's old quote about his 'sadness' was true. He did put his work first and it did kill his relationships. 'I kept taking jobs and the jobs kept taking me further away,' he says. 'Did I treat my relationship with her too cavalierly? Yes. I suppose I blew it because I didn't want to deal with the issue of how all the time we were spending away from each other was hurting her. I admit it, I blew it.

'She was a really nice girl; wanted nothing more than was normal. Just to go out a few times and go to dinner. And I couldn't do it. She lasted as long as I think she was going to last. It was frustrating for a minute because you think, "Am I sort of relegated to three-year relationships for the rest of my life?" Trying not to be a dick takes work.'

Others had seen it coming, including his friend Michelle Pfeiffer. When she had witnessed how much in love George and Céline were, she knew it was only a matter of time before one of them wanted more. George's response at the time had been to bury his head in the sand. If he foresaw the problems, he did not admit it. 'He's got this new girlfriend and they're hot and heavy,' Pfeiffer said during the European press tour for *One Fine Day*. 'I was like, "So, George? Does she want kids?" He wouldn't answer.'

Céline knows the answer only too well. Shortly after the split she confessed to a French newspaper, 'I wanted to have a real family with children. It will never be the right time for George.'

Thanks to his obsession with being a 'guy' and doing the right thing, George busied himself making sure that Céline would be OK financially. He couldn't give her what she wanted, but he could give her security. 'She pulled up roots and came here for me,' he says, 'so I made sure that she had a great place to live. And I made sure she had cash.' Totalled together, he was rumoured to have handed over $4 million in property, cars and hard currency. He even suggested a good lawyer in case, as a French citizen, she had problems staying in the US.

But treating the problem as a business proposal could not hide the fact that he was really hurting, for probably the first time since he and Talia had split up. Casa de Clooney had been transformed by his girlfriend over the last three years. Every room George went in betrayed Céline's presence. Sometimes it was the furniture or the decoration that she had chosen. Sometimes it was just the memories of the times they had shared that haunted him.

His head was in a tailspin and all the money in Hollywood could not help. What he needed was friendship. Fortunately he had it in spades. George went to stay with Grant Heslov for a few weeks to get his head together – 'It's always after break-ups,' he laughs. The Boys would get him through it.

The Boys could only do so much. Ironically, considering it was what had got him into trouble in the first place, George found the best medicine for most emotional ailments was work. Even with ER finishing, he looked like having one of his busiest years yet. With Céline no longer around, he could throw himself into it with gusto.

There were a couple of small things to occupy him. His old friend Robert Rodriguez was putting together a big-budget James Bond spoof featuring children and he was calling in the favours. Antonio Banderas had already signed up and now it was George's turn. No problem, he said, no problem at all. In the largely uncredited role of Devlin, he actually turns in one of the campest performances of his career – which is saying something. It was a good commercial move, too. *Spy Kids* would become one of the biggest films of the next year.

George took an even smaller role in another film. *South Park* had become one of the hottest TV shows in America, infiltrating daily life in all manner of ways. In one of George's last episodes on *ER*, for example, there was a story line involving a dog named – you guessed it – Sparky. Everyone was getting in on the act. As usual with a hit show, there were calls for a film. Trey Parker and Matt Stone would only do it if they could find an original way of doing it. They succeeded; they made a musical. *South Park – Bigger, Longer and Uncut* was ninety minutes of unbleeped mayhem surrounded by fantastic old-fashioned show-tune orchestrations. There was a vague plot of a nuclear war against Canada for poisoning American kids' minds, plus a stunning cameo from Saddam Hussein as Satan's insatiable sex-slave. With his role kicking Saddam's butt in *Three Kings*, George had to get involved here. He pitched in with two voiceovers, both of them doctors (one looked uncannily like himself): Dr Doctor and Dr Gouache. Another five minutes of his time, more commercial dynamite.

For his next full-time big-screen role, though, George would be a little more choosy. He was happy to lend his weight to friends' projects, but if his name was going to be used to sell a picture, it would have to meet certain standards. He had set a personal precedent with the calibre of his two recent films. One had not made money, the other could still fail if it was not marketed properly, but both made him proud to be involved and that feeling would not change. 'If for some reason no one wants me to do a movie or anything, then at least I've got a few good ones in the bank,' he says, ever the fatalist. 'Ultimately it's not about how good the box office is. The money stuff, the numbers, doesn't matter to me anymore. It used to. It used to be devastating, but not any more. If I'm 85 years old and somebody sees *Out of Sight* or *Three Kings* and goes, "Man, I really love that movie," and I can go, "OK, thanks, that's cool," that's what I want.'

Working with the right people was crucial to getting a film that would stand the test of time. Soderbergh, Russell and Malick were all provocative film-makers first and commercial players second. That is what George admired about them, that is why he wanted to work with them. The collaborators on his next picture certainly met this criterion.

19. I'M A DAPPER DAN MAN

It's not every writer whose work is filmed almost three-thousand years after his death, but a 2000 picture by writing/directing/producing team Ethan and Joel Coen opened with the words 'Based on *The Odyssey* by Homer'. Who says there are no good plots around anymore?

In reality, the Coen brothers, Hollywood's most arch independent film-makers, have always done things differently. Didn't they, while still in their early twenties, raise capital for their first film by making unsolicited house-calls to the wealthy residents of their home town Minnesota? Don't they credit editing duties on their films to the fictional 'Roderick Jaynes' (a fact only exposed when Jaynes was nominated for an Oscar)? Hadn't they made stars of Nicolas Cage, Frances McDormand (who would become Joel's wife) and Holly Hunter? And with *Raising Arizona*, *Blood Simple*, *Miller's Crossing*, *Barton Fink*, *The Hudsucker Proxy*, *Fargo* and *The Big Lebowski*, haven't they made some of the starkest, funniest, most bizarre audience-challenging films of recent years?

Aptly, given the brothers' first hit, George Clooney was on location in Arizona with *Three Kings* when he heard that they were interested in him. He had never met the Coens before, but obviously their reputation spoke volumes. They were up there with Soderbergh, if not above him on the list of modern, innovative auteurs. One phone call later and he was driving from Casa Grande to Phoenix for a meeting that was simplicity itself, he says.

'Joel and Ethan came over to see me and said, "We've got this part for you. It's about an idiot. He's about the dumbest guy you'll ever meet. We think you're perfect for it!"' George laughs. 'I'm like, "I'm flattered. Thanks guys. I'm in."' George accepted the part even before he had read a word just because he admired all their other work. Of course, being George there were superficial doubts, especially following the commercial failure of *Out of Sight*. 'I was a little bit afraid that it would be their first bad movie,' he says, 'but when I read it I couldn't believe how lucky I was. They are incredibly brilliant.'

'We didn't write the part for George, but he was the first person we thought of to play it,' Joel Coen says. 'We'd seen him in *Out of Sight* and we really liked him in that. He was the only actor we considered for the part, for reasons that are hard to pin down.'

If he was hooked before bothering to turn a page, when he did settle down for a little night reading George was blown away. 'As soon as I read the title, I said, "This is the movie that Joel McCreas' character wanted to make in Preston Sturges's movie *Sullivan's Travels*," ' he says. 'I'm a huge fan of Sturges and *Sullivan's Travels*. I checked into a hotel room because I didn't feel like driving back, and I read the script. First page it says it's based on Homer's *The Odyssey*, and I realise I'm playing Ulysses. And it's a musical, and it has a little sex in it. I couldn't believe my luck!'

He was in. As with *Three Kings*, he turned down his budget-breaking appearance fee in exchange for a share of the profits. 'Pay me one million and I'll take a back-end,' he told the Coens. 'If the movie makes money, I make money; if it doesn't, then we got to make the movie.' With that deal done, everything else fell into place with the brothers' customary lack of fuss. 'The whole thing made me laugh,' he says. 'It took a couple weeks to set up the movie and we were off and running.'

Production started in the first week of June on location in the Mississippi delta, where the film is set. After the gruelling *Three Kings* shoot, and the void left by both *ER* and Céline, George set off hoping for a better second half of the year. He would not be disappointed.

The reference that so caught George's attention when he picked up the script was indeed culled from *Sullivan's Travels*, the 1941 Preston Sturges comic vehicle. In it, Sturges's character aspires to make a film in the hope of redeeming himself. Its title: 'O Brother, Where Art Thou?'

Redemption runs heavily throughout the Coens' movie of *O Brother* . . . Its plot centres on wise-cracking, fast-talking convict Ulysses Everett McGill who breaks away from his boulder-hacking life on a chain gang to prevent his ex-wife's imminent re-marriage. Fellow felons Pete (John Turturro) and Delmar (Tim Blake Nelson) are roped – or, more accurately, chained – into going along with McGill on account of the fact that, being bound to them night and day, he literally can't get away from them. Since they would have little interest in risking their parole chances for his marital bliss, he spins them a yarn about the stash of swag he has buried near his old house, a stash soon to be lost forever when the area is flooded in a few days' time.

Which is where the links to *The Odyssey* come in. McGill and Co. have to embark on a journey across dangerous lands and against time, pursued throughout by a mysterious marshal. A chance meeting with a blind soothsayer alerts viewers, if not the characters themselves, to the moral/metaphorical trials ahead of them: 'Yes, you will find treasure,' he predicts, 'but not the treasure you seek.' En route, they are seduced by sirens and attacked by a cyclops (Coen brothers stalwart John Goodman, another film star alumnus of *Roseanne*, as a one-eyed, mugging Bible salesman). Just like Ulysses, in fact.

The allusions to the script's source material don't end there. On one level, *The Odyssey* itself is about a man fighting to return to his wife – called Penelope – before she is swept off by suitors; George's character needs to prevent his ex-wife Penny's new marriage (she has convinced his six – sorry, seven – daughters that their daddy has been hit by a train – 'lots of good people get hit by trains'). Throw in politicians called Menelaus (corrupt governor 'Pappy O'Daniel') and Homer, the appearance of bewitching Lotus Eaters and each doubting wife's endgame 'test' for her returning husband – shooting a bow for Ulysses, finding a ring for Everett – and there's enough historic nods to intrigue the keenest classicist.

Of course, being the Coens, *O Brother* ... is based on *The Odyssey* like *Hot Shots* is based on *Top Gun*. A lot of the enjoyment from the film comes from spotting the knowing references to the earlier productions; but if you don't see them it doesn't matter. The film still works. Which is just as well for George, considering he missed every single reference to *The Odyssey* on his first reading (unlike classically trained Tim Nelson who read it in English and Greek). 'I hadn't read the damned thing, so they told me that after and I thought they were kidding,' he says. 'I thought it was just a joke when the script said, "Based on Homer's *Odyssey*". So I didn't get all of the references, like John Goodman is the Cyclops, the Sirens and the Seer and all that stuff.'

For others like George who skipped Greek legend at school, there are plenty of other references to pick up on. The film is alive with twists and turns, subtle ironies and slap-in-your-face belly laughs as a result of its homages to other legends. All are immaculately framed. An aerial camera, for example, films the fugitives picking up a hitch-hiking 'coloured' musician at a four-way intersection. The musician had been there since midnight, having sold his soul to the devil in exchange for musical prowess. At the crossroads. Get it? But does it matter if viewers don't spot the reference to the world's first guitar hero, Robert Johnson? No more than if you miss the majestic sight of a Ku Klux Klan festival descending subtly into a murderously tinged visual pastiche of *The Wizard of Oz*.

A gag that would not have been lost on audiences, though, is the sight of world-famous hearth-throb George Clooney sending up his celebrated 'film star' looks and locks. His character is obsessive, to the point of paranoia, about the condition of his hair. In prison, he is meticulously coiffure-conscious. On the run, he can give full rein to his beauty regime. He wears a hairnet to sleep and slams a store as a 'geographical oddity – two weeks from everywhere' because it can't supply his preferred brand of hair pomade for a fortnight. 'I'm a Dapper Dan man,' he rages with wild-eyed disgust at the suggestion of using an inferior rival hair-care product. Police dogs sniffing Everett's discarded tins of Dapper Dan form a recurring image of the movie, but despite his precarious status, the fugitive's first thought on being suddenly awakened is always 'my hair!' George attacks the part with aplomb. The question is, were the Coens sending him up for comments he'd made earlier in his career? Not many people can say things like 'I have good TV hair' without it coming back to haunt them at least once.

Of course, if anyone could pull off looking the part of the follically-fetished jailbreaker, then it is George. You need a handsome, comic actor with great hair? He's your man. (Although 'his hair was too short when we started filming because he was doing *Three Kings*,' Joel reveals.) And not just on his head. He was also required to grow a pencil moustache for the part, giving him an instant 30s movie-star look. Tabloid pictures, news shows, as well as promotional interviews he gave in 1999 for *Three Kings* and *The Thin Red Line*, all made mention of it – Actor Grows Facial Hair! – and no prizes for guessing who they compared him to. Even the film's writers saw it. 'You put that little thin moustache on him and you've got the matinee idol look, that mix of Clark Gable and Cary Grant,' Ethan says. Even

George sees it. Sort of. 'Clark is turning in his grave right now,' he jokes. 'Actually I think I look like a lot of the guys who were doing movies in the 40s and 50s, bigger chin and everything exaggerated a little. But you never saw Clark Gable act the way I do in this – he was always a lot more subtle.'

For all his modest denials, George's light touch throughout the movie more than justifies the comparisons; Cary Grant-style charm mixed with Clark Gable looks. More so than the former, though, when the occasion calls for something less subtle, he doesn't disappoint – those parts on *Golden Girls* and *Baby Talk* had taught him something. The look of bewildered innocence on Everett's face as he is smited to the ground by John Goodman's branch-wielding Bible salesman is a moment to treasure. Even better, the sight of George's strained larynx and popping eyes as he belts out (mimed) lead vocals on The Soggy Bottom Boys' 'I Am a Man of Constant Sorrow' is a triumph of comic performance. The fact that the second rendering of the song is performed behind fake ZZ Top-style beards only increases his chance to mug to the camera.

Physical humour aside, Cary Grant would probably never have taken on the role of a fool, which McGill undoubtedly is. 'My character is an idiot,' George says. 'He has unshakeable optimism and gets through difficulties saying to his buddies not to worry because everything would be OK.' McGill is a fast-talking faux lawyer, although sadly his tongue is forever writing cheques his brain can't cash, coming up with a string of ten-dollar phrases for ten-cent sentiments. But for all his bumbling naivety, he is charming and persuasive and ready with an answer and an alibi at the drop of a hairnet. In their leading man, the Coens signed someone more than capable of delivering the goods.

'George is an interesting combination,' Joel says. 'He's got that leading man, movie-star thing you need to carry the movie but also he's a real actor, he can inhabit the character. He played this very vain character as a goofball and did it with a light touch that was just right for it. He has no vanity. From George's sense of humour it was apparent he'd understand the material.'

Occasionally the material allowed George to freewheel. A perfect example is the bearded Soggy Bottom Boys performance where not only are they singing the song, but they are meant to be entertaining on stage, too. For inspiration George turned to his country roots.

'I'm from Kentucky where we have this tradition of "cloggers",' he says. 'It's a bit like *Riverdance* where they keep their arms tight by their sides and only kick their legs.' If the resulting impression of a strait-jacketed coal-walker is anything to go by, then it will be some time before this particular Kentucky tradition breaks into the mainstream.

There was another reason for George to call home before filming began. The part called for a strong southern accent of the type he had spent his youth trying to lose. In his next film, the decision would be taken not to try an authentic accent; but for *O Brother* ... it was all or nothing. He needed that talking-through-teeth, tobacco-chewing twang of his past. 'I wanted to rediscover the Old South accent that I listened to in my grandmother's house when I was growing up,' George says. First port of call was his mother's brother, Jack, whose tobacco farm George used to work on in summers. 'It had been a while since I'd been in Kentucky and heard the accent,' he says, 'so I sent my uncle the script and said, "I want you to just read the script into the tape recorder, the whole script. And then I'm going to use that. I'll get you a credit and pay you some money." And now, at the end of the movie, there's a special thanks to Jack Warren.'

With the accent in place, George could go to town on some of the oleaginous McGill's more high falutin' phraseology. If he didn't share his character's hubris, he certainly didn't share his dumbness. 'You have to be pretty smart to play somebody dumb,' Joel adds. 'There's long takes with reams of dialogue. George pulls it off effortlessly.'

Not always, though. There were one or two occasions where George just could not get his words out. For scene twelve, where the felons approach Wash Hogwallop's house, he dried on the first take. The same with takes two and three. Each time Turturro and Nelson nodded sympathetically at their co-star, glad that their monosyllabic cretins didn't come with the same convoluted lines as George's. As for the Coens? No shouts, no gesticulations of temper, just paternal pats on the back and quiet words of advice: 'Remember to talk like someone who enjoys talking,' Ethan suggests. To everyone's relief, take four goes perfectly – except a bottle being shot at was not in the frame. Take five ...

After the frantic antics of David O Russell, the Coens' approach to directing was a welcome change for George. Not only were they unflappable in the face of human and mechanical error, but their professional serenity extended to the way they ran their set and the way they treated their stars. 'They never panic,' George says. 'They're friendly and funny and easy-going and they never disagree. There was never a harsh word on set – it was great.'

They don't overpower with their 'vision', either, unlike some directors. 'They don't direct you a lot,' George says. 'They advise.' For one scene, they suggested to George that he approach it like Popeye. Now that's an instruction the master of impressions can relate to (his 'Ethan' and 'Joel' often had the set in stitches). 'Like this?' George said as he slipped into an uncanny take of the spinach-chomping sailor. 'Or maybe this?' The directors chose the second option. For another scene where McGill is robbing a bank, they suggested he hop up and down as though needing to go to the bathroom. 'They play dumb a little, but they let you figure it out,' George says.

Another way the Coens effortlessly get the best out of their team is by being one jump ahead. Their preparation is remarkable and everything is done to minimise the stress on their actors and crew. This starts with the script. 'I got the script in February, and in June when we shot it there was literally one page of changes,' George says. 'I've never seen anything like it. Every film I've been on has changed a lot – sometimes too much, *Batman* not quite enough. But this one didn't change a bit.'

For ease of referral, the brothers ensured that each actor had not only their 'sides' (script pages that have been reduced to fit a back pocket) but also a set of miniaturised storyboards so that everyone knew what was meant to happen. So on the ball were they, in fact, that even an inveterate tinkerer like George was more often than not at a loss for suggestions. 'They're open to trying things,' he says, 'and you can suggest things and they say, "OK, you can try that," but they've already covered all the bases.'

Even when it comes to the all-singing, all-dancing set pieces of the film, the Coens are equanimity personified. Big budget does not have to equal big pressure as far as they are concerned. Take the great water baptism scene where Tim Nelson's character is lured to his own moral cleansing; a cast of two-hundred extras, a crane and pages of dialogue meant that setting up took the best part of a day. Execution, however, went seamlessly. 'We did it one time and the Coens looked over and said, "OK,"' George recalls, still bemused. 'We all kind of looked around like "that's it?" And it was.' After 44 takes in Steven Soderbergh's boot, you can see how George would be surprised.

For his own part, George approached the shoot with his usual all-embracing enthusiasm. Night shoots in particular are silent affairs until the man shows up, still perky at nine in the evening, with a day's shooting behind him and several hours ahead. With Céline no longer around to boss him, he admits that the catering table is the only way he can get through the long hours. 'You walk by and those apple fritters start calling "George!"' he laughs.

His upbeat demeanour won over his co-stars pretty quickly too. 'He's really a gracious guy,' John Turturro says. 'He has a very boyish quality. He's more like a young colt. He loves to fool around and I think overall it's a good thing as long as you're serious about what you're doing – and he is.'

'He's a wonderful man,' Tim Blake Nelson states. 'He made my life really easy.' On one occasion, he made it physically easier too. After a few days of long walks from the location accommodation to the shoot, George presented his cast-mates with brand new mountain bikes. 'He just showed up at my trailer one day and said, "Here. It's a long way to the set every day, and I want you to have this,"' Nelson recalls, still impressed by the gesture. 'It was so natural the way he did it and so low-key.'

While George was happily chalking up points for personality, looks, accent and dexterity with a hair net, there was one area in which he just did not come up to scratch: singing. And with Rosemary Clooney his aunt, too. One of the central plots of *O Brother* ... involves the fugitives inadvertently recording a hit record, 'I Am a Man of Constant Sorrow', lead vocals courtesy of Ulysses Everett McGill. Sadly, despite his heritage, George's efforts in the studio were far from what the Coens had in mind.

'I rehearsed for weeks,' George complains, 'and the Coens said, "It sounds pretty good."' But then he went to do it for real. 'The first bad sign was when I looked up, and I couldn't get any eye contact from anyone. It was actually a very embarrassing moment, because I had worked really hard on it.'

'We were both staring at our shoes,' Joel laughs. 'George has a good voice,' he adds seriously, 'but it's not suited to that kind of mountain music, which is hard to just walk into. You have to be brought up in it because it's a very particular sound.'

'I got singers in my family, you'd think I'd be able to pull it off,' George shrugs with mock moroseness. 'I guess it skipped a generation. My version is probably streaming around on the internet as we speak.' It's unlikely. Clooney personally supervised the destruction of each copy of his debut. 'I was like [Nixon's secretary] Rosemary Woods, erasing tapes everywhere!' he admits. In the final film, George lip-syncs to Dan Tyminski's bells-and-whistles vocal.

The Soggy Bottom song aside, O Brother . . . is almost a musical in its dependence on the tunes of the period, a fact that passed George by, just like the Greek references. 'At first, I didn't realise the music's importance,' he admits. 'I understood that we sing some songs, but not that the music was the real frame of the movie. Joel and Ethan – but especially Ethan – know the music of this period very well.'

T Bone Burnett was employed to put together the most authentic-sounding bluegrass soundtrack possible, but there were also many moments when the songs took centre stage in the movie. One set-piece sequence sees Delmar and Pete blessed in a mass river baptism, to the accompaniment of the white besmocked congregation's plaintive rendering of 'Down to the River to Pray'. Another scene has the trio seduced by ululating sirens (or 'sigh-reens'), dashed against the rocks by the harpies' dulcet tones like Ulysses' namesake. The success of Burnett's soundtrack would later lead to Grammy awards, a concert tour and a music film called Down from the Mountain – none of which featured George's dulcet tones.

If the soundtrack seemed authentic, the film's visual style more than matched it, thanks to the efforts of long-time Coen associate and cinematographer Roger Deakins. Despite filming in and around the verdant fields of the Mississippi, the brothers wanted to capture the look of photographs from the period: ochres, sepias, yellows and browns. Thanks to the wonders of post-production, Deakins was able to oversee a global tinting of all the backgrounds, the result of which is there to be admired.

Work on O Brother . . . continued through the summer, winding up in LA for final additions. The film was finished in October. With only the violent death of another innocent cow to remind him of the horrors of his Three Kings experience (and this cow didn't cost him a penny), it was undoubtedly one of George's happiest filming experiences and a welcome change of pace after the first half of his year. What's more, he had got to work with Joel and Ethan.

'The reason you work with the Coen brothers is that you say to yourself, "It'd sure be nice to do one of their movies and have it sit around awhile," ' he says. 'Even movies of theirs that everybody else hates, *The Hudsucker Proxy* and *The Big Lebowski*, I just love. When they hit – *Blood Simple*, *Fargo*, *Raising Arizona* – they're shockingly good.'

20. THAT'S A BIG WAVE!

So much for taking things easier post-*ER*. After probably the easiest film shoot of his career, George flung himself immediately into what would be, physically at least, the hardest – and that was just the facial hair. Where *O Brother . . .* called for a bit of stubble and a girly pencil moustache, his new role demanded a full beard.

The first the public saw of this new look was at the Hollywood premiere of *Three Kings* in October 1999, halfway through filming. Smart in a dark suit and with his long hair slicked back, George's new look was the subject of as many red-carpet interviews as the film – 'Those grey tips are so cute!' There were times when this would have been a relief, but not this night. For all their personal problems, George knew that David O Russell (still wielding his hand-held camera like a gurning Greg Rusedski lookalike) had an amazing movie on his hands. Even before a single critic had cast an opinion, he was confident of the verdict.

He was right. There was no doubt that the film touched a nerve with a lot of writers, especially when George's Major Gates delivers the line: 'Bush told the people to rise up against Saddam. They thought they'd have our support. They didn't. Now they're being slaughtered.' This was a major studio picture moving hardened critics. How often did that happen?

'When it comes to rousing action, whip-smart laughs and moral uplift that doesn't blow sunshine up your ass, *Three Kings* rules,' sang *Rolling Stone*. 'This dark comedy manages to be both disturbingly powerful and powerfully funny,' raved the previously misled *Newsweek*. 'Off-and-on cynical and sentimental, Russell's darkly comic tale shows how much can be done with familiar material when you're burning to do things differently and have the gifts to pull that off,' opined the *Los Angeles Times*. *Variety* praised its 'impudently comic, stylistically aggressive and, finally, very thoughtful manner'. 'George Clooney could be the next Humphrey Bogart,' said *People* magazine.

After the recent intermittent schmaltz of *Saving Private Ryan* and the starkness of *The Thin Red Line*, it was refreshing to find a film that had so many goals, that strove to tackle so many genres. 'The main proposition is to have a cinematic experience that grabs you and doesn't let go of you until the end and constantly surprises you,' an enthused Russell says. 'And then at the end you realise, "Jeez, there was this historical political exposé along the way." You want to put people in spin cycle.'

The film won one special fan. HBO had run a 'making of' documentary of the film and President Clinton had seen it. On 16 October, Russell sat down in the White House screening room as Bill and forty associates watched *Three Kings*. It was nerve-racking but Russell loved every minute of it, especially when the President used the film for the basis of a two-hour seminar on US foreign policy.

Sod's law, of course, that the very thing that commended the film to critics would serve as its main weakness. Promoting a film that went in so many directions is never easy, but George felt that the marketing department had shot themselves in the foot this time. 'I wish they wouldn't sell it as an action movie,' he said shortly afterwards. 'We've been doing interviews in different cities and everywhere we go people say, "It wasn't the film I thought I was going to see." That can work against you a lot of the time. You can't bring an audience in for one thing and then give them something else. They resent it. They think you're insulting them.' Somehow it had worked on *From Dusk Till Dawn*.

When *Three Kings* opened in Europe the following spring, the verdict would be the same. Revered film expert Pauline Kael summed up the problem for the movie-makers when she said it was 'the best American movie I saw last year, but it didn't have much of a following, even with George Clooney in the lead and he was very good'.

American box office was healthy but not spectacular, not considering the weight of the press backing. The movie's first weekend saw almost $16 million handed over at sales kiosks; 25 per cent more than *The Peacemaker*, *Out of Sight*, *Thin Red Line* and even *South Park* mustered. Lifetime US sales would be just over $60 million, almost double *Out of Sight* and *Peacemaker* so not bad at all. Even though it opened at number one and made money for Warner Bros, no one could call it a big hit. George still had yet to have that pleasure as commentators were beginning to snipe with increasing regularity. Maybe his new film would be The One?

When Sebastian Junger's book *The Perfect Storm* landed on the *New York Times* best-sellers list in summer 1997, it caused more than a little consternation at Warner Bros. Why? Because more than a year earlier, production company Spring Creek, which has an agreement with Warners, bought the film rights to the book. That in itself is not so unusual; major studios acquire rights to more books than they know what to do with, just like they buy scripts by the dozen for their intellectual property bank. Even if they don't touch them, the logic runs, it stops anyone else. *The Perfect Storm* book was different, though, by daring to be such a success. If ever there was a bandwagon to be jumped onto, this was it.

With almost obscene alacrity, industry telegraphs were soon rattling with names of possible directors. Steven Spielberg was the first choice, but after *Jaws* he had sworn never to film in water again. The studio's second choice had also had his fair share of wet success but unlike Spielberg was itching for more.

Wolfgang Petersen was best known for his disturbing marine drama *Das Boot*, although he had recently helmed blockbusters such as Harrison Ford's *Air Force One* and Dustin Hoffman's *Outbreak*. He leapt at the chance of translating one of nature's most savage moments into a watchable movie. Natural disaster pictures were in vogue again, with *Volcano* and *Dante's Peak* chasing each other around cinemas. But *The Perfect Storm*, Petersen realised, had everything those films offered, and more: thrilling action, unstoppable natural fury, great characters and, the ace up its sleeve, a heartbreakingly unhappy ending. As in *Das Boot*, *The Perfect Storm* ends in tragedy for its protagonist. Immediately there were calls from within the studio to change the ending. Hollywood does not do death well; audiences don't like it. Petersen refused, and with one very good reason. The tragic events covered in *The Perfect Storm* are true.

At the end of October 1991, the swordfishing boat *Andrea Gail* set sail from Gloucester, Massachusetts, in the hope of landing the season's last big catch. They could not have picked a worse time. Hurricane Grace had torn through the Caribbean and was on her way out to sea when she was met by the cold winds of a northern Atlantic storm and an arctic cold front moving in from Canada. The resulting convergence took everybody by surprise. Pressure gradients went off the scale, wind speeds of 120 m.p.h. appeared seemingly from nowhere, creating 100-foot waves. The greatest storm of the century had been born and the *Andrea Gail* was trapped in the heart of it.

George Clooney joined the project early on. As usual, his radar system at Warner Bros had intercepted an early draft of the script. He liked what he read, in particular the character of Bobby Shatford. He met with Petersen who was singularly unimpressed with the idea. He was the wrong age for a start. 'I said, "Come on – he wants to do that?"' Petersen recalls. 'Shatford is in his twenties and Billy Tyne is 38 years old – a little rough around the edges, a little dark. I got pretty excited about going with George that way.'

'I didn't think of a captain of a ship as 38,' the actor explains. 'You think of them as fifty-odd.' It just so happened that George was 38.

Of course, before he could get the part of Billy Tyne, he had to wait for Mel Gibson to drop out of the running. (Gibson eventually opted to do *The Patriot* instead.) This was getting to be a habit, but one that George could appreciate. 'If I were a producer or director trying to put a project together, I'd go with Mel Gibson, too,' he says. 'If Harrison Ford had been in *Out of Sight* or Mel Gibson was in *Three Kings*, those movies would have made more money. It's a reasonable consideration.'

Petersen was impressed with George from the start. 'What I needed for this role was the commanding presence of a man who was unquestionably in charge,' he says. George proved how in charge he was when it came to filling the now vacant role of Bobby Shatford. 'They were talking about guys they were going to go to and I called up Wolfgang and I said, "You know, it's weird, because we just did a movie together,"' George says. He was talking about Mark Wahlberg. They had had a great time on *Three Kings* and George rated him as an actor. 'You can't take your eyes off Mark, he's so good,' he enthuses. But there was another reason. Wahlberg was signed to a two-picture deal with George's Maysville, starting with 2001's *Metal God*. The bigger a star Wahlberg was by then, the bigger business that movie would do. Clever? Just the sort of lateral thinking that George applies to his career on a daily basis.

Fortunately Petersen agreed. 'I met him – boom! We fell in love right in that brief instant,' he says. Wahlberg was equally smitten. 'Wolfgang,' he said, 'anything you want me to do, any stunts, anything you wouldn't normally ask an actor, I'm your man.' The director's response should have set alarm bells ringing. 'Vee'll see,' Wahlberg laughs as he does the impression.

Shooting of *The Perfect Storm* took place at Soundstage 16 at Burbank and on location in Gloucester. Each leg of the operation had its own specific problems. Recreating the effects of a raging ocean in a Force-12 gale indoors had obvious technical demands. When the operation moved to Massachusetts, however, there were more human concerns. The six men who sailed to their death on the *Andrea Gail* were all real people with real families. For authenticity's sake, filming would take place on a replica ship at the very same harbour where Tyne moored; town scenes would feature the exact streets where his crew walked, the houses they lived in, the bars they drank in, the church they were commemorated in.

'The tricky part about this movie is that we're walking a very fine line between entertainment and also dealing with real people's lives,' George says. 'So you can't just go, "My ex-wife's an idiot," because the lady actually lives in this town.'

For the Gloucester locals, the idea of re-opening old wounds almost a decade after the tragedy was daunting. From what everyone had heard of Hollywood types, their town would soon be swamped by limos, Ray-Bans, dark suits and cellphones; by streets being closed without notice and by rudeness at every turn. They reckoned without the inclusive sensibilities of Wolfgang Petersen and the down-to-earthness of George and Mark Wahlberg.

To immerse himself in his part, Wahlberg arrived in town weeks early and took a small room above a bar called The Crow's Nest. It was the same room where Shatford had lived. Shatford's mother, Ethel, was a bartender downstairs. Like everyone else, she viewed suspiciously this young man who had been dropping his trousers with Marky Mark And The Funky Bunch in the year her son perished. But she was soon won over by his dedication to doing his best to keep Bobby's memory alive.

Petersen was equally determined to make the production's hosts feel as involved as possible. He hired local fishermen as advisors and even cast Bobby Shatford's brother Rick as an extra. At nights, Petersen and his stars would spend hours in The Crow's Nest drinking with friends and relatives of the dead sailors, hearing personal accounts, memories and theories about what happened. Petersen would soak up all the information and make script changes the next day. Wahlberg would take on all-comers at pool, George would drink as long as he had a companion. The movie's producer, Gail Katz, remembers one night being invited to see a band featuring one of Bobby Shatford's brothers at another venue. 'And there was George,' she says. 'He was already there, drinking with everyone in town.'

George claims that Mark Wahlberg was the big talent in *Three Kings*; his own role was 'getting the film made in the right way'. That is the sort of thing he cares about. It certainly made an impression on the townsfolk in Gloucester, in particular on Rusty Shatford (Bobby's other brother) who watched George meet Bobby's son John. 'He put his arm around my nephew and walked off with him for about an hour, just talking to the kid,' Rusty says. There were other such acts. Long impromptu autograph sessions, photographs willingly posed for onlookers, jokes with Ethel Shatford, basketball games outside his trailer with anyone who happened to be passing. When George went walking, traffic ground to a halt. What did he do? He apologised.

Forging a relationship with the family of Billy Tyne, however, was fraught with problems. In the film, Tyne comes across as the least sympathetic character. He is also largely blamed for the disaster when he opts to face the storm for the sake of selling their swordfish haul. 'In the original draft it was much more Billy Tyne's decision,' George says. 'But Wolfgang thought that this should be much more about all their decisions. We don't know what happened in the boat in real life. What we do know is they had a hold full of fish, a broken radio, an ice machine that's down and a storm ahead of them.

'I was happy with this because I was friends with Roberta, Billy Tyne's sister. Her main concern was not to make him out to be a Captain Bligh or a Queeg. And the way you do that is by making the decision democratic.'

(It turned out not to be enough. In August 2000, members of Tyne's family would file a lawsuit against Warner Bros for defaming their good name and for impugning the character of their dead relative for financial and entertainment ends. The studio would fight the claim.)

For Wolfgang Petersen, it was refreshing to work with a star who seemed comfortable with the trappings of his success, without letting them affect him, even when hundreds of girls would line the harbour of Gloucester hoping to catch a glimpse of the star. 'They were always screaming when George was there and he was very sweet to them,' Petersen says. 'I've seen other guys who were really annoyed by that. But that's part of his popularity. People feel he's just a very friendly guy. He's nice to people and doesn't want to hurt their feelings.'

George was encouraged to see Petersen leading the mood from the front, reminding him of the great atmosphere on the *Batman* set. Every day the director would serve soup, he encouraged visits from locals and he went out of his way to get every detail as close to the truth as possible. Even Sebastian Junger was impressed. Petersen's coup de grace was to track down the *Lady Grace*, the sister ship of the *Andrea Gail*, to play the stricken vessel. 'If they had used another boat that was basically the same size, no one would have known,' Junger admits. 'The people in Gloucester wouldn't even have known.'

When the 'fake' 72-foot *Andrea Gail* pulled into Gloucester harbour that first time, one can only imagine the emotions it must have stirred in the grieving locals. 'I just stood looking at it for about an hour,' Rusty Shatford says, overwhelmed at the memory. 'When I saw that boat again, I was blown away. It was like a ghost ship sailing back into port.'

In the face of all the raw emotion, George was usually equipped for a little light relief. He took great pleasure hamming up his 'boy from Kentucky' background by parking the *Andrea Gail* as badly as he could for comedic effect. When no one was looking, however, he was proud of his piloting achievements. 'I grew up cutting tobacco,' he says, 'so it was a big leap to suddenly be steering a ship. I'd never sailed before, and fortunately, I didn't screw up badly enough to wipe out any docks.'

One can only guess at the behaviour that Petersen is used to encountering from his leading men because his gratitude to George's on-set influence seems unfakeable. He seems genuinely flabbergasted that George should actually queue for his food with the rest of the crew. And as for any so-called movie-star attitude – there was none. 'This man has an amazing sense of humour,' Petersen enthuses. 'Maybe it's to get rid of stress, but between takes he always starts to joke around and play practical jokes.' On one occasion he recreated his Harry Hamlin stunt. When a photographer had to run to the side of the boat to throw up, George gave her camera to someone and posed with his pants down for a picture. The photographer had no idea until she developed the film a couple of days later. 'He did that kind of stuff all the time,' Petersen says. 'I like a set where people are in a good mood, and boy, if you have a partner like George on the set, it's just fun all over.'

Whether Petersen was aware of it in advance or not, he soon discovered that if you hire George, that is what you get for your $12 million (and for the first time, he was finally being paid his rate on this $100-million production). It was just as well.

When Steven Spielberg had turned down the chance to direct Junger's book, it had been for the simple reason that films and water are not a happy marriage. No film shot with water had ever come in on budget; no other type of shoot is likely to result in as much sickness and injury to cast and crew; and there is nothing like water for destroying expensive camera equipment. For the three months of shooting in Gloucester, everyone involved in the movie was put through the most testing time of their lives.

'Filming was six months of hell,' George says. There was the constant cold, the wear and tear on the actors' skin from actually working the fishing boat, the fact that Petersen's instructions were often inaudible over the elements around them, plus the added hindrance of having to act and physically pilot a ship at the same time. And then there was the vomiting. Lots of it. From everyone except George, in fact, although once he came very close.

'Hurricane Floyd came by while we were filming,' George says. 'It had been downgraded to a tropical storm, and Wolfgang said, "Let's go. We have a storm." So, we went out, and everybody got seasick. The crew was throwing up like crazy. Mark was throwing up like a mad man.

'But it never got me, even though I have sort of a delicate stomach. I had given everyone else such a hard time about getting seasick that I knew if I threw up, I was dead. At one point I started to get a little queasy, and they were all looking at me and laughing. I said, "I'm telling you, before I throw up, I'll throw myself in the ocean."'

'It was a tricky day,' Mary Elizabeth Mastrantonio, who plays Billy Tyne's rival and girlfriend, confirms. 'People were turning purple below stairs.' It didn't help George that the storm came before he had fully mastered his ship.

The main threat to George, however, was his co-star and shipmate Wahlberg. Despite his weeks of acclimatisation spent on fishing boats, and despite the fact that he grew up only forty miles along the coast, Wahlberg had a problem with seasickness. A big problem. One day, it is said, he vomited 52 times. 'I was desperate to get my lines out before I had to throw up,' he laughs.

'It was actually hysterically funny when you saw the dailies,' George says. 'There's one scene we filmed out on the ocean and it was choppy, about five or six feet, and Mark was throwing up every five minutes. I'd never seen anyone throw up for five hours straight. We're in the wheel house and the camera is on me and you can hear him say, "Skipper, you promised you'd find us fish . . ." and then "Uuuughhh" as he throws up and you see me get out of the way pretty damn quick. It was the best acting I ever did, trying to avoid getting barfed on.'

As it transpired, the seasickness and authentic chaos in Gloucester were the least of the cast's problems once the production moved back to LA. Since the start of the year, work had been going on to transform Soundstage 16 into the biggest water tank on earth. By the time the crew arrived in autumn, they had succeeded. Even Spielberg was impressed. Legend has it that his jaw visibly dropped when he sneaked an early peek at the set-up. Petersen had taken the tank used for *The Old Man and the Sea* and – to be technical for a moment – made it bigger. As Spielberg looked on, the sheer scale of the 100-foot by 92-foot tank slowly sank in. And at 22-feet deep, it was large enough to hide a vast gimbal capable of carrying the entire *Andrea Gail* and replicating the effects of anything Mother Nature could come up with. Wind machines primed to crank up 100 m.p.h. gales were positioned at every corner, there were numerous hoses stationed to douse the entire ship on cue, and surrounding the whole affair was a 360-foot blue screen, onto which George Lucas's Industrial Light & Magic team would later superimpose realistic backgrounds.

At the start of the day, the cast had to be ferried to their ship by motor boat. Then they were on their own, monitored by cameras fixed in the water, on the ship and on land. If Petersen needed to speak to them, often he could not be heard above the fake elements so he, too, had to go out in the boat to reach them. It was a slow, gruelling process. And this was indoors.

At the end of the day, though, a 50-foot wave is a 50-foot wave. Whether it is out at sea or created in a California studio, the effect is the same. And it is the response to those effects that Petersen was determined to get out of his cast. Only now did Wahlberg come to regret being so open with the director at that first meeting. 'We didn't have to fake a moment of it,' George says. 'Simple truth: if you're not strapped in with a cable that screws you down, you're literally blown from one side of the boat all the way off the back.' Wahlberg nearly drowned on more than one occasion and was hit so hard by a mechanical water jet that his earplug was lodged inside his inner ear.

'We'd get up at seven in the morning, get in the tank, and then they'd hit you with this dump tank of water,' George recalls. 'There's actually a photo of Mark and I standing there between takes where we've just been hit, and we look like we couldn't be more miserable. Wolfgang's standing right next to us with a big smile.'

Both leads did their own stunts, but Petersen reserves special mention for his star. George, he says, was 'the guy who was most ready and willing to go the whole way. For the actors, it's a bit frightening when these huge masses of water come all over you, but George was probably the least intimidated. I think he actually enjoyed fighting the elements, so to speak. And imagine these fishing boats: they have these things like wings that go out left and right to stabilise the boats. In one scene at the height of the storm, he has to crawl out and fix something at the very end of the wing, and most of these shots he actually did himself. It was pretty astonishing.'

Of course, George refuses to take any special credit. 'It's not the hardest job in the world but it is miserable,' he demurs. 'Wolfgang, though, made a lot of jokes and really kept it fun all the time. His sense of fun, and the fact that he loves what he does, was infectious. But there wasn't a day when I got up and thought, "Wow, I can't wait to get wet!" '

Despite campaigning for the part, George had been concerned by the original script. Why, for example, when faced with a big wave, did Billy Tyne, experienced fisherman that he was, need to exclaim, 'That's a big wave!'? After the Coens' tight scripting, George had no choice: out came the Magic Marker. But how to tell the director without sounding like a big-shot jackass?

'I was going to sit down with Wolfgang when I felt comfortable with him,' George says. 'You don't want to come in and jam around, "This is what we're going to do" or "This is what I want." So I was waiting. On my first day, we had to shoot one of the scenes that I had a lot of notes on. I walked up to Wolfgang to say, "OK, it's going to be weird, but I've got a shit-load of notes on that scene, just editing, chopping down lines." And he goes, "Before you say anything, listen, way too many words in this, here's what we're chopping down," and he hands it to me. And I went, "Perfect." '

There was the further problem for George of Billy Tyne's character. Or, more specifically, his voice. Tyne was a local boy, born and bred. George had willingly gone back to his roots for the authentic Delta accent of Everett McGill, but this would be trickier. And would audiences accept it from him? 'I'm pretty good at accents,' he says, 'but I've also reached that stage where people know me and the Boston accent is the hardest one to do.

'I don't want the audience spending the first fifteen minutes of this movie like the RCA Victor dog, trying to figure out what I'm doing.' For co-star Wahlberg, however, it was less of a problem. Having been born in Boston he knew he could get the twang right; he had, after all, spent long enough trying to get rid of it.

Shooting on *The Perfect Storm* finished in January 2000. It had been the most gruelling six months of George's professional career, but it had been worth it. Not only had he taken the lead role in an out-and-out summer blockbuster (unlike in *Batman* where he played second fiddle to his costume and Arnie), but his co-stars and fellow industry professionals were rushing to commend his amazing work ethic and personality. That would do future business no harm at all. Author Sebastian Junger had been a regular presence on the set, much to George's pleasure – 'having him around made us feel like we had his seal of approval' – and fittingly Junger gets the last word on the man who made his novel a cinematic reality. 'It's guys like Clooney who are the successful captains,' he says. 'The kind who can charm the work and the courage out of the men, who understand that the men are lonely, they miss their girlfriends, they're scared. The other kind of captain is a tyrant. He'd have been a terrible tyrant.'

He'd have been a terrible prima donna, too. Unlike a lot of celebrities, George is open with the press, willing to do interviews and cognisant of his part in the media game. Consequently, he suffers little compared to, say, Tom Cruise or

Michael Jackson, both of whom the press feel are hiding something. But still there is the interest. They always want more. During the Gloucester shoot for *The Perfect Storm*, a Boston paper ran stories about George's blossoming 'relationship' with former *Melrose Place* actress Brooke Langton. Back in LA there were revelations that he was returning to *ER* for a Thanksgiving special. 'News to me,' George said. Obviously it never happened. By Christmas he was 'definitely' contracted to marry Hathaway during Julianna Margulies' last episode for a $2-million fee. 'I saw that in *USA Today*,' he said, 'and I called everyone I knew and said, "I'm rich!" '

You cannot blame the press for attacking the *ER* story. Since Doug Ross's exit, ratings for the sixth season had dropped by 22 per cent. George, of course, refuses to shoulder any of the (flattering?) blame. 'The ratings were dropping while I was there as well,' he vainly points out. 'The quality of the show was slipping. It happens after five years. Things get tired, and it's time for something new.' He even denied that the producers would like him to return for the occasional shot in the arm. 'They sort of have to say they'd really like me to come back, but I have a feeling they want to move on,' he bluffed. 'I don't think they want to have these nostalgia shows.'

Christmas for George that year was again spent in the collective bosom of The Boys. It was his first New Year without Céline for some time, and he was glad of the company for the holidays. As a result, he wanted to make sure everyone remembered it. They would. On 25 December, each of his friends woke to find a brand new Indian motorcycle parked in the drive. Those Sunday morning rides would never be the same again.

Business-wise, 2000 was busy. Maysville was going through a weird period. On the one hand George's production of *Fail Safe* was scheduled to debut on 9 April on CBS and Jennifer Aniston was being linked with playing opposite Mark Wahlberg in *Metal God*. On the other hand, George was itching to do other things. He had enjoyed working with Steven Soderbergh so much on *Out of Sight* that he wanted to formalise some sort of partnership. With his contracts with Robert Lawrence and Pam Williams drawing to a close, he took the opportunity to officially dissolve Maysville Pictures. In its place would come Section Eight. Partners: G Clooney and S Soderbergh.

Without missing a beat, George had already secured the company's first production. It would be a remake of an old Rat Pack film, hopefully to be released in 2001. To do justice to the spirit of the original, there would need to be an impressive roster of talent to come close to the appeal of Frank Sinatra, Dean Martin and Sammy Davis Jr. No problem. The fervid imaginations of the Hollywood media set to work, announcing dozens of names as signed up for the project, often with little or no basis in fact. Still, it kept his name in the papers as a producer, George thought. That was no bad thing.

Despite the imminent developments in his production set-up, George had no intention of dishonouring his CBS obligation, signed back in 1998. He had been planning *Fail Safe* for some time, but he was just waiting for the right format. 'Usually I hate people who take a good film and say, "Let's go and do it again," ' he says. 'You should just re-release good films. But if you can do it again in a different medium, I think that's more interesting.'

Originally he was planning just to produce the show. Old friend Leslie Moonves, the president of CBS television, had other ideas when George put the deal to him. 'I sat down with Les and I said, "OK, here's the deal: *Fail Safe* . . . live," ' George recalls. 'And he goes, "Mmm hmm. Mmm hmm." And I go, "Black and white." And he goes, "Mmm hmm." And then we kind of looked at each other for a minute, and he goes, "You're going to be in it." And I go, "Mmm hmm." And then we both kind of laughed and I said, "OK, fair enough." Which is fun. I'm glad we're doing it that way.'

Moonves was just as happy with the deal. 'It was a no-brainer,' he says. 'We're always looking for event TV. So, George Clooney in a great piece of material done live? If that ain't an event, I don't know what is.'

In 1964, Sidney Lumet's *Fail-Safe* (complete with hyphen) shook the world. When a technical error orders a squadron of armed bombers to drop nuclear bombs on Moscow, the President of the USA, played by Henry Fonda, is forced to destroy New York as a gesture of parity and admission of error. When George saw it as a child, he was hooked. 'I can remember when I saw it the first time,' he says. 'I couldn't believe what they were doing. I sat there with my mouth open for the last hour of it. It's a very personal story about several million people being killed. That doesn't happen very often and that's an amazing event. It's my favourite film of all time.'

It would be the first live CBS drama for 39 years, since *Playhouse 90* had stopped running before George was born. As well as not using colour, George had other ideas about keeping his new broadcast faithful to the original era. 'We're going to try to use the older-style lenses as much as possible. Maybe by taking a step backward and tipping our hat to TV's past, we might make TV today a little more interesting.'

Whereas *Playhouse 90* had pretty much transmitted theatre productions live, with just a couple of cameras following actors around one room, *Fail Safe* represented the first time a full-scale movie had been attempted. It was no small concern. Seven sets built over two soundstages hosted everything from a colonel's bedroom to the Omaha war room and the President's office. Twenty-two cameras, some disguised as on-screen computers and operated by cameramen in soldiers' fatigues, were in place to allow for multiple angles, something else the old dramas never managed. Given the precision required, there was a chance of actors drying up, although 'cheats' were in place. The giant electronic map in the war room doubled as a prompt. 'We have a guy with a keyboard ready, so if an actor misses a line, he can instantly update the map,' George revealed, hoping it would not be necessary.

The map would not have been required by him, however. Since his character Colonel Jack Grady (George's third 'Jack' in his short film career) spends the entire film in a plane, George was able to wear an earpiece under his flying helmet. The other actors were more exposed. Fortunately, George had corralled quite a cast of heavyweights to minimise risk. For a start, he drafted in a few old pals. Noah Wyle from *ER* (who took over Larry Hagman's original role), Don Cheadle from *Out of Sight* and Harvey Keitel all signed up. Recreating the Henry Fonda part was Richard Dreyfuss while the excellent Brian Dennehy played General Bogan. Although cousin Miguel Ferrer was originally billed to appear, the only person to turn down George's personal entreaties was someone even closer to home – Nick Clooney. 'I said, 'Come on, come on, be a senator or something,'' George recalls, laughing. 'But he won't do that. He will never do it.' The show was directed live by Stephen Frears and set in its original era, although updated slightly by original screenwriter Walter Bernstein. (Because Maysville had rights to the book but not the film, Bernstein rewrote the screenplay from scratch.)

From the moment at 9 p.m. Eastern Standard Time on 9 April 2000 when George Clooney's voice announced to the world, 'Coming to you live from CBS, your host, Mr Walter Cronkite,' the network was committed to two hours of seat-of-your-pants broadcasting (unlike the *ER* live event, this was only performed once). Ironically, it was the hugely experienced Cronkite who made the largest error, stumbling over a writer's name; on the actors' part, things went as close to without a hitch as could be hoped for.

Watching at home, thirty-million people had the chance to see some of the biggest movie names performing without a safety-net. There was off-screen coughing, an audible hiss in many scenes, the occasional panicked look in an actor's eye, and the over-loud clunk of some serious 60s furniture (those phones!). But the overall result was a feeling of a risky shot pulled off. 'Frears makes a sterling job of reviving the original film's taut, monochrome claustrophobia,' *Sight and Sound* approved. *Empire* was equally impressed, wading in with four stars. The programme even received a Golden Globe nomination.

George had done it again and he deserved every credit. 'He is not a vanity producer,' Moonves says. 'Every single piece of that project was overseen by George.' For better or worse. 'I got the network to do it in black and white, a letterbox format and live, got all the guys to work for nothing,' he says, reaming off the positives. On the other hand, 'I slept on the couch for three months and I lost money on it. It was the most exciting thing I ever did in my life.'

21. WHERE ARE THE GIRLS?

Rarely does anything happen on a major TV programme that is unexpected. The whole business of television these days is less about surprises than about expectation. For the suits who ultimately run the networks, there seems no point in having a major guest-star or a skilful plot twist on your show if no one knows about it. If viewers aren't tipped off that the surprise is coming, they might not watch. So companies trail the best bits of each show and leak the story lines in order to maximise the audience potential. At the same time, though, any semblance of kinship and shared experience between the viewer and the programme is lost. Everyone knows they are pawns in the marketing department's crass numbers game. But it says a lot about television's power that we put up with it.

It says even more about George Clooney's increasingly awesome power that he was able to thwart this procedure on one very special occasion.

Thanks to the traditional leaks and pre-press system, viewers of the penultimate episode of ER's sixth season tuned in fully aware of the night's plot: Hathaway, played by Julianna Margulies, was set to flee the Emergency Room for Seattle in search of the father of her twins, Dr Ross. As the teaser clips had promised, Hathaway's exit would be tearful and dramatic.

Nobody was prepared for just how dramatic – not even the powers that be at NBC. With barely sixty seconds left on the show's broadcast time, viewers saw Hathaway stare out at a lake and ponder her life. A noise makes her turn and Doug Ross, unshaven and smiling, enters the scene. 'Where are the girls?' he enquires, they hug and kiss to the strains of Don Henley's 'Taking You Home'. Roll credits.

So there it was: George Clooney had returned to ER and the first thing anyone knew about it was when the moment aired on 11 May 2000. Viewers in their millions would have pinched themselves on their way to bed that night, but it was true. To prove it, NBC's Today show was forced by public demand to re-run the entire scene on Friday morning.

The episode caught out a lot of people, in particular the

network itself, but that was part of the deal. There had been a lot of public pressure, doubtless originated by the station's money-men, who had seen the show's ratings share slide by a quarter, for George to give some kind of closure to his character's relationship with Carol Hathaway. He had always refused because he did not want to be seen as some big star riding in to save the day; that isn't his style. If he were to return, he always thought, it would have to be on his terms, it would have to be subtle and it would have to be intrinsic to the story. The suits would never swallow that.

But what if they weren't told? As the sixth season of *ER* slipped quietly towards its finale, George spoke to the show's executive producer John Wells. Between them they hatched a plan: George would put in a small appearance as long as it was kept secret. He didn't want his return to overshadow what should be the grand farewell for his friend Margulies, who was turning down a reported $27-million contract to pursue theatre and film work. Deal.

Less than a week after *Fail Safe* had aired, on 14 April 2000, George and Margulies found themselves in Seattle, reunited once more for his blink-or-you'll-miss-it scene. 'We fixed a date and sneaked up with the producer, director, a camera guy, a sound man and Julianna,' George says proudly of the subterfuge. 'We rented a private house from a couple for $10,000 and they were given a post-dated cheque so if they sold the story then the cheque could be cancelled.' The same deal applied to everyone else. Only those who were involved in shooting the encounter were told about it, and they were sworn to secrecy. In case that didn't work, there were also financial inducements for the crew – bribes by any other name – of the same kind as the house owners received. 'John gave everyone cheques and said, "If no one finds out, these cheques are good," ' George reveals.

For his own part, George played his cards very close to his chest. 'It was all very sneaky,' he says. 'Even my agent didn't know until I told him as we took a plane to Cannes. He was talking into a phone saying, "He'll never do it." I said to him, "Well, I did do it."

'We flew up to Seattle and shot it in four hours in the rain,' he says. Fittingly for the actor who famously refused to take a pay increase, George did the work for a union scale fee: $596. 'That's not bad for a couple of lines,' he says.

It's fair to say that by Friday morning, NBC's switchboard was buzzing with various parties demanding to know why they hadn't been informed. The stock answer was the same one that George gives: 'We thought if we could keep it quiet, we wouldn't take away anything from the show completing Julianna's character,' he says. Actually, the execs were tipped off the night before, just in time to put out a subtle teaser. Warner Bros, which makes the show, found out on Thursday morning.

Credit for keeping the cat in the bag has to go to John Wells, who went to extraordinary lengths to protect the secret. Apart from the bonus payments to the crew, he filed false scripts to the network and hid the film in his refrigerator. 'It's so difficult to keep anything quiet anymore,' he admits. As NBC spokeswoman Barbara Tranchito says, 'None of us knew. I saw the script and he wasn't in there.'

Wells was eventually forced to release a press statement to appease the media throng: 'We shot the sixty-second scene several weeks ago in Seattle before George had to leave to promote his new Ethan and Joel Coen film at Cannes. George came back to help us conclude the six-year love story between Doug Ross and Carol Hathaway. He did the scene for scale, for old friends and for the many fans of this long-running story line.'

Apart from endless speculation in the press – presented as fact – there had been serious talk of George returning to the show late in 1999 when Hathaway gave birth to Doug's twins. 'Julianna got quite upset when I decided against it,' George admits. 'She got madder and madder at me.' To be fair, it was not entirely his fault. George was aware that his character's returning so soon and for just one episode would not do the show any favours in the long run. It so happened that Dr Mark Greene agreed. 'I talked with the other actors and Anthony Edwards said that he didn't want me to come back,' George says. 'We talked sensibly; there was no argument. He said: "This is not about you and I, because we're friends. But we've had to spend a year addressing how the show was going to survive without you. We did very well, despite hiccups along the way. It doesn't seem fair for you to come back for one episode. If you're coming back for four or five, then that's a different story." I said: "Fair enough."'

By returning unannounced, he reckoned, Margulies would have her big exit, Hathaway would get closure to her life, Edwards and Co.'s noses would remain in joint and the fans would get a massive treat. 'It was the only way to do it that seemed fair for the people on the show,' George reflects. 'It didn't take attention away from them. Doug and Carol are now going to be looking after the twins in Seattle.' To live happily ever after.

In overnight ratings, the episode generated a 38 share in its final half-hour – making ER the highest rated programme on Thursday night. The tactic also propelled the show back up the water-cooler discussion charts where it had once resided. More than anything, though, it rammed home just how powerful George Clooney had become.

While the true extent of his influence had yet to dawn on most people, other aspects of George's life were more transparent. People magazine's list for the month of June was '100 Most Eligible Bachelors'. Yankees star Derek Jeter was number two, George Dubya's nephew was number three. No guesses for who came in at number one.

It was not the first thing George had won that year, however. In February he, Ice Cube and Mark Wahlberg had joined David O Russell in Berlin for the city's International Film Festival to launch Three Kings in Europe. Among the other gongs, George picked up a prestigious Golden Camera award for 'Best International Movie Star'. Sadly though, he told the audience, he was not holding out for any Oscars. He was right not to. The Golden Globes also overlooked the film although the screenplay was nominated by the Writers Guild of America. On the bright side, George got to hob-nob with other megastars, particularly delighting at having a dinner with another German director, European film legend Wim Wenders, and Bono who had just collaborated on Million Dollar Hotel. 'Well, that was pretty cool,' George says. 'I'm drinking with them, thinking, "Man!" and Wenders is like, "So, vy don't you come here and do a vilm vit us?" I told him, "I will! I will!"'

From Germany to France . . . Most American film moguls don't have a lot of time for non-US promotion, but the Cannes Film Festival is an early entry in the diaries of the biggest companies. As well as the prestigious and lucrative Best Film award, the festival also offers distributors the chance to premiere films outside of the competition. That way, major stars can still turn up and surf the perennial tsunami of media interest without the ignominy of being seen to lose. Everyone wins.

The Coen brothers, of course, are not afraid of a little bit of competition. In 1991 they won the coveted Palme d'Or for Barton

Fink, and have returned most years either with a film or as guests. May 2000 found them opening the festival with *O Brother . . .* and so they called on the film's big guns to support it. Clooney and Coen stalwarts John Turturro and Holly Hunter were drafted in to begin their promotion duties even though the film wouldn't open until the end of the year. Speaking before his trip, George was excited by the experience. 'The Coen brothers warned me it will be a little crazy,' he said. 'But I can't wait to go because I'm going with a movie that I'm proud of.'

(Actually, George had two movies premiering at Cannes that year, although he was only aware of one. He also appears in *The Book That Wrote Itself*, a £20,000-digital movie by enterprising Irish director Liam O'Mochain. Posing as a journalist at 1999's Venice Film Festival, O'Mochain was able to film himself interviewing the likes of George and Kenneth Branagh; the results were then spliced into his film. Since press conferences are considered 'public domain', he argued, there was nothing anyone could do to stop him. Given his recent shows of strength, if George had been bothered by the film, you can almost believe that O'Mochain would have been turned back at the airport.)

The Coens' prediction wasn't wrong. When the Clooney entourage descended on the Riviera there was mayhem of a kind that even the former Batman hadn't experienced. In Cannes, the press (all four thousand of them) behave like overexcited fans. The real fans meanwhile were even worse, blockading roads and pounding car roofs and windows. 'It was like Nixon arriving in China,' a flushed George recalls. Ever the professional, he took the red-carpet stroll in slo-mo, maximising the time he could spend signing autographs, posing for photos and slipping in the odd two-line interview. In the distance, a largely unheralded supporting cast was seen slipping inside the building. Forget that there were Oscar-winners among them. This was George's show.

If he was feeling nervous outside the theatre, he didn't let on. But the Cannes screening was, after all, the first time he had seen the completed film. 'That's normally something you'd want to do alone,' he says. 'With a bottle of whiskey and a shotgun.' He thought it had turned out great, though. The critics were not so sure. Neither were the judges, who overlooked it for the prizes.

On the plus side, however, George did get to drink a lot of vodka and flirt with plenty of girls. Coming less than four weeks since he and The Boys had partied in Phoenix for his 39th birthday, May was turning into a good month. Unlike a lot of stars, who paranoically keep their antics to themselves, he was happy to drink at the public Terrace bar of his exclusive $1,700-a-night Hotel du Cap at Cap d'Antibes. He had tips for fellow drinkers. 'You've got to keep it simple,' he lectured. 'Stolly, Stolly, Stolly' – and to think at home he is more of an Absolut man. Always one to follow his own advice, George spent a lot of the mornings-after nursing a fragile head – and other organs. 'I was up drinking vodka last night,' he started more than one conversation. 'They keep these bars open far too late for me. I ground up my liver this morning. I'm going to get a new one from an internet auction house.' Eventually he caught some sleep. 'I had to,' he smiled apologetically the next day, slightly disappointed that his 39-year-old body had told him to slow down. 'I've been drinking on behalf of the late Oliver Reed for the last three days and it was time to take a break.'

The break came a little too late, not that he probably remembers much about it. After one particularly pleasant Stolly-fuelled session with Poison Ivy herself, brave man that he is, George was seen following his six-foot *Batman* co-star hungrily out of the Terrace bar. When he returned again almost immediately – alone – he declared to the room, 'I am an alcoholic. This is the second day of alcoholism. I'm going to stay up all night.' He lasted till three.

Considering his aversion to asking girls out, it must have taken a lot of Dutch courage to pursue Uma Thurman so blatantly, however inebriated. With his ego pummelled, he reverted to modest type when back in the bar. 'There are sixteen guys around that girl,' he mused to a friend. 'But I can't be bothered by the competition.' Does anyone really believe that once George had thrown his hat into the ring there would have been any competition? Funny boy.

There was better luck to be had elsewhere, it seemed. His *Batman* co-star may have been out of bounds, but the press eagerly reported how husky-voiced TV presenter Mariella Frostrup and light-fingered movie star Winona Ryder appeared in less of a hurry to evade his company. Added to the fact that before arriving in Cannes, he had been photographed cruising with actress Traylor Howard on the back of his Indian motorbike (not to mention being linked with Charlize Theron and Lucy Liu) and you get a picture of a man taking his title of 'world's most eligible bachelor' seriously. Very seriously. A worthy champion indeed.

While *O Brother* ... was done and dusted by October 1999, film company scheduling meant it would not hit the movie theatres until late 2000. Hence its appearance at Cannes. It would not be seen, in fact, until after *The Perfect Storm* had done the bulk of its box-office business.

Promotion for *The Perfect Storm* in America started with a stunning personal coup for its star: he made the cover of fashion bible *Vogue*, the first man to do so since 1992 when Richard Gere and then wife Cindy Crawford shared the space. Playing Cindy to George's Gere eight years later was Brazilian supermodel Gisele Bundchen, recently partner of Leonardo DiCaprio. For all his playboy reputation, George was quick to make the first dig at the stunt: 'I kept saying to [the photographer] Herb Ritts, "Herb, do I look like her father?" ' he recalls. 'After all, I am 39 and she is 19.' If only he believed that.

After three – soon to be four – films where George had done his movie legacy no harm at all but had hardly broken audience records, he was faced with a very different proposition with Wolfgang Petersen's wet epic. Lukewarm critical response but a massive hit. What's a guy to do? The *New York Times* captured the media mood: 'Once the movie leaves the shore, a story that began as a richly hued mosaic of life in a New England fishing town quickly succumbs to its own technological wizardry and becomes water-logged.'

The Perfect Storm took $41 million on its opening weekend, only slightly down on *Batman & Robin*. The Caped Crusader was soon left trawling, however, as *Storm*'s US box office tallied at $183 million, almost double the Batfilm's take. Worldwide it won by a healthy $100 million. For the first time in his career, George had a summer blockbuster hit on his hands and, boy, did it feel good.

The figures are even more impressive when you consider what the movie was up against, namely Mel Gibson's *The Patriot* – the project Gibson had turned down *The Perfect Storm* for. Since Mel and George are widely touted as appealing to the same demographic audience (largely women over 25), even George thought he would lose out to the bigger star's pulling power. *The Patriot* was due to open two days earlier than its rival in the run-up to the Independence Day holiday period. 'In truth, if you and I were sitting at a bar and having a drink, I'd say my guess is that opening weekend, Mel might take us,' George reflected before the showdown. 'He hasn't done a movie in a long time and it's a big film and I hear it's truly wonderful and I will go see it. But there is room for two or three or four films in the summer. I think we'll be standing. I think it'll be around for a long time.'

He was too modest. *Storm* beat *The Patriot* outright and he was graciousness personified in victory. 'I wasn't competing with Mel,' he insists. 'That was just something that came up because there were two big movies opening against each other.'

Although he said his responsibility to the movie ended with his acting part, George was secretly relieved to see the figures build up. 'It's nice to have a good movie that's actually made money under my belt. Because although it didn't seem to matter as much to me, it did seem to matter to a lot of other people. I found that out when it made money. "Wow," they said, "and you were on your way out." I wish people had told me earlier.'

The film was a hit everywhere, in particular in Massachusetts. In a brilliant stroke of marketing, the world premiere of *The Perfect Storm* took place in the New England town of Danvers on 28 June. A lot of film-makers would have forgotten the region at the centre of their story as soon as the pantechnicons pulled onto the highway. But Wolfgang Petersen and George were adamant that they pay their debt to Gloucester publicly. Tickets to the event were invitation only and cost $150 – with all proceeds going to the Gloucester Fund, a local fishing charity.

Fans started queuing outside the Loewe's Theater in Danvers twelve hours before the scheduled 8 p.m. launch. This little movie about the area's swordfishermen seemed to have really captured the local imagination. Of course, it did not hurt that it happened to star a certain character actor called George Clooney. When he arrived, with Mark Wahlberg and Co. shortly before the start, the place erupted. The noise he and Wahlberg had had to contend with in the wheel-house of the *Andrea Gail* was nothing compared to this. Screaming, sobbing, shouting and pleading poured from the amassed fans. Wolfgang Petersen looked suitably non-plussed, Mark Wahlberg laughed his head off and George – well, George just smiled that smile and looked faintly surprised by it all, which only made the screaming worse. He waved, sparking off more screaming; he shook some hands, which was the cue for formation fainting; and he said 'Hi' to the people in the front row. And that was it. For that, people had called in sick to schools and offices just to get prime positions behind the barriers. Few people alive wield that kind of power. And George, as he had proved in Cannes, was one of them.

Inside the auditorium George and his co-stars joined the director in speaking about the film. 'I hope that we did a tribute to their life here,' Petersen said. 'I want to give people a feeling of what's behind the swordfish on their plate.' George agreed. 'We thought that if we did it right, we could come back and say with any luck we served their story,' he said.

On reflection, it was a brave move showing the film in front of the friends and family of the dead men. If they failed, George thought, they would soon know: the faces of the people they had come to know as friends would not be able to lie. He was right. When the movie reached the point of the memorial service in honour of the lost men – filmed at the same church where the original ceremony had taken place eight years earlier, and featuring actual locals – the sound of crying filled the cinema.

Wolfgang had set out to present 'Reality. Reality. Reality'. Looking at the red eyes of the friends and family of the missing crew of the *Andrea Gail*, he knew they had succeeded.

'It was very difficult,' Rusty Shatford said after the screening. 'It was like a white-knuckle ride, holding on. I wanted it to end, but I didn't want it to end. I was happy with the outcome.' 'They did a wonderful job,' his sister Mary Anne agreed. 'After seeing this I am proud to be Bobby's sister, and proud to be from Gloucester.'

The emotion of the event finally caught up with George a few days later when the premiere circuit hit Europe. When time came to face the glitz and glamour of the UK launch, he was lain up in bed with flu. Ever the trooper, he struggled manfully from his suite at the Dorchester long enough to enough to give a press conference downstairs. Then it was off to the premiere. As in the US, the venue for the grand unveiling was a little different. So different, in fact, that it could have explained George's sudden illness.

A short helicopter flight later, and he and Mark Walhberg landed at the Star City multiplex cinema, just off the M6 motorway in Birmingham. However groggy he was feeling before he set off, the sight – and sound – of two-thousand fans, many hanging from lamp posts and standing on cars and buildings, all screaming his name brought a smile to George's face. For 45 minutes he signed autographs, posed for pictures and attempted to chat to the masses beneath the deafening roar. 'I'm enjoying the sunshine,' appeared to be most fans' recollection of their conversations. While Wahlberg amused everyone by nipping into a McLavatory during his walkabout, George undertook the honoured task of cutting a ribbon and proudly declaring this brand new Warner complex open. Job done, he was back in the chopper and swanning around the Dorchester before the final credits rolled up in Brum. Despite the fact that he was there for less time than the movie took to play, he was the first major Hollywood star to visit the town in years. At least two-thousand people wouldn't forget him.

Maybe it was because they felt snubbed, but the majority of the London-based press agreed with US critics about the film's substance. Most criticisms boiled down to this: you've got six men in a boat and they all die. Where's the drama in that? It's not in the waves, because we all know it's just special effects. It's not in the shark that grips its teeth around Wahlberg's leg, because we know no real animals were used in filming. It's not in the characters, because we hardly get to see them before they're plunged into the tumults of the deep.

'Hollow but thrilling,' wavered *The Times*. 'The characters mouth dialogue that you wouldn't wish on a ventriloquist's dummy,' savaged the *FT*. 'You can't hear what anyone says (not that it matters); but worse you don't care what happens to anyone,' this courtesy of the *Evening Standard*'s Alexander Walker, George's most ardent non-admirer of recent times. 'Though the storm sequences are long and loud, they are in danger of being drowned out by the sound of snoring in the auditorium,' said the *Guardian*. And so it went on, just as in America. But just as in America, punters chose to vote with their wallets. *The Perfect Storm* blew everything else out of the water, *The Patriot* included. Was George becoming a bigger star than his hero (and friend) Mel Gibson? It didn't bear thinking about.

After the thrills and spills of the high seas, it was almost an anti-climax to come back to talking about a good-quality, well-scripted, original piece of film-making. But that was the next job in George's schedule. *O Brother, Where Art Thou?* (to give it its full title) was released internationally to world-wide acclaim – the word from Cannes proved prematurely negative. In particular, the star himself was singled out for more than enough flattery to make up for the critical drubbing he took in *The Perfect Storm*.

'Mr Clooney not only looks like Clark Gable, with his hair slicked against his scalp and his carefully etched Art Deco moustache, but he also gives the kind of detached, matinee idol performance that used to be Gable's trademark,' panted the *New York Times*. 'Mr Clooney's self-conscious line readings and leisurely double-takes are like a wink to the audience. We never forget that, whatever else the script may demand, we are watching a movie star.' 'He produces a novel, raffish charm as the silver-tongued rogue, and a certain old-fashioned masculine mass and substance, which he wears lightly, but in such a way as to signal unmistakably his arrival in the big-screen big league,' said London's *Guardian*. The only vaguely dissenting voice, in fact, came from *Village Voice* who likened the leading man's charisma to 'the oily charm of middle-period Burt Reynolds' – which can be a good or a bad thing, depending on whether you are Sally Fields or not.

With the reviews generally getting George's name talked about in the most high-brow of circles, something *The Perfect Storm* never pulled off whatever its literary origins, it was time to look at the box office. George was not hopeful for his homeland, despite coming on the back of his summer monster. 'We'll have a tough time with it in the US,' he fretted. 'It's a funny country. We like a little cheese in our soufflé, so we cheese it up. It's hard to sell unique, different things.'

His fears proved spot on. Over its entire run, the US takings for *O Brother . . .* were just a couple of million short of *The Perfect Storm*'s opening weekend rout. With takings of $3 million, the Coens' opening salvo was easily the worst of George's post-1994 career. But it still made money (for him and them) and *look* at the reviews. A 70-year-old in a bar would be proud to be reminded of this one.

When you're on a roll, you're on a roll. Buoyed by the professional fillip that the Coen experience had given him, he immediately started pestering the brothers about new projects. Luckily for him, they are not averse to re-casting their favourite actors (John Turturro, John Goodman, Holly Hunter . . .). Even more fortunate, they had something in mind, an idea called *Hail Caesar*. Not a promo piece for *O Brother . . .* went by without George letting slip a detail or two. He was not going to let his critical momentum slide by an inch. 'It's about an old 30s movie star who is a total idiot, who has grown up in the studio system and is hateful to everyone,' he raved, before setting up the self-deprecating punchline. 'I'd play that guy and it's really funny, I'm ready for it. I've been preparing for that role my whole life.'

He was also talking about a new Soderbergh project now that his partnership with Robert Lawrence had been dissolved. *Out of Sight* seemed so long ago and since then the director had been working with Julia Roberts on *Erin Brockovich* and Michael Douglas in *Traffic*. There was talk of Academy Awards for both. The best bet at the moment, after their own film to be shot next year, was *The Jacket*, a time-travel drama about a Vietnam vet framed for murder. But that was for the future, as it were. After *Out of Sight*, all George could talk about in the press was *Leatherheads*, and what happened to that?

Apart from the Rat Pack remake, George was also lined up for a part in *Confessions of a Dangerous Mind*, the autobiography of game show host Chuck Barris. Johnny Depp, the king of quirk, would be his co-star. On top of that, Alan Parker wanted him to star as the anti-capital punishment campaigner on death row in *The Life of David Gale*. 2001 was shaping up to be another busy one after a slack 2000.

With no other filming to be done until late January, George took a little time out from his *O Brother . . .* promo tour to go to Barcelona for a slightly smaller project. A TV commercial.

Europe had been taking up more of his time than usual that year, and France in particular had been a recurring haunt. Could it have anything to do with hoping to find another Céline, by any chance? Men have done stranger things out of loneliness and regret. A month after Cannes, he had vacationed on a yacht in St Tropez with a few of The Boys, much to the amusement of other tourists. A few got more than they bargained for when they approached too near his boat. He'd done it on the *Andrea Gail* for the unsuspecting photographer, he'd got Richard Kind to do it for Harry Hamlin – why shouldn't holidaymakers in the South of France see his ass? It made the day of at least one witness. 'I glanced up and thought it was just a bunch of lads pulling moonies,' the unidentified tourist said. 'But the bloke was absolutely gorgeous, so I had a second look and realised it was George. Naturally, I swam closer to enjoy the fantastic view!' Pictures of the grand unveiling appeared in British tabloids under the banner 'George Mooney'. So much for building on his critical mass.

As well as putting a few pesetas in his pocket, the Spanish trip also gave George something else: a new girlfriend. If he had been looking for a 'new Céline' in France, he was in the wrong country. And so, in fact, was the object of his desires. In the ad for Martini, filmed for Spanish and Italian broadcast only, English MAW – model-actress-whatever – Lisa Snowdon has to open a door to welcome a man into her house. Nothing very demanding, even for a model. During rehearsals an extra played the part of 'the man'. When George arrived at the set halfway through one run-through, he couldn't resist a bit of fun. As Snowdon flung open the door as she had done already a dozen times that afternoon, she was confronted not by the stand-in but by George Clooney: International Man Of Movies. The squeals could be heard all over Catalonia.

Within weeks Snowdon was visiting LA, staying at Casa de Clooney and being indoctrinated into the ways of The Boys. First there was Max, then there was the weekend barbecue, then there was being paraded around the snazziest parties. In this case, George took her to see *Friends* being recorded – his pal Ben Weiss had recently directed his first episode. Very romantic, of course. But hadn't it all been done before?

As he always claims, George does not like to date Hollywood girls because they don't seem real. He originally fell for Céline for her lack of pretence. (It is also fair to say he does not like the competition offered by a girl working full time. His life is too full to fit in with another person's schedule unless they are flexible.) As far as pretence went, Snowdon seemed to be a girl after his own heart? 'I love running off in the middle of the day to make love,' she once famously said. 'That really burns up the calories. Sex keeps me in shape. I don't diet, I eat what I like. I love Mars bars and I smoke and drink.'

For all her charms – and Snowdon had shot to fame in the UK as the 'Special K' girl wearing a well-filled red swim-suit – George most liked her sense of humour. If he didn't, then his instructions to his houseguests before introducing her were a little risky if not downright rude. As far as George was concerned, her teeth, perfect by English standards, were Austin Powers-esque compared to Californian dental ideals. As for her accent: 'When you meet her, you mustn't laugh,' he teased. 'And speak slowly – don't use any big words.' What a gent.

22. ARE YOU IN OR ARE YOU OUT?

Up, down, up, down, up and down. How hard can it be to be filmed going up an escalator? On 13 February 2001, George found out as, again and again, he rode the electronic staircase at the Trump Plaza in Atlantic City. The man behind the madness, of course, was Steven Soderbergh. The reason was his new collaboration with George, a modern remake of the Rat Pack romp, *Ocean's 11*. While the earlier film is remembered mainly for the fact that its cast – Frank Sinatra, Dean Martin, Sammy Davis Jr, Peter Lawford and Joey Bishop – were obviously more interested in having a blast off-screen than putting together anything worthwhile on celluloid, the Section Eight edition was aiming higher. And why shouldn't it? The *Ocean's 11* of 1960 might have had three of the most charismatic entertainers of the twentieth century, but the 2001 version boasted Golden Globe winners and multiple Academy Award nominees.

On 21 January, George had turned up to the Beverly Hilton Hotel with the task of awarding one of the prizes for the 58th Golden Globes. He was also nominated, for his role in *O Brother . . .*, for 'Best Actor in a Comedy or Musical'. When Nicole Kidman took to the stage to announce the result, Clooney fans started celebrating. Event organisers are not subtle people. Best Actress in the same category went to Renee Zellweger for her role in *Nurse Betty*. Who stepped up for the handing-over ceremony? Her good friend and recent *Bridget Jones* co-star Hugh Grant. So who of George's competitors – Jim Carrey, Robert De Niro, John Cusack and old rival Mel Gibson – had recently filmed with Kidman? Not only that, but who had recently been gossiped about as a major factor in the break-up of her marriage to Tom Cruise?

After the usual inane autocue introduction, Kidman opened the golden envelope as the TV director cut between the nominees present and the still photographs of the absentees. 'George Clooney,' she announced, smiling. Through a field of proffered handshakes, George bounded up onto the stage to embrace and kiss his *Peacemaker* co-star, doing nothing to quell those rumours. For the first major award of his career, George thought a little humility might be called for. Then he changed his mind.

'I think when you list the names of the actors in this category that you've got to figure I'm going to win this,' he deadpanned to the corpsing crowd. Running through the array of vanquished talent, he added: 'What have they done?'

Backstage for the media interrogation of winners, George and Nicole continued to give off more sparks than they had mustered during their ninety movie-minutes. It was so hot that George's PR guy Stan Rosenfield was forced to make a statement to kill off the rumours. 'George and Nicole co-starred in DreamWorks' *The Peacemaker* and had not seen each other in two years,' he insisted. 'That accounts for their happiness at the Globes. And the fact that he had just won a major award.' He also pointed out that the 'friends' separated as soon as they left the press room.

How disappointing. Is that any way for the 'Most Erotic Actor of All Time' to behave? Just a few weeks before picking up his Globe, George had picked up an amazing 36.5 per cent of the votes in a poll conducted by Germany's *Cinema* magazine. Pamela Anderson walked off with the female equivalent. Coming so close to his selection as condom-maker Durex's 'Hunk of the Year', George was amused to see the direction his decision to do 'serious' work had taken him in.

He was also amused to see the Kidman 'affair' dominate the gossip columns. It proved an interesting smokescreen for his brief liaison with fellow winner Renee Zellweger. As usual, nothing was admitted. George passed this one off as just neighbourly friendship.

Back at the Trump Plaza, Golden Globe winner George had news for his director. Word had just come in that the Oscar nominations were out and Soderbergh was up for Best Director for *Traffic* and *Erin Brockovich* and both films were possible Best Pictures – a quadruple first for an individual film-maker. (*O Brother . . .* somehow got the nod for a Best Adapted Screenplay vote – someone at the Academy is either very smart or very dumb.) George had the pleasure of revealing the news. After a short round of high-fives and hugs from everyone present, Soderbergh pulled his cap slightly further down over his bashful face and it was back to work. Considering that one of George's new co-stars, Julia Roberts, was also nominated for Best Actress, 'It's going to be hard to live with that group up there,' George said to crew members as he stepped onto the 'up' escalator for take 15.

Of course he was joking. George has always been comfortable in the company of winners: surround yourself with the best people and you look good. It's obvious. There is also no one better at deflating egos. When the rest of the cast met up later that month in Las Vegas they would soon find out. George was as excited as everyone else when Roberts eventually took the prize for *Erin Brockovich* and Soderbergh won for *Traffic*; he led the speeches at the set's celebratory caviar banquet at the Bellagio a few days later. Roberts wore a long-sleeved jersey with Soderbergh's face on the front and the partying went through the night. Congratulations to whomever decided to put back the following day's start time till 4 p.m.

For all the talent involved, though, recreating a Rat Pack film brings with it a truckload of baggage, and George admits to having a few early qualms. 'In pre-production people were coming up and saying, "So, you're playing Frank Sinatra," ' he says. 'And I'd go, "No, I'm not playing Frank Sinatra. I'm doing a movie that he did." '

The end results bear this claim out, not that many believed it at the time. 'The truth is we had a really good script,' George says. 'Frank didn't get to say the lines I get to say in this movie, and he didn't get the director I got. So I won't be as cool as Frank, but I will have a better piece of material to work with. So I figured I'd be all right.'

Ocean's Eleven Soderbergh-style is a completely different proposition from the original, and not just because it uses numerals and not words. The essential premise of eleven guys planning the greatest heist Las Vegas has ever seen stayed the same, but as for everything else ... Where the original was obviously just something for the Rat Pack to do during the day while they earned serious money at night performing at the Copa Room, Soderbergh would not settle for anything less than the best. After all, he had his Oscar-nominated reputation to think about.

Fortunately, his partner in Section Eight was in total agreement throughout. 'George and I read the script at the same time and decided we wanted to do it,' Soderbergh says. Coming off the back of three hits in 2000 between them, the timing just felt right. 'We both had a great year, and suddenly this company was in a position to get pretty much anything we wanted made,' George explains. 'Steven is a film snob, he doesn't like too many things. So when he says, "I know how to do it," you pay attention.'

One of the areas crucial to Soderbergh's vision was casting. 'We thought it was one of the few movies that could really justify getting a lot of movie stars,' he explains. 'George said, "Well, the only way to do that is if everybody cuts their fee. I'll cut mine and everybody's got to go the same way." ' In the film, Danny Ocean persuades his gang members with the words 'Are you in or are you out?' Soderberg's tactic was not quite so abrasive, but the result was the same. 'We made our wish list and they all wanted to do it,' he says proudly.

Top of the list was Brad Pitt. But as soon as Pitt said 'yes', George was thrown into a quandary. Should he give up the lead role of Ocean for the bigger box office draw? 'Brad's a bigger star, and I was cognisant of being delicate with the egos involved,' he says. 'But it seemed to me that I was really made to play Danny, because I look too old to play the other part. I'm only a couple of years older than that fucker, by the way, but Brad looks 25 and I look 45.'

Next stop was Julia Roberts for the part of Ocean's estranged wife Tess. Man of letters Clooney was onto it. 'I sent her a script with a $20-bill and put in a note saying, "I hear you get twenty a picture. Would you like to do the film?" ' George says. She did, although she is quick to play down the actor's part in the event. 'That money was from George and Steven,' she points out, 'so obviously George only put in ten bucks.'

Matt Damon, at the same stage of his career as George when he took *Batman* although carrying an Oscar for *Good Will Hunting*, accepted an offer to play pickpocket Linus Caldwell without even reading the script. 'Just tell me when to show up,' he told Soderbergh. Andy Garcia was similarly eager to step onboard.

While almost everyone said 'yes', a couple of people were ruled out by other circumstances. Mark Wahlberg (of course) wanted to get involved but was still monkeying around on his remake of *Planet of the Apes* when *O11* started. Alan Arkin also had scheduling difficulties but his replacement more than compensated. 'There are no stars in this movie except for Carl Reiner,' George enthuses. 'Carl would stand in the middle of all of us. Julia, Andy, Matt, Brad and me would stand there and Carl would tell stories. He is a star. We couldn't wait to be around him.'

With Elliott Gould, Casey Affleck and *Fail Safe* and *Out of Sight* alumnus Don Cheadle (who had once played Sammy Davis Jr in a TV film) also signing up, the cast list came close to matching the Rat Pack line-up on star status. More importantly, though, it was every bit the earlier production's equal in terms of camaraderie. 'We only wanted to have people who play nice and want to have fun,' George admits. 'We're way into the life's-too-short theory.'

When you're a producer, you can do these things. Getting everyone to invest in the film long-term by slashing their up-front fees with the chance of a large slice of the profits at the end was the biggest factor in gauging his co-stars' attitudes. 'There was a feeling of participation, because you'll have some percentage of the film in the back-end, and we'll put it into a pot and split it up,' George recalls. He had done it with *O Brother . . .* and *Three Kings* and never regretted it. Now, as a producer, he was getting others to do the same.

'I've been a producer for forty-some years and I've never had an actor cut his own salary,' Jerry Weintraub, whose idea the remake was, says. 'And I've never had an actor say that in order to get the cast we wanted, he would talk to each actor. George became the first to cut his salary, then Steven and George went after our cast.'

For everyone to invest so heavily in the picture, there was pressure on George and Soderbergh to ensure it delivered, both in terms of quality and employee enjoyment. They did. While Soderbergh worried about the on-screen product – 'this is a perfect piece of light entertainment, a big movie with big movie stars in it that's fun, that you don't feel insulted by,' he says – George took it upon himself to make sure things stayed the right side of fun away from the cameras.

'The pranks here are akin to *Animal House*,' Weintraub muttered. He should know. As a figure of authority and the man who had originally given Soderbergh and George the *O11* script, he seemed to bear the brunt of George's humour. One night he returned to his villa at Vegas's Bellagio hotel – one of the buildings looted in the film – to find Vaseline smeared on every door handle. 'Clooney!' he roared as he set off, baseball bat in hand, looking for suspect number one. Then there was the time his toilet was wrapped in cellophane – 'When I came in to pee one night,' the producer recalls, 'it went all over!' – or he was covered in M&Ms while napping or woken at 5 a.m. by the hotel reception following up 'his' request for a wake-up call.

That Weintraub had swung neighbouring villas for the talent and himself just made the practical joking even easier. With Matt Damon and Julia Roberts, George started nipping out at night to rearrange the hotel's plant life and statue displays, inching everything closer to Weintraub's door at night. 'Every day he'd have something else outside his door so he couldn't get out,' George laughs.

While Damon and Roberts cosied up to the arch prankster, Brad Pitt took him head on. Sometimes it was subtle: like telling interviewers that 'George is very witty but go easy on him – and don't mention his hairpiece'; or spreading rumours about how desperate the former Sexiest Man Alive was desperate to reclaim his title for a record-breaking second time. Other times it was public and the fall-out affected everyone. The farting contest between the pair on a small Warners jet was a particular low for screenwriter Ted Griffin. 'When you're at thirty-thousand feet and you can't crack a window, it can be particularly upsetting,' he says. 'Brad came up with the winner, which absolutely flattened all of us.'

Away from the frat house, George and Weintraub took turns in keeping spirits up. Seeing how well it went down on *O Brother* . . ., George bought the cast red bikes with their names engraved into the side. He played golf every morning before work and of course there were the scratch ball games ready to kick off at a moment's notice as soon as an opponent was found outside his trailer. 'It was just fun, fun, fun,' says Brad Pitt, who plays detail man Rusty Ryan. 'Off-camera it was basketball games, backgammon, playing poker – jokes.'

George also led the line into the Vegas restaurants and bars, although Weintraub was often the one picking up the tab. Over six weeks of shooting, no club went unvisited by George and the hardcore Damon plus varying supporting stalwarts (only Soderbergh was a habitual no-show, but then he was also working on a script for what would be his next film, also starring George). Big-dollar haunts like the Foundation Room at the top of the Mandalay Bay hotel and the V Bar at the Venetian were just two of the targets.

Although happy to recreate a little of the Rat Pack approach to partying, George was painfully aware that it could not pass onto his work: his film had to be better than theirs. To be honest, if he had turned up for work drunk, then he would still have been better prepared than Frank and his posse. On one occasion, he put that to the test. 'I had changed my theory about drinking, I was having vodka and soda and nothing sweet, so there's no hangover,' he recalls sheepishly. 'When I got back at like four in the morning, I had a message that said I had to work the next morning at 6 a.m. And when the alarm went off two hours later, I felt pretty good. I was going, "My theory works." When I went in the bathroom and looked at myself, I realised I wasn't hung over because I was still sauced.'

The fun continued into the actual filming, much to Soder-bergh's bemusement. Put insatiable joker George opposite laugh-ing-bomb-waiting-to-go-off Roberts and you get slow shooting with lots of breaks.

'It was really hard acting with George, because we have similar personalities and are like brother and sister,' Roberts says. 'I'm supposed to be steely and serious and I was laughing like a twelve-year-old. Around three in the morning one night, I think Steven was beginning to ask himself why he had brought these two people to the table together.'

'Our scenes are really fun,' George says, 'because they're like an old Howard Hawks film where we're both going at each other and nobody really wins. Which is the way it should be.' Out-takes of the pair show George forever smirking as his co-star tosses her head back and shows arguably one of the widest mouths in Hollywood, thanks to one of his unscripted com-ments. Soderbergh, more often than not, just smiles and asks his team to regroup for one more time. *One* more? Nobody believes him.

'Steven would say, "If having a great time making a movie translated into a good movie, then *The Cannonball Run* would have been the greatest movie ever made," ' writer Ted Griffin reveals. 'We all had a consciousness that even though we were in Vegas, it shouldn't be one big screw-off.'

Just occasionally, George's ad-libs gave Soderbergh more than they cost him. His character, Danny Ocean, starts the movie winning parole. He enters blinking into sunshine wearing a full tuxedo. Gaudily dressed Pitt meets him and their first words set the tone for the whole film. 'I hope you were the groom,' Pitt laughs as he sucks on a lolly stick. George bats back: 'Ted Nugent called: he wants his shirt back.' Both lines were made up by the actors as they laughed at each other's costumes. Soderbergh liked the digs and kept them in. A happy set is a productive one.

But there are limits and George was harder on himself than anyone when he let the side down. For the scene where Ocean outlines his heist plan to his ten men, the dialogue just would not flow. 'George did the speech over and over, and I think he got really pissed at himself for not having it solid,' Griffin says. 'I saw him pretty much punch a wall because he flattened a line. I think the problem was that he's a guy who tries not to be self-absorbed when he's working, and on set he's focused quite often not on what he's doing, but on the whole shebang, on making sure he's in a good movie.'

Shooting in Vegas ran from mid-March to the end of April. There was a day in Chicago to get George recruiting Matt Damon's character on the city's Van Buren elevated train, then a couple of days in St Petersburg, Florida. While there, George dropped in at Tampa's Legends Field to watch the Yankees train. 'He was like a kid in a candy store,' team manager Joe Torre recalled. The same could be said of his happiness at being in Atlantic City. When he was not mastering the Plaza's complex escalator system or shooting at Caesar's and the White House Sub shop, George and friends hit the town big time, according to the ecstatic local press. After an evening enjoying the delights of strip club Naked City, George was flagged by *People Weekly* magazine moving onto the Atlantic City Bar & Grill at 2 a.m. flanked by three of the club's dancers and at least one pal. 'They were beautiful girls, dressed really well – not cheesy,' Bar & Grill owner Gino Garofalo said. And George's meal of choice? Chicken fingers with hot sauce washed down with Jack Daniel's. Was the vodka off?

No sooner had shooting on George's first film under the Section Eight umbrella drawn to a close, than it was time for another landmark. On 6 May 2001, he turned forty and for a moment he was $10,000 richer. He woke that morning to find Nicole Kidman had been as good as her word and sent her cheque for losing the 'babies' bet. Ever the sport, George returned the cheque with a note: 'Double or quits for fifty.'

For the actual celebration, George invited a few close million-aire friends over to his home the night before, a Saturday. Noah Wyle, Brad Pitt and Matt Damon represented the beefcake side of the guest-list; Jerry Weintraub, though, proved that you don't need youth to make an impression. Dragging the birthday boy outside Casa de Clooney for a moment, he handed over his present: a restored 1974 Cadillac station wagon worth about $30,000. The sound of grown men kissing could be heard for miles around as George was totally bowled over by the gift. Obviously Weintraub was hopeful of making some money from *O11*.

Of course, tabloids leapt at Kidman's uncanny recollection of not only the bet but George's birthday and deduced that there had definitely been something between them. The good news for him, though, was that the gossip did not last long. The bad news was that they had fresher fish to fry. Following a series of increasingly wild public bust-ups, Julia Roberts and her fiancé Benjamin Bratt announced the end of their engagement. Numerous sources put the fault squarely at George's door. 'George and Julia put on a steamy show on the dance floor' at the *Ocean's Eleven* wrap party, the *Las Vegas Review-Journal* reported. For Bratt, apparently, their 'deepening friendship' was the last straw. 'Ben felt a little threatened by George,' a friend of the actress said. 'What man wouldn't? Let's face it, he's got quite a reputation with the ladies.'

George at first refused to comment. Then came the denial. Of course, it was couched in the most flippant terms possible. Did he split the happy couple up? 'I didn't have time,' he insisted. 'I was too busy breaking up Tom and Nicole's marriage.'

Touché.

Anthony and Joe Russo had come to Steven Soderbergh's attention at the 1997 Sundance Film Festival where Soderbergh had enjoyed their no-budget *Pieces* and offered to help them in the future. Four years later, they had a budget of $8 million, a stellar cast (courtesy of G Clooney's contacts) and a distribution deal for the following year. Not only that, but, for their remake of the Italian heist comedy *Big Deal on Madonna Street*, they even got one of their producers to play the role of Jerzy, the wheelchair-bound safe-cracker (Jerzy is Polish for 'George'). It was, it seemed, the only way to get the project green-lighted.

'The fact that George chose to play a small role was very influential in Warner Bros' decision to finance the movie,' Section Eight's Ben Cosgrove reveals about the Russos' *Welcome to*

Collinwood. Not only did he swing the investment, but George also helped out on a very personal level. 'Everybody across the board took a significant pay cut to do this film, including George Clooney,' Cosgrove says. 'He was actually the lowest paid person on the production. He made less than the production assistants did. In fact, George and Steven contributed their entire producing fee to the production. So they're investors as well as producers.'

As a disabled former felon (he lost the use of his legs in a bungled Toledo robbery), Jerzy teaches the local youth. His specialist subject 'Lockpicking and the Finer Points of Larceny' proves so popular that an extra Sunday class has to be arranged. Enter Sam Rockwell and friends, eager to learn the rudiments of holding up a bank.

The role of the tattoo-covered Jerzy offered George the chance to dominate the film in one intense burst. Locked into his wheelchair and looking good in a vest and, less impressively, a Liam Gallagher-style fishing hat, he got to spin around the Cleveland set with his students hanging on his every word. When Jerzy says, '. . . and that is why I favour the circular saw method', people listened – if George got it right, that is. According to his co-producer, he certainly did.

'He's a better actor than he thinks he is,' Soderbergh says. 'He's now starting to build a body of films that indicate that he has very good taste. He's really funny in a seven-minute performance in *Welcome to Collinwood*. It's a glimpse of something he doesn't normally do or is asked to do. And when the time comes, he's going to pull one out that's really going to surprise people.' (At the time he said this, Soderbergh had lined George up for a project the next year that could well offer that 'moment'.)

When George arrived in Cleveland for his two-day contribution to the filming side of things in late May 2001, he single-handedly invigorated the entire area. The local populace, intrigued early on by the sight of a camera crew all around town, was suddenly alive with people gossiping about whether they had seen 'him' or not. Crowds of a hundred or more gathered at the various locations in the hope of spotting him. When he was seen, dozens of fans screamed his name but he carried on walking. Could this be the George that everyone had heard about? Was this really the nicest man in movies? Obviously not. A few minutes later, the real George Clooney strolled out of a trailer –

the earlier guy had been his double, Bill Piper. The real deal was happy to immerse himself among autograph hunters and well-wishers for as long as it took to get through everybody's requests. Now, that was more like it.

It was not only the locals who were charmed by George's arrival. His former *ER* co-star William H Macy reveals how George revived some seriously flagging spirits among the crew. 'He's the real deal,' Macy says. 'He swept onto the set and it was like a tornado. We were about three-quarters of the way through and people were tired and George was like a shot of adrenaline. He took the whole crew out the first night. I, being older and wiser than these guys, didn't go. The next morning they looked like they'd been run over by a truck. If George had worked one more day, we would've had to hospitalise the actors.'

Although he never fails to enjoy himself at work, once his part in *Collinwood* was out of the way, George could go back to some serious fun. Despite the rumours about his relationship with Julia Roberts, he was not afraid to show that he was still close to some of his other *O11* pals. He popped up in June at the Armani fashion show in Milan, Italy next to Brad Pitt, his wife Jennifer Aniston and *Out of Sight* cameo-star Samuel L Jackson. Apart from acting alongside the two men, George had also produced *Rock Star*, formerly known as *Metal God*, which starred Aniston alongside Mark Wahlberg and was due out soon.

George had actually been in town for a few days before the show. He had shown up as guest of honour of the Running Heart Foundation charity, aimed at promoting prompt first aid to people struck by heart attacks. At the Il Ragno d'Oro restaurant, he spent the evening giving interviews. Commitments done, however, and it was party time.

For the annual Boys trip, someone had come up with the idea of a bike ride across Europe. Three weeks of driving across the continent, tasting every aspect of the local delicacies – perfect. The trip started at Lake Como and wound up in St Tropez, George's European home town. En route, there was a scary moment when his bike broke down outside the northern Italian village of Nuova Olonia. Goaded by The Boys he got down and greasy trying to fix the problem himself, but eventually he had to admit defeat.

Passing farmer Bonifacio Ferraro offered to call the village mechanic and invited George back to his house to have something to eat while he waited. Only when the farmer's kids appeared did anyone realise that something out of the ordinary was up. 'My son couldn't quite believe his eyes when he walked through the front door to see George Clooney sitting at the kitchen table,' the farmer said. 'He told me who he was but, to be honest, I've never heard of him.'

Elsewhere on the trip there was better luck. At the Palace Hotel in St Moritz, the crowd met a bunch of party people, among them Prince Alexander Schaumburg zu Lippe, who played piano. Used to being the most famous face around, the prince watched as George's presence dominated the night. It was the same story in St Tropez. George was surrounded by women. According to most sources, he did not seem to mind.

After three weeks of touring Europe, it was time to pack up the bikes and head home. Between his own and his Section Eight commitments, George had a full diary. After a rapid turnaround, *O11* was slated to hit the screens on 7 December, going up against the big hitting Will Smith vehicle *Ali*. Shortly afterwards he began location work on his directorial debut *Confessions of a Dangerous Mind* in Canada, followed by a starring role in Soderbergh's 2002 remake of *Solaris* for James Cameron's production company.

Before then, however, was *Rock Star*, the first and last feature from George's production company Maysville Pictures. Starring Wahlberg and Aniston, it tells the story of a tribute band singer who gets to join his favourite band when the original singer quits. Originally based on the true story of Judas Priest and singer Tim 'Ripper' Owens who replaced gay singer Rob Halford ('Metal God' was a Priest track), sources were obscured when the heavy metal outfit demanded a say in the script. Judas Priest became Steel Dragon and Ripper became Chris Cole. George Clooney, meanwhile, became boss.

'George-the-actor is a really great guy because he wants you to help make him look good on screen,' Wahlberg says. 'George-the-producer is a hard-nosed businessman who wants to make money. I wasn't George's first choice to be in this film.' Number-one choice was Brad Pitt, Aniston's husband.

Reviews following the film's 5 September premiere at the Westwood Theater were not great. 'A gruelling and pointless endurance test,' carped the *New York Observer*, the first among many critics. The *Detroit News* was loud in its encouragement. 'Rock Star isn't okay junk or merely good junk, it's great junk.' A first-week take of $6 million would earn it the tag of 'the season's first flop'.

While Wahlberg and Aniston riled at the criticisms, its producer was faced with a new dilemma. It had been so long since George had been poorly received in anything – his personal press had been good even in *The Perfect Storm* – that the scorn heaped on *Rock Star* seemed quite breathtaking and hard to deal with. Everyone agreed that the performances of Aniston and Wahlberg and, in particular, English actor Timothy Spall, had been exceptional but the movie still flopped. That left the fault entirely at the producer's feet. George dealt with it as best he could. He started to make noises about Maysville being wound down and Section Eight having better product and suggested that the film was being misinterpreted. Then, less than a week later, he stopped talking about it altogether. Like all Americans, he suddenly had better things to worry about.

23. YOUR BIGGEST FAN

When American Airlines Flight 175 cruised serenely over Manhattan harbour on a direct collision course with the South Tower of Manhattan's World Trade Center, it was tracked every inch of the way by TV news cameras. Eighteen minutes after AA Flight 11 had exploded into the North Tower at 8.45 a.m. Eastern Standard Time on 11 September 2001, the second 767 impacted against the neighbouring building. The event was broadcast live to disbelieving millions around the globe. In that single moment, the face of America changed forever, in no small part thanks to the endlessly repeated television images.

Fittingly for such a 'made-for-TV' event, modern media's fascination with celebrity meant that the tragic consequences of the Al-Qaeda attacks were soon intercut with shots of the famous mingling with other mourners at Ground Zero, all trying to get through it in their own way. There was Tom Hanks helping out at a shelter. There was Tom Cruise shaking hugging strangers. George Clooney was spotted riding round on a motorbike, handing out Stars-and-Stripes flags as a mark of solidarity. On the night of the attacks, The Boys and their families had gathered at Casa de Clooney to light candles and read off the names of those who had died on the planes.

It did not take long for Hollywood to realise that a bigger gesture was required. America needed to show the world that it would not be cowed by terrorism. It would rise again and Tinseltown would lead the way, just as it had always done. On 15 December 1941, just eight days after Japanese planes had bombed Pearl Harbor, the great and the good of US entertainment had gathered to pay tribute and rally spirits as best they knew how. Humphrey Bogart, Judy Garland and Orson Welles led a cast who performed free in the radio broadcast of a drama honouring the 150th anniversary of the ratification of the US Bill of Rights. Unusually, this never-before-seen spirit of patriotism was carried by all the major entertainment networks.

Within a few days of the 11 September attacks, rumours started to circulate that something big was in the pipeline, but like so much other news at that time it was subject to misinformation and rumour. Gradually some consistency emerged. It would be a fund-raising telethon designed to attract donations from a watching public and big corporations.

On 15 September 2001, the heads of the major TV networks, speaking across the country on a conference call, hit upon the idea of a joint production. Costs for the night would be borne by the four major networks: NBC, ABC, CBS and Fox. Presenters and performers would donate their time freely. The show would be two hours of prime time on 21 September. It would include the biggest names in entertainment. It would feature no credits or ad breaks – unheard of in the hotbed of American media commerce. Most significantly, it would be a simulcast – that is, broadcast simultaneously on every channel that would take it. Just like sixty years earlier.

In many ways, getting the means of broadcast was the hardest aspect. Now they just had to put on a show. Joel Gallen, former producer of the MTV Music Awards and veteran of negotiating around the joint minefields of multiple egos and live television, was charged with putting the event together. A night of music – live music only – was conceived of as the most direct way to try to entertain a distraught public. As soon as word of the show got out, Gallen was inundated by offers from singers and other stars. Within 24 hours he was close to drawing a line under his list of contributors. The fact that Michael Jackson, vocal in his rallying cry for a charity single, did not appear on the final running order led to rumours that he was turned down. It was that big a deal. 'Too many people wanted in,' Gallen says. 'By Tuesday, I was asking myself, "What do I do with all these people?" '

According to Gallen, it was George Clooney who came up with the solution. One of the first names to pledge his time and energy, George suggested a celebrity phone bank. Get the likes of Robert De Niro answering phones, he said, and the pledges will flood in as folk try to give their credit card numbers to their favourite stars.

'It's been overwhelming,' George acknowledged at the time. 'They made the mistake early of asking a couple of people, and then it got out and now everyone wants to be involved, which is amazing. Brad Pitt's showing up, people are just showing up to get on the phone, just answer phone calls,' he added. 'It's always nice when you see people coming together.'

Apart from manning the phones, the actors and celebrities would make short speeches, George explained. 'I'm going to read,' he revealed. 'We're going to talk about heroes – real heroes – and a lot of us will read something about that. And there's going to be a lot of music – a lot of the musicians are going to be here to sing. It seems to be always the great salve in these situations.'

Details of where the show was being performed from were kept secret for security reasons, but it soon emerged that studios in Los Angeles and New York would share hosting duties. The exact addresses were released to performers on the day of the show. 'Well there's always security issues, and certainly they're heightened right now,' George explained. 'But if we become too cognisant of it then they really do win. Everybody's showing up not afraid. You go on, and you do your job.'

Called *America: A Tribute to Heroes*, the show was broadcast live at 8 p.m. Eastern Standard Time on 21 September. Bruce Springsteen was chosen to open the show with 'City Of Ruins', his paean to Asbury Park, now given horrific new meaning. Calling upon his audience to 'come on, rise up', the song set the perfect note for an evening of national self-discovery and resilience. The Boss also set the agenda for the commercial aspect of the evening. He was not introduced by name, his song was not introduced, his identity did not appear on the screen in any caption. There would be no claims of artists' self-promotion on this night.

Tom Hanks, ever the face of trust and hope in American entertainment, again set the tone for the evening with his words: 'We are merely artists and entertainers here to raise spirits and, we hope, a great deal of money to ensure that victims' families are supported.' The real heroes, he said, were those whose lives were lost and those who were working at Ground Zero. Hanks also revealed the format for the evening: musical performances, intercut with readings from celebrities and short films about the fund-raising.

By way of illustration, a sombrely dressed George Clooney took to the stage unannounced to speak of a New York cop from the Fortieth Precinct in the Bronx who went to work Tuesday morning to file his retirement papers and then lost his life in the rescue effort. Like all the other readings that night, it was a tearful moment, powerfully delivered. George then introduced the night's celebrity phone bank as Jack Nicholson, Al Pacino, Halle Berry, Whoopi Goldberg, Salma Hayek, Andy Garcia,

Adam Sandler, Brad Pitt, Goldie Hawn, Kurt Russell, Sylvester Stallone, Tom Cruise and others appeared to take pledges of donations.

To emphasise the international effect of the attacks, Sting and U2 performed their songs live from London. Celine Dion, a Canadian, performed 'God Bless America'. The moment showed how inclusive the evening's mood was – everyone felt like an honorary Yank.

The show was broadcast by all seven commercial US networks – ABC, CBS, NBC, Fox, WB, UPN and Pax (it was carried live in the Eastern and Central time zones; recorded for the rest of the country). It was also taken by PBS, the public broadcaster, and Univision and Telemundo, the country's two largest Spanish networks. Cable channels HBO, MTV, Showtime and almost twenty others also devoted their airtime to the show as did more than eight-thousand radio stations around the country. Internet portal Yahoo! ran a live feed and set up a web site to accept audience pledges during and after the event. International interest was huge. At least 156 countries took the show and American Forces Network carried it live on TV and radio to US troops in more than 175 countries.

Some critics in America – and yes, there were a few, even for this most charitable of events – missed the point in spectacular fashion. Can't these overpaid actors read autocues? Were Julia Roberts' tears real? And look at her standing with Brad Pitt and George Clooney, some said. Are those people not in a new movie due out soon? Yes, they were. They also happened to be very good friends who sought each other's company at a time of pain.

It is only afterwards that the degree of George's involvement can be assessed; perhaps it will never really be quantifiable. But what is known is that George worked quickly behind the scenes to get the idea of some sort of celebrity-driven fund-raiser together. He pledged his availability even before there was a vehicle. He is credited with the notion of the celebrity phone bank. And of course he delivered his speech about the policeman with real emotion.

Sadly, though, George's involvement did not end with the telethon. On 31 October, Fox News Network presenter Bill O'Reilly accused the 11 September Fund of holding out on payments to victims and their families, claiming the 160 charities involved in collecting funds after the tragedy had been slow to the point of cruel in their distribution. In particular, the Red Cross, The United Way and the mayor's Twin Towers Fund were called to book. Over several nights on his show, *The Factor*, O'Reilly grilled the leaders of each charity, getting commitments from each that they would release funds immediately to get to those in need.

On the face of it, a worthy enterprise. But of course there is another side. The 11 September Fund had raised $266 million of which $35 million had been immediately released by November. The remainder was designated for longer-term aid, for rebuilding programmes, for education and help for years to come. With the added factor that the death total was thankfully falling for many weeks as missing people were found alive in hospitals, charities could not even be certain of exactly who should be receiving their aid.

Another aspect of O'Reilly's criticism, though, was that it attacked the work of the *Tribute to Heroes* telethon and patronised the stars who took part. He accused them of either being duped by the process or not caring enough about events after the broadcast to stay involved. In other words, people like George and Tom and Brad and Bruce were only in it for their own publicity. They had all since reneged on their civic duty to keep checks on the money they had raised.

After the initial salvo, George entered the debate with O'Reilly on behalf of all those who took part in the charity show. 'We've all been personally involved, and I've been personally involved for a long time,' he explained. 'I'm not an accountant but do I get a list every week of how much money is being spent? Yes. And do I basically know what they're doing? Yes. Am I there at Ground Zero doing it? No.'

Was it any coincidence that O'Reilly made his comments at a time called 'the sweeps' in American TV, when ratings are at their most crucial? George thought so. On 6 November, he was back at his Selectric and firing off a more measured response to the Fox presenter. On 7 November the letter was carried on the front page of the *Washington Post*. O'Reilly also read it out on his show, taking side swipes throughout.

As he did with his campaign against *Hard Copy*, George was careful to ensure the debate was never personal. O'Reilly could say what he liked about him and his fellow celebrities, but what mattered was the effect on the people of America, the millions who had dug deep and donated their hard-earned income to the various charities in response to the telethon and other appeals. Those people needed to feel they had been useful.

'Here's the problem,' George said, 'and why I'm forced to respond: people are coming up to me and asking if it's true that the telethon was a fraud. That means the next time we try to raise money, like when the CD from the telethon comes out this month, fewer people will participate. Because of your unsubstantiated, untrue statements about the 11 September Fund, you, Mr O'Reilly, will be taking money away from people who need it. And all because it's the first week of sweeps.'

There was more: O'Reilly had committed the cardinal sin in George's eyes: he had postured entertainment as news. He was no journalist. 'The fund is intact and has already handed out some $36 million to victims' families (fifteen-thousand cheques), with over $230 million more to be allocated as The United Way sorts through the complicated process of who is in the most need,' he went on. 'To have given out all of the money only six weeks after it was raised, would truly be irresponsible. If you were a journalist you would have known that. It took one phone call to find this information. One phone call you did not make.'

Most embarrassingly for O'Reilly, George ended with a dig at the presenter's claim that the stars were running scared of him. Not at all. It's just that everyone knew that Fox were just trying to whip up debate as a ratings ploy. If people like Tom Cruise, Tom Hanks and Brad Pitt were 'too busy' when Bill called, there was a reason: 'You're right, Mr O'Reilly, we lied, all of us. Of course we weren't too busy. And if you were Peter Jennings, or Dan Rather, Tom Brokaw, Charlie Rose, the *Washington Post*, the *New York Times*, the *LA Times*, or pretty much anybody else, we would have dropped everything and explained what we know. You see, Bill, these are journalists. So, yes, we lied when we said we were too busy to do your "entertainment show". We were just trying to not hurt your feelings.'

The letter was signed 'your biggest fan'.

O'Reilly remained unimpressed and uncontrite. 'What can I say?' he said. 'I believe Mr Clooney's tone speaks for itself. I believe that all the celebrities involved in fundraising for the families have a responsibility to care about what happens to the money they asked for. Mr Clooney can call me any name he wants, but facts are facts. And his letter is silly.'

George was aware that by entering into a dialogue with O'Reilly he was stoking the newsman's own ratings fire. There was also a chance that he would come out of it badly. Yet again, though, these were concerns that had to be sidelined. If just one 'real person' thought that the telethon was a fraud then that was one too many.

The next move was to make public statements. Two TV appearances in particular got O'Reilly talking about slander. The first, a spot on *The Late Show* with David Letterman, found George unwilling even to talk about his combatant for fear of boosting his ratings. 'I don't really want to help that guy out at all,' he said. 'He just makes up stories and hurts people.'

Talking to Katie Couric on NBC's *The Today Show*, he was more forthcoming. 'Less money is being collected because he asked the wrong people and ran a story that was three weeks old,' George said. 'The last time he talked to anybody was 9 October at United Way, when we had raised $150 million. By the time he ran the story on 31 October, we'd raised $266 million. It would have helped his story to say $266 million, but he didn't do it. All of his facts were wrong or three weeks old, in a six-week-old story.'

Not only was George appalled at O'Reilly's perceived lack of professionalism, but there was the matter of being a decent human being, a deserving member of society. 'There is a responsibility, you know, to be a good citizen,' he said. 'You can't run into a crowded theatre with no sign of smoke at all, and start screaming, "Is there a fire in here?" That's not being a good citizen. That is exactly what he's done.'

O'Reilly hit back. 'George Clooney is stunningly misinformed,' he insisted, setting his opponent up perfectly. 'Hey, did he say I was stunning?' George shot back. 'I've been all wrong about this guy. He's a stunning man, too, actually.'

On 12 December, George took part in a press conference alongside Franklin Thomas, the chairman of The United Way's 11 September Fund. They announced a new $75-million Cash Assistance Programme to be distributed before Christmas. 'Nothing we can do can change the events of September 11,' George said, 'but our hope is that we can alleviate some of the financial burden and help victims begin to rebuild their lives. As one of the participants in the telethon, and as a concerned citizen, I'm proud to come here today and support the tremendous work that the 11 September Fund has already done and is continuing to do.'

Both George and O'Reilly took the press statement as vindication of their efforts.

It was not just the 11 September charities that got George's support in the run-up to Christmas. The Screen Actors' Guild had waged a six-month strike the year before, calling for its members to boycott the commercial industry. Famously Elizabeth Hurley, Tiger Woods and Shaquille O'Neal broke the picket line and worked for Estée Lauder, Buick and Disneyland respectively, for which SAG fined them $100,000 each. However, there were three other cases where unknown actors also broke the strike conditions and worked. These members, Gerry Donato, Mario Barbieri Cecchini and Robert Kalomeer, were not only fined but also expelled from the union.

On 24 October 2001, George sent a letter to the SAG's national board-members calling for them to rescind the decision and reinstate the actors. It was the same old story, as far as George was concerned. The big organisation punishing the little guy and turning a blind eye to the indiscretions of bigger names. 'All right, we set the rules,' he wrote, 'we have to live by them, all of us. But if we're going to punish people, punish all of the offenders. That means Elizabeth Hurley, Tiger Woods, Shaquille O'Neal and every one of the celebrities who worked during the strike.

'I suggest in this time of healing that we accept all of the actors' apologies, attach fines appropriately and fairly and let people go about the business of chasing their dreams. This union was created not to protect the famous (they can take care of themselves) but to protect the struggling actor, even if that means from themselves.'

The letter was reprinted widely across the industry press, as was George's offer to pay the expelled three's fines.

On 5 December, *Ocean's Eleven* premiered to the usual overwrought fanfare at Mann's Village in Westwood. George, Julia, Andy, Matt, Brad and Jennifer, Don, Carl – the whole gang turned up for the red carpet treatment. Warner Bros had spared no expense in its first big launch of the season. A parking lot near the theatre had been tented and decorated casino-style, with a giant roulette-wheel carpet laid underfoot. Witnesses likened it to the return of Beatlemania or Elvis's second coming as the screaming and jostling and shouting which greeted the stars' every appearance reached intimidating proportions. Commentators pointed out how the crowds seemed more emotional post-9/11, as though more intent than ever on enjoying the good times. When was the last time so many stars of this calibre turned out together?

Twenty-four hours later, they did it all again – this time for a very restricted audience. Jerry Weintraub had had a plan and he put it to his old friend George W Bush. It was decided. As soon as the Westwood party finished, Weintraub, Soderbergh and the cast would board a US Airforce jet to be taken to an American military base 'somewhere in Turkey' for an unorthodox worldwide launch of *Ocean's Eleven*. Weintraub wanted to give a public 'thank you' to the US and coalition forces stationed for the conflict in Afghanistan, just like Bob Hope and other stars had done during World War II. And what could be better than giving the troops their own Hollywood premiere?

'We want to bring them a little bit of home for Christmas,' Weintraub explained. 'We really wanted to do something for these kids. We can pat them on the back, sign autographs and tell them we care.'

George had other plans – and probably he was more in tune with the boys on the ground. 'We'll drop Julia Roberts over an aircraft carrier,' he promised. 'We're going to fly to Turkey and do the world premiere for the troops. We all want to be there doing something.'

Although the military screening was in place of a European launch, Warner Bros arranged for the cast to return to America via extensive press junkets in London and Paris. *Ocean's Eleven* was their first big gun and no opportunity was overlooked. And with all the stars' financial deals riding on the end box office, everyone was more than happy to pull their weight – even at the cost to their own health. Only dedicated troupers like George and co-star Pitt would have bothered turning up to the Dorchester Hotel press conference on 9 December looking so obviously under the weather thanks to a spectacular night out in London.

But the life-threatening effort paid off. Danny Ocean's team took the number-one spot on their first weekend with $38 million. At $183 million, the final American figure was slightly up on *The Perfect Storm*'s take; but at $412 million, its world-wide haul eclipsed the sea adventure by almost $90 million. George's love affair with Europe, and his regular holidays there, were paying off financially.

Unlike *The Perfect Storm*, *O11* won mostly positive press. Everyone agreed with Jerry Weintraub that the only reason for seeing the 1960 version was its cast. 'What people went to see in the original film was Frank Sinatra, Dean Martin, Sammy Davis, Jr, Peter Lawford and Joey Bishop on screen together,' he says. 'They could have been reading the telephone book and it would have been exactly as successful.'

Premiere hit the spot with its review: 'Soderbergh, Ted Griffin and their playmates are up to nothing more than an entertainment, and this is a very good one, one that wears its hipness loosely and doesn't overdo the charm; beautifully shot by Soderbergh.' 'Brave, brilliant, audacious and preposterous,' cooed New York critic Rex Reed. 'Pitt is in fine form: playing a quick-on-his-feet card-shark who's been reduced to teaching bratty Hollywood actors how to play poker, he's loose, charming and funny. Clooney had deeper notes to strike in *Out of Sight*, but his relaxed suavity makes him the perfect host of this larcenous party,' said *Newsweek*.

24. I WOULD BE MASSACRING A LOT OF FILM

By the end of its run, *O11* would cash three times the haul that Ocean and his crew set out to steal from Andy Garcia's Terry Benedict, recouping its $80 million costs four times over – easily enough for the cast to be grateful they signed up for George's sweet 'back end' deal. Yet again he had proved a shrewd businessman and a film-maker prepared to take risks. At the end of 2001, however, his biggest risk was still to come.

In agreement with Soderbergh, George wanted their Section Eight company to pursue projects that might otherwise struggle within the major studio system. This meant backing movies which might not have star names or star directors, the two 'must haves' on any studio's wish list. 'We're trying not to put movies through the terrible process that studios put movies through,' George admitted. This was good news for *Memento* director Christopher Nolan, who found his Al Pacino thriller *Insomnia* backed by Section Eight, Todd Haynes, whose *Far from Heaven* now got green-lighted, and *Welcome to Collinwood*'s Russo brothers. 'We won't be able to do this forever,' George admitted, wary of his fame's shelf-life. 'But we can do it now. The only thing you can try to do is make good movies as long as you can – and stick your neck out.' By the end of 2002, George's power showed no sign of fading. *Entertainment Weekly* named him and Soderbergh jointly as the twelfth most powerful voice in Hollywood; *Premiere* voted him 27th – a fantastic achievement for the men responsible for *Grizzly II* and *Schizopolis*.

Asked once whether he would ever direct a film, George shot back a 'no' couched in his customary self-deprecating style. 'I would be massacring a lot of film,' he said. But something changed. He started working with Steven Soderbergh, he started caring more and more about the type of film he wanted to work on and, as Ted Griffin had observed, he was always thinking about the overall look of a production, even as an actor.

After a fitful birth over several years, during which time George was due to co-star variously with first Mike Myers then Johnny

Depp under the direction of *X-Men* helmer Bryan Singer, *Confessions of a Dangerous Mind* took on a new lease of life on 17 December 2001 when it started filming in Montreal, Canada. Depp had since been replaced by the lower-profile Sam Rockwell while Singer had also been superseded by a first-timer. After a lot of soul-searching and encouragement from Soderbergh, George had thrown his hat into the ring as director. 'I wasn't the guy sitting around going, "I want to direct." I just knew how to tell this particular story,' he says honestly.

Confessions is based on the 'unauthorised autobiography' of *The Gong Show* and *Dating Game* host Chuck Barris who claimed he was covertly doubling as a CIA agent during his prime time success. Despite comparisons with the previous year's fantasy-fuelled *A Beautiful Mind*, *Being John Malkovich* scribe Charlie Kaufman turned in a starkly original script which, although even more fanciful than the book, Barris was pleased with. As for asking Barris whether any of it was true, George decided not to. 'I didn't want to know and I didn't want to ask,' he insists. 'I thought it was interesting if it was true and I thought it was interesting if it wasn't.'

Originally given a budget of $38 million, George said he would do it for $30 million. The casting of newcomer Sam Rockwell was a start – producers Miramax fought the appointment on 'status' grounds, but George dug his heels in having worked with Rockwell on *Welcome to Collinwood*. 'I had to put up a hell of a fight to replace Johnny Depp with Sam Rockwell,' he says. 'Johnny's just too cool to play a nerd.' There was a price for Miramax chief Harvey Weinstein's blessing. 'He thought I'd gone insane,' George laughs. 'I had to give away a large portion of our production company to get this green-lit.' He eventually agreed to maximise his own screen time for the company in return.

George also selected the cost-efficient location of Montreal to represent New York, Philadelphia, Helsinki and, in a particularly ingenious piece of construction work around the MandrakeSoft offices on Place Royale, even the Berlin Wall, consigning him to at least three months away from his beloved LA. Most tellingly of all, he also took just $500,000 as his combined acting and directing fee. It was no surprise move. He and Soderbergh had already pooled their joint $1 million fees for producing *Insomnia* to stabilise the *Collinwood* budget. As Soderbergh says, 'He is putting his money where his mouth is, and he is working his ass off.'

There were further signs of George's frugality on location. For a start he had called on as many of his A-list friends as possible to play (cheap) cameos in Barris's various shows alongside old favourites Gene Gene The Dancing Machine, The Unknown Comic and even Pee Wee Herman. (A lot of the film's enjoyment comes from looking out for Brad Pitt, Julia Roberts, Matt Damon and Drew Barrymore among the obese tap dancers and the tone-deaf folk singing Chinese.) His hotel room was a thousand miles from the comfort he would normally expect and it took him no time to crowd the floor space with thermal underwear, videos, scripts and other evidence of hectic daily life. A mini-bar full of chilled soda to accompany his Absolut was just about his only luxury (his latest drinking theory: 'hydrate while you dehydrate'). At meal times, he seemed happy to grab a sandwich and take the bag back to his room to work on storyboards with the production artist. His own personal script had been covered with his cartoon sketches of Rockwell, himself and Julia Roberts since before Christmas. Other times he would dine alone in the hotel restaurant, lost in plans for the next day's shoot, or go with a couple of friends into town where the conversation would inevitably return to the just-seen dailies. It was a 24-hour job: no wonder Soderbergh never used to come out to play with the guys in Las Vegas.

'I'm in way over my head,' he admitted early on. 'But on every job I've ever liked, I've been in over my head. Pop flies are no fun. It's fun to toggle back and grab one off the fence.' As usual, he had given himself the best possible chance. Conversations back in LA left friends feeling like they'd been hit on the head by *Making Movies*, Sidney Lumet's book about directing, as his enthusiasm bubbled over.

As usual, George had his personal crew with him during the freezing Montreal shoot to help out with his incredible precision. Amy Cohen, his long-time assistant and listed executive producer, was on hand to keep the new hyphenate's (director-actor) schedule as realistic as possible. And to make sure George's self-cut hair was up to scratch, of course Waldo was an ever-present figure around the town.

One way to minimise problems was to work with as many known quantities as possible. Apart from acting spots from *O11*'s Roberts, Pitt and Damon, and *Collinwood*'s Rockwell, George hired *Three Kings* cinematographer Newton Thomas Sigel and *O*

Brother . . . storyboard artist John Todd Anderson (who also got to cameo as a game show contestant). And then there was his encyclopaedic knowledge of film to draw upon. 'I wanted to steal from guys I loved,' he admits. 'People like Alan J. Pakula, Sidney Lumet, Mike Nichols, Hal Hasby and Bob Fosse.' The Coens and Soderbergh should also check their stylistic wallets.

The first scene to be shot required Rockwell to be *sans appareil*. 'The very first day of shooting I had Sam standing completely naked in front of a TV set,' George reflects. It was ultimately unnecessary. 'Up until the very last cut we had a full-frontal nude shot of him because it was the right moment at the right time and place.'

Despite the unnecessary strip, Rockwell, like all the cast, was impressed by George's approach. 'I don't know if people realise how really intensely smart and creative he is,' he says. 'The film is really beautifully crafted. He did an amazing job. It's great because he's an actor, he knows actors. So he created a really fun set, a really safe environment.'

Drew Barrymore, who plays Barris's girlfriend Penny, gushes further. 'George came so well prepared,' she says. 'His cultural references, his love of film, his instincts as an actor and a director, the way he articulately spoke to the actors – he had a vision and he stuck with it consistently. He was a brilliant film-maker.'

Brad Pitt, of course, can always be relied upon to counter any fawning where his buddy George is concerned. 'First of all, I don't think he came off effeminate in this movie,' he deadpans. 'I don't know what people are talking about. Second of all, he's not five-foot-two – he's about five-foot-four. And the halitosis – it's not true. It's just not true.'

While Julia Roberts' role of *femme fatale* Patricia is crucial to the plot, Pitt and Matt Damon were only drafted in to play a couple of 'bachelors' on an edition of Barris's *Dating Game* – that and to release a serious amount of captive Montreal alcohol back into the wild.

However much Pitt misbehaved, he didn't cause George as many headaches as directing himself did. 'Horrible,' he says. 'It's embarrassing because you can't do more takes on yourself than you do on the other actors, you know, because they'd just hate you. So, most of the time, I'd just rattle off two takes in a row, then look over at the sound guy and kind of shrug my shoulders. He'd go, "Eh?" and then I'd walk away.'

Ever cognisant of his split responsibilities, when it came to editing the movie later, George would anguish over cutting people out. The first most actors know of their deletion is usually when they take their proud family to the premiere. George decided to do something else; he was an actor, after all. Obviously he sent letters to everyone cut. 'A lot of people were cut because we came in over time,' the notes said. 'This has nothing to do with your abilities. I wanted you to hear it from me first. Until another time, I hope, George Clooney.'

Acting-wise, he was required – by himself, admittedly – to play a shady CIA agent who 'converts' Barris from Mr Light Entertainment to assassin. Apart from greased-back hair, his character Jim Byrd sported a hideous Tom Selleck-style moustache. As a consequence, George's directorial debut was made with him looking like a 1970s German porn star. 'I was stuck with it for six months,' he growls. 'I looked like a biker from The Village People.'

Some people didn't seem to mind the 'tache. One of them was Maria Bertrand. The couple met when Bertrand waited George's table at the Globe restaurant on St Laurent Boulevard. It was not the first time he had dated a part-time bar worker with a French accent (Bertrand is French-Canadian), of course, and soon they were spotted playing basketball at her health club and dining at the BIS restaurant and the Hotel Vogue bar.

Like Céline, Bertrand was a part-time model, described as not overly glamorous but 'very, very good looking' by a friend; she was also an actress, contributing to six low-budget local films. On 7 March, her acting career took a turn for the better when she played a Dating Game bachelorette. The role seemed to go to her friends' heads. There was soon talk of her being 'the one' for George. He was not so sure. Within a fortnight the production had finished in Montreal and he was seen dating other women.

After enduring three months of the worst weather conditions since The Perfect Storm, George's Confessions wrap party took place on 23 March. Next stop LA for various exterior shots and a party scene filmed at Hugh Hefner's Playboy Mansion, recorded on 11 April. Although Hef did not appear, Jerry Weintraub, maybe as George's thank you for his Cadillac on his 40th birthday, did pop up as an extra. It was his task to watch Rockwell's Barris realise that a cold shoulder was the only part of the Bunnies' bodies he was likely to score.

After LA, it was off for two days in the searing heat of Nogales, Mexico, for what was the biggest earning day of the town's year. Involving three hundred people during the Monday shoot featuring Rockwell and Daniel Zecapa, an estimated $50,000 was ploughed into the local economy. The all-important West Coast wrap party took place in Arizona after a short shoot there.

And that was that. George had directed his first picture, bringing it in one day early and under budget. He was soon to realise the adage that a director doesn't 'finish' and film as much as 'abandon' it. 'Every two weeks you look at it and go, "God, what was I doing? What was I thinking?"' he said in winter 2002. 'But at some point it's pencils down, hand in your homework, done. In a way, it's very good. It's a good thing to walk away and not be able to change things.'

Spring 2002 saw mixed fortunes. *O Brother* . . . may have been passed over for the Academy Awards, but it fared a lot better at the 44th annual Grammys. In the face of stiff competition from the likes of U2 and Bob Dylan, the film's soundtrack walked away with the prestigious Album of the Year award. 'It's a sweet defeat,' The Edge said of his band's loss to a record he so admired. The honours did not stop there but surprise of the night was the fictitious Soggy Bottom Boys picking up the very real gong for Best Country Vocal Collaboration. The only downside to the evening, as far as the Clooney family was concerned, was that Aunt Rosemary was in hospital following surgery to fight lung cancer and so was unable to receive in person her Grammy for Contribution to Music.

There was at least some good news for another George film that spring, however. In May, US Federal Court Judge Anne C Conway finally threw out the lawsuit that the *Perfect Storm* relatives had brought against Warner Bros. In a twelve-page ruling, she said that the film was protected by the First Amendment and that the studio was totally within its rights to fictionalise the account of the ill-fated trawler and her crew.

When George was relayed the good news from the courthouse, he was already a fortnight into his next film, a remake of the 1972 space chiller *Solaris*, based on director Steven Soderbergh's own script. Production was scheduled to start on Monday 6 May, George's birthday, so his parents flew into town for a small friends-and-family celebration on the Friday, having just come from daughter Ada's birthday celebration two days before (George's maternal grandmother celebrates on 1 May – it's a busy month). Although shot entirely on Stages 19 and 20 at Warner Bros' lot as opposed to the wintry environs of Montreal (which afforded him plenty of time to be photographed in LA with new belle Krista Allen, a former Miss Texas and an actress in *Confessions* as well as *Baywatch* and *Emmanuelle*), in many ways George's first foray into sci-fi would be the most taxing role of his career.

A remake of Andrei Tarkovsky's 1972 Russian-language *Solyaris* ('but not nine hours long' – George), based on the novel by Stanislaw Lem, the movie's action takes place aboard the claustrophobic atmosphere of space station Prometheus orbiting the planet Solaris. George plays Chris Kelvin, a psychologist sent to investigate the disturbing behaviour of the station's scientists. On docking, he discovers the crew's leader is dead and the survivors have been driven mad by an oceanic life-form that grants repressed desires. Kelvin's greatest wish is to be reunited with his suicide-victim wife but when she appears, it is only a matter of time before he goes insane. With a small cast featuring Natascha McElhone, Jeremy Davies, Viola Davis and Ulrich Tukur, the emphasis of the film is on the subtle transformation of George's character and in particular his displaced grief for his wife. It would take more than the occasional 'Diana' look or lantern-jawed grin to get through this one; it would require everything that he had learned since 1994 to just not suck. And then some.

'This is by far the hardest acting job I have ever had to do,' George admits. 'Every single scene is like, "OK, this scene may be the last moment of your life." '

The part of Kelvin is such a departure for George that he was not originally in the director's thoughts at all. Daniel Day-Lewis was Soderbergh's top target, but then he received a call . . . 'A woman who works with him called me up and said, "I have a letter from George that I'm to put in your hand," ' Soderbergh says. 'I thought, "Oh God!" – I'm trying to run through my mind, "Did I say something in an interview or what?" That was my first reaction because I know George usually writes letters when something's gone wrong.'

He needn't have worried. 'I'd read the *Solaris* script and I was really turned on by the idea of it, but I also didn't want to put Steven in a stressful position,' George explains. 'He is my friend and my partner. So I thought the best way to give him the out was for me to give him some space by writing and saying, "Look, I'd love to take a shot at it, but only if you think I can do it." And he basically said, "What the fuck? Let's try." '

'To work with somebody you know well, and to have them surprise you, is really exciting,' Soderbergh says. 'I've worked with him twice before and I know him pretty well, and he was doing things on this film that really surprised me.'

On reflection, Soderbergh could see how George might be suited to at least one aspect. '2001: A Space Odyssey meets Last Tango in Paris' is how the director describes the movie, and George could definitely light up a screen with Natascha McElhone, with or without Lurpak. But like Brando in Paris, George would be required to divest himself of his cute dark green space suit at least once. Considering his reputation as a screen heart-throb, this would actually be his first nude scene. 'It's not an easy thing to do when you're 41,' he says. 'I not only had to clear the entire set, I had to clear the director out.'

Joking aside, the prospect of George's naked butt had serious consequences for the film's financial viability. If it received an R rating because of it, the film would have a more restricted audience than intended. On the other hand, think of all the ER fans who fall well above the R age limit. The sight of George sporting a neat light-looking haircut, parted on the left-hand side, and playing the first overtly sexual role of his career meant box-office hopes were high before word got out that the Clooney buns would be on display. In the event, it was certified R then pegged back to PG-13 with no cuts.

'I don't quite understand the ratings board,' George confesses. 'I always thought I had a sort of G-rated, Barney kind of butt. What's really weird is, I fell asleep the other night with the TV on. At four in the morning, I woke up and some guy was on TV talking about my butt – which is a really weird thing to wake up to. I didn't quite know what was going on.'

Seven short weeks later, Solaris wrapped and guess what? George was on to his next project.

On 20 June, production began on the Coen brothers' Intolerable Cruelty, a film noir about a serial bride who has built a financial empire thanks to the divorce laws of America. George plays Miles Massey, a womanising lawyer who successfully saves his client's fortune, only to be seduced by the gold-digging ex-wife who is out for revenge. Marylin Rexroth, the scheming wife, is played by Welsh beauty Catherine Zeta-Jones. Geoffrey Rush and Billy Bob Thornton, the star of the brothers' recent *The Man Who Wasn't There*, also appear.

With divorce at the heart of the movie and George's name linked in the press with every failed celebrity marriage, he was quick to check his co-star Jones's status. 'I said, "I hope your marriage is OK because otherwise I'm going to get the blame." '

The bulk of shooting took place in LA. Fittingly for a movie about matrimony, the production soon decamped to the world's wedding capital: Las Vegas. For a week in September, George and his leading lady were filmed playing the tables at Caesar's Palace (where they drew a crowd of seven hundred spectators), dining in the Terrazza restaurant (it was closed to the public that day) and honeymooning in suite 8316, the same rooms where Tom Cruise taught Dustin Hoffman to dance in *Rain Man*. For the actual wedding sequence, where better than downtown's Wee Kirk O' the Heather Wedding Chapel? (Interior shots were already completed in LA.)

Having spent so long in Vegas the previous year, George felt more than qualified to give his co-star the guided tour. Saturday night at the Whiskey Sky seemed an ideal way to commemorate the picture's presence in town, and judging from the pictures of the night, Jones agreed.

Of course, some pleasures you just have to have on your own. For the round trip to Vegas, George shunned the usual jet. Instead he tore up Interstate 15 in his latest toy, a brand new Porsche. Was this the end of his love affair with BMW? Seeing the exhilarated look on his face as he pulled into the Palace parking lot, it sure looked like it.

Shooting on *Intolerable Cruelty* finished in autumn. George's verdict? 'That's the scariest performance I've ever given,' he grins. 'It makes *O Brother* . . . look like Kafka.'

The end of June saw the news that the Clooney clan had been dreading: Aunt Rosemary died. At 74, the recurrence of her lung cancer, thought to be in remission following her surgery earlier in the year, had proved a hurdle too far, and she passed away shortly after 6 p.m. local time on 29 June 2002, at her home in Beverly Hills. Her five children, Miguel, Maria, Gabriel, Monsita and Rafael, husband Dante Di Paolo and her ten grandchildren were with her at the end.

A week later, on Friday 5 July, her family gathered once again to pay their final respects at her funeral in Maysville, Kentucky. They weren't alone. A throng of eight hundred mourners – among them Hollywood stars Al Pacino and Beverly D'Angelo – filled St Patrick's Church and many more of the town's 8,900 population observed the proceedings with deferential tears and silence from outside. As pallbearers, son Miguel and nephew George helped carry Rosemary's casket to its place before the altar.

Her brother Nick addressed the congregation with his customary ease – and maintained his poise almost until the end. Producing a pocket watch from his jacket, he recalled how he'd made a pact with his sister some fifteen years earlier. 'We agreed that whichever of us went first,' he explained, 'the other one would say a few words at their funeral – for no more than three minutes by Papa Clooney's watch.

'There isn't a person here this morning who isn't saying, "I knew her the best", and they're all right. She wrapped us up with affection and humour and allowed us to believe that everything would turn out all right in the end.' His voice finally beginning to break, Nick ended his speech with seconds to spare. 'I've avoided so far the two words we came here to say,' he said. Then, looking at his sister's coffin, he added, 'Goodbye, Rosemary.'

A few weeks later, there was a happier church event for George to get involved in. After broken engagements to Kiefer Sutherland, Dylan McDermott, Liam Neeson and Benjamin Bratt, and a brief marriage to Lyle Lovett, Julia Roberts finally tied the knot with Danny Moder, with George in attendance.

Twenty years after arriving in Hollywood (and the same year he attended a gala celebrating his father's fifty years in broadcasting), it was time to sit back and take stock of wheels George had set in motion earlier, personally and professionally. Chosen to advertise the Police brand of sunglasses in the US over summer, following in the footsteps of footballers Gabriel Batistuta and David Beckham in Europe, and finally succumbing to his dream of buying a home in Italy, an impressive white brick, three-storey mansion in Laglio, just outside Lake Como, life was good. Even parting company with his long-time CAA agent Michael Gruber could not derail the momentum.

In September he was awarded the prestigious title of 'Most Beautiful Person in the World' by *People* magazine. As if to prove his appeal, reports from the *Intolerable Cruelty* set had had him wooing Elizabeth 'EG' Daily towards the end of summer. More reliable sources pinned his affections to the mast of Jennifer Siebel, a close friend of Céline Balitran's. While magazine psychiatrists fussed about what it all meant – Céline had just got married to screenwriter David Rosenthal: could George be trying to let his ex know that he wants her back by dating her physically similar friend? – George quietly went about his usual dating tactics: he flew Siebel out to watch him at work in Vegas; there were bike rides through the Hollywood Hills; he introduced her to Max and The Boys. Another textbook seduction, in other words, not that George admits such things. 'Jen's a good friend,' he said in November 2002, 'but I'm not dating anyone right now.' *Ouch*.

After a season of excellent reviews for his production stable – *Insomnia*, *Far from Heaven* and *Welcome to Collinwood* ('The funniest film of the year,' according to the *Boston Globe*) – Thanksgiving saw the unveiling of George's new work as an actor. 'A mind-bender in the best sense of the word: the spell it casts follows you all the way home,' was *Rolling Stone*'s take on *Solaris*. '*Solaris* is a rich, repeatable experience,' said the London *Guardian*. 'Besides being one of the high points of Soderbergh's fascinating career, *Solaris*, no less than Tarkovsky's version, is a landmark in cerebral sci-fi, a likely cult-movie for decades to come.' Following a performance which sees his features shown to their brooding fullest in the half lights and shadows of the space station, George impresses the *Chicago Sun-Times*: 'Clooney has successfully survived being named *People* magazine's sexiest man alive by deliberately choosing projects that ignore that image. Here, as Kelvin, he is intelligent, withdrawn, sad, puzzled.' Even *Variety*, which found the film disappointing, could not fault him: 'Clooney's star shines in Soderbergh's *Solaris*.'

As feared, given its dark, cerebral outlook, *Solaris* did not set registers ringing – despite the Clooney backside's screen debut. By the end of the year the film had grossed only $14 million in the US – admittedly enough to earn it 131st place in the best performers chart. Hopes were higher for Europe where Soderbergh and George would be carrying out a full press tour.

Meanwhile, George's other little project was attracting very good feedback. Despite a very restricted early release (to make it eligible for various awards), *Confessions* was voted the Las Vegas Film Critics' Best Film of the Year. The National Board of Review agreed, honouring the novice helmsman with a Special Film-Making Achievement award for his first outing. Soderbergh had won the Cannes prize with his first picture and George was following suit. Next stop an Oscar?

Buoyed by the critical response, even the film's premieres seemed more upbeat, despite George turning up to the LA event on crutches following (yet another) basketball injury and appearing at New York's Paris Theater sporting a flat side-parting and an unpleasant blue roll neck sweater beneath his trademark black suit. At least the moustache had gone. Even London got a star-studded Christmas preview despite the movie not opening there for another two months. The advance word justified the moves. 'Clooney's sense of composition and framing is unusually developed for a first-timer,' commended *Screen International*. 'Clooney has absorbed his time with the Coen brothers, David O Russell and Steven Soderbergh to create an enveloping world that only rarely teeters into excess or self-seriousness,' agreed *Variety*. George Clooney: heart-throb and now award-winning auteur. Not bad at all.

25. GEORGE, MARRY ME!

If George Clooney had learned anything in his lifetime in the media business, either as an onlooker or a player, it was that nothing lasts. No sooner had the good notices for *Confessions* arrived than the backlash started. At first there were just a few annoying comparisons made, notably comparing the morals of Rockwell's Barris with one of Nick Clooney's early employees, Jerry Springer. Never happy to give the oxygen of publicity to outsiders, George was quick to clamp down on any rumours of a 'tribute'. Despite an earlier relationship – 'there was a time when we were friends', he said on *The Richard and Judy Show* – he was keen to stop any link between his current work and Springer's show: George was quoted in the *Sun* as saying, 'He's smart enough to know better than put wireless mikes on people and setting up fights.'

There was worse to come. Stephen Hunter in the *Washington Post*, while actually praising the film, accused George of having less than a firm hand on *Confessions*' helm. 'The credits say George Clooney, but the movie says Steven Soderbergh,' he wrote. 'It's the story of a man who wasn't there by a director who may not have been there either.'

A couple of obvious courses of action present themselves at times like these. One was court action for libel – especially with Soderbergh saying, 'I was on set only once for 20 minutes, and I was busy making my own movie.' The other option, certainly the more George-like course, was the strongly worded and – let's be honest – sarcastic letter. Sure, George had borrowed from his peers, but Soderbergh was one of many. In fact, other letters had gone out to Alan J Pakula, Mike Nichols and Sidney Lumet, this time apologising for appropriating their various styles. Even David O Russell received a nod in interviews for influencing the 'saturated' look of the picture. The tone of the letter to Hunter was somewhat more abrasive, however. Making sure his point got home with a joke, George ended the document with the words 'letter written by Steven Soderbergh'.

By the time the mail was sent, the damage had been done. The Oscars, it transpired, had no interest in *Confessions* and certainly not *Solaris*; Rockwell's amazing performance would go un-rewarded after all, it seemed. More importantly, ticket sales for the movie were slow. On the back of *Solaris*'s poor box office, it meant a cold Christmas over at Section Eight. 'Neither of us was accustomed to having people not like what we were up to,' Soderbergh admitted to *Vanity Fair*. 'But ten years from now, we'll both be glad to have made those films.'

George is glad already. 'You win some, you lose some,' he told the *Chicago Sun-Times*. 'You just have to do good work and not take it personally. I'm really proud of *Confessions*, and I hope people will check it out someday.'

Even before the bad news had started to trickle in, George had been saying to anyone who would listen that enough was enough. He had pocketed a mere $125,000 for his debut stint behind the cameras, and now it was time to get back to his day job. And yet . . . Ever since teaming up with Soderbergh on *Out of Sight*, George had been talking about making the NFL flick *Leatherheads* with the director. But, with Soderbergh announcing a hiatus for 2003, suddenly George was toying with the idea of shooting it himself. 'I think I may end up directing,' he admitted. 'It's about 1925 football, and it's a real Preston Sturges–Howard Hawks comedy. So I've been boning up on *Hail the Conquering Hero* and *Sullivan's Travels*. I have to understand why those things work.'

Within a few months, a clearer picture emerged. 'Steven Soderbergh did a draft of it and was going to direct it with me in it for a while,' he told the *Independent*. 'I think I still might be in it, which is gonna be the harder part.' But, he revealed, 2004 would be the starting point at the earliest, pushing release back to at least 2005.

There were plenty of things to occupy George's thoughts, however, especially those related to Section Eight matters. As 2003 got underway, he finally started looking into bringing *Gates of Fire* in all its *Gladiator*-style glory to the screen, no doubt pleasing prospective star Bruce Willis no end. Also on the production line were *Revelation* for Warner Bros and the adaptation of John Saul's latest novel, *Midnight Voices*. Even *The Good German*, Soderbergh and Clooney's first look at World War II, was finally slated for production. Another Elmore Leonard adaptation, this time of *Tishomingo Blues*, was also scheduled. If it could combine the performances of *Out of Sight* with the selling power of *Get Shorty* then the future was perking up immensely. There were even rumours that George was 'looking at' a script for a big-screen version of *The A-Team* as well as holding out for a Ferrari of his own before signing up for a similar-scale remake of *Magnum* – surefire box-office winners both.

Meanwhile, over in Great Britain, word had it that a certain Hollywood heartthrob was scoping out locations for another picture in Basil Fawlty territory. According to the *South Devon Herald Express*, Torbay was being scoured for a site that looked like an asylum and could house a full movie production crew. A spokesman for Section Eight revealed how they were looking for 'a three-storey stand-alone building or buildings in grounds, a solid brutal looking exterior and completely empty' in order to house their eighteen sets.

Although names were strictly on a need-to-know basis as far as the locals were concerned, the film being scouted for was *The Jacket*, a futuristic psychological thriller involving a Gulf War veteran with amnesia accused of a murder he did not commit. Unfortunately for the good burghers of Torbay, the perfect building was found almost as far away as possible, in Glasgow. By the time the asylum had been located, Jennifer Jason Leigh, Kelly Lynch, Kris Kristofferson and Daniel Craig had signed up to star opposite the gorgeous *Pirates of the Caribbean* and *Love Actually* star Keira Knightley and *The Pianist* Oscar-winner Adrien Brody. Fittingly, the 'jacket' of the title is of the distinctly 'strait' variety and George revealed that filming would commence early in 2004, overseen by Section Eight's Ben Cosgrove.

Also in George's stars at the beginning of the year was Jerry Weintraub's oft-dreamed-of *Ocean's Twelve*. The team were reuniting in Europe, this time to steal, among other things, one of the fabled Fabergé eggs of *Octopussy* fame. Another target for them, according to an interview Jerry Weintraub gave to a Dutch newspaper, will be Rembrandt's *Nightwatch*, currently hanging in Amsterdam's Rijksmuseum. As Julia Roberts's Tess was an art gallery curator, there are definite possibilities for that story. But, millions would like to know, would Roberts actually be appearing in the follow-up?

Oh yes, says George, 'Everyone is coming back.' Not only that, but they'll even be cheaper. 'We all decided to take five per cent less up front than we did the first time because we all made good money off the profits of the first one.' Filming, he revealed, would start on 1 March 2004 in Paris, Amsterdam and Rome.

Linking up with Brad Pitt again was something George was looking forward to. After all, in Pitt's presence, he realised how 'unfamous' he was. If ever he was hassled by press on the original *Ocean's Eleven* tour in Italy, he merely had to point out where his co-star could be found and suddenly he'd be alone. 'Thanks, dude,' the fleeing Pitt would be heard cursing.

That's not to say, of course, that George Clooney could pass unnoticed through Italy. No sooner had knowledge of his Lake Como purchase become known, than paparazzi stalkers had a new address to add to their haunts; endless travel pieces for the region also started appearing in international papers, all from the angle that you could 'see' Clooney (some even claimed they had, despite him not being there at the time). For George's summer holiday throughout August 2003, he was almost a prisoner in his own (second) home, but at least he had the company of up to fifteen guests, plus the villa's four ducks who kindly took on the role of Max when George is in Europe. As he told anyone who would listen, it was still the best investment of his life, despite a farcical series of break-ins while he was in the US.

'It was a life-altering time for me,' he said to *OK!* 'I still have that "stop and you'll be unemployed forever" mentality, but I spent three months doing nothing, and it was the best thing I could have done in my life. Everyone should have a villa in Italy.'

Lake Como also managed, coincidentally, to be quite convenient for George's work. On 3 September he and a radiant-looking Catherine Zeta-Jones were in Venice for the world premiere of *Intolerable Cruelty*. Given the Coen brothers' track record, it was no surprise to find their film launched at a European film festival; although it wasn't in the competition and it wasn't even quite complete ('it's in an unfinished state', George revealed), it was important to the Coens for it to be there. It was also important for George and his co-star to be very prominent in front of the world's media.

At a press conference for the movie, George took part in a conversation that would make headlines the world over – what could be better for the film? Taking her place in the queue along with everyone else, the woman called 'Victoria' waited until bade to speak then yelled, 'George, marry me!' Throwing on a veil and approaching the star's seat, she was joined by a conveniently on-hand vicar, who promptly supplied two rings for an im-promptu 'ceremony'. George, of course, took it all in good spirits. 'Is he really a priest?' he inquired as organisers dragged off the interlopers. ('Victoria' later revealed to press she had been stalking George for a while; their last encounter had seen her 'dressed as a pig' to impress him.)

Nuptials aside, it was during the Venetian press for the film that George revealed how he and the Coens had only worked together so soon after *O Brother* because of a failed project with another actor. Even with no clues, George would instinctively have known the calibre of actor and celebrity who could cause so much upheaval to his life: it had to be Brad Pitt.

It was only after the Coens' proposed production of *To the White Sea* featuring Pitt fell apart that the brothers moved for George and another project. 'I'm their go-to guy,' George laughed. 'I'm their Buddy Hackett. If you can't get Burt Reynolds, give me Buddy Hackett.'

As with *O Brother*, George was more than willing to send himself up at the Coens' hands. After the jokes about his pomade obsession, now in *Intolerable Cruelty* he was playing an ultra-smooth tooth obsessive. Miles Massey's choppers are pristine white. So white, it seems, that the Clooney pegs did not quite pass muster. 'They were stunt teeth in the opening scene,' he laughs. Ethan Coen confirmed, 'We were trying to introduce his character, so it was like, well, let's see his teeth.'

While the first set the audience sees are not real, the offer of free cleaning to get his own set up to scratch was always there. 'They kept offering it,' George says. 'I wanted to come in eating Oreos after that, just to get them off my back.' Whoever they belong to, there was no doubt when the movie reached non-Venetian shores later that month that George could expect to hear comments on his orthodontic extremities. 'If I do another film with the Coens, I'm afraid because I'm running out of body parts to mock,' he says. 'Maybe I'll have to wax my back.'

Teeth aside, audiences in the US and Europe fell for the film. The slowly thawing relationship between Zeta-Jones's multiple divorcee and her next notch won hearts everywhere. George's character's sentiment that 'It's a challenge', as he shamelessly pursues her through court buildings, hotels and elevators, is powerfully delivered and with all the comedic punch you'd expect from the team that brought us Everett McGill. 'Despite the influence of its mainstream stars,' the *Evening Standard* agreed, 'Intolerable Cruelty retains the atmosphere of a film that might be about to rocket off into something very eccentric, and that is impossible to dislike.'

Almost a month after the Venice preview, the rest of the world got its chance to see what the fuss was about, starting with the LA launch at the Samuel Goldwyn Theatre. London and the rest of Europe followed, supported by George and his co-star on full beam tooth-wise, wowing media audiences wherever they ventured. The on-screen chemistry between the pair was thankfully as alive in reality as all audiences hope. (Asked by the *Calgary Sun* who they had based their characters on, George shot back, 'Ben and Jen' – was this a dig at his *Out of Sight* co-star, the media wanted to know? George, of course, denied any such slur.)

One question from the *Chicago Sun-Times* highlighted George's fondness for Ms Zeta-Jones. When she was asked whether her opinion on prenuptial agreements was the same as Marylin's, there was barely enough time for her smile to flicker before George chivalrously leapt in. 'I'll take that one,' he said. There was no way he was allowing Catherine to be rail-roaded by any interrogation about her famous agreement with husband Michael Douglas. 'Why, yes, I think a prenup is very important,' he began. 'I have a prenup and I'm not even married.' 'He has one with his dog,' the relieved Zeta-Jones chipped in. 'Actually I have a prenup with anyone I take out to dinner.' Many a true word said in jest . . .

Clearly the sparkling on- and off-screen pairing was having some effect. *Intolerable Cruelty* quickly reached the $90 million mark (and counting), aided by strong international performances. Even South Korea chipped in with $531,000 from its 76 screens, replicating the 'number one hit' status achieved the world over (rivalled only by *Finding Nemo*).

Everything was rosy, then, in the Coen garden. Actually, that isn't strictly true. As George joked to *USA Today*, while he hadn't pulled any of his famous *Punk'd*-style practical jokes on Ethan and Joel, he had been responsible for something worse. 'I made you guys sell-outs,' he laughed, and there were more than a couple of Internet sites buzzing with grievances that *Intolerable Cruelty* had seen the brothers jettison their film roots. They will have none of it, however. 'We've worked with studios from the very beginning,' Joel says. 'So it's actually a little bit irritating being sort of associated with "independent cinema" in quotation marks. Because it's not something that has a lot of meaning for us.' As Ethan adds, 'We've been trying to sell out for years. Nobody's been buying – that's the problem.'

Speaking of sell-outs, George was more than qualified to comment. As well as agreeing to star as the 'face' of Spanish chain El Corte Inglés, part of his summer had been spent filming a new TV commercial (only for viewing outside the USA, of course) in Canada. Shot by an Italian company to cash in on his Villa di Georgia back home, the ad shows George crashing a dull party full of beautiful women and ordering drinks to liven things up. The product being placed is Martini Spumante. His closing line? 'No Martini, no party.' The ad aired all over Italy from late December, guaranteeing the star all-year-round coverage in his adopted homeland. (Rumours that he was paid almost $2 million for a day's work were loudly denied.)

That little Italian job aside, George's summer break saw him revitalised and ready once again to take on a project at the opposite end of the 'sell-out' scale to *Intolerable Cruelty*. Reunited with Steven Soderbergh, they had come up with *K Street*, a hybrid docu-drama set in the corridors of government and mixing real politicians, like Hillary Clinton, with actors who front a 'consulting' firm for the Washington players. To further mix things up, political pundits James Carville and Mary Matalin get to play themselves, while actors such as Mary McCormack and John Slattery play characters.

For its ten-week run, the US capital was besieged by the Section Eight team, led by George and Soderbergh, as they directed real people in fake scenarios, and vice versa, taking over offices in the Capitol building and senators' favourite eating establishments. The weekly pattern was the same: on Monday the team would brainstorm what DC was talking about then, according to its star McCormack, 'We would relate it to our PR consulting firm then go out and actually talk to political notables. It is all improvised. No script, no hair, no make-up.' After three days' filming and two days of editing, the show would be aired that Sunday night. No easy task, especially given the slight production difficulties suffered when certain Republicans successfully got the crew's access rights to a lot of the normally off-limits areas rescinded.

Premiered on HBO on 14 September, *K Street* initially won strong audiences – not surprisingly, its Washington share was double the national average. From there, however, figures went downhill, with many viewers disappointed that George did not step in front of the camera rather than work so hard behind the scenes (he even got a union card to qualify for working as the show's cinematographer). When the ten-week run came to an end in November, it was to rumours that HBO had pulled the project. The word from Section Eight was different. The workload was not what George or Soderbergh had expected; neither of them had anticipated becoming so engrossed in the subject matter that they'd be working that closely with the project. 'They were working nonstop for six days a week,' a spokesman said. 'Their level of commitment was overwhelming, but midway through it became clear they'd have to stop once they told a complete arc in the first ten episodes.' A vague plan for HBO and the duo to team up again on another limited-run series to be shot in the same way but set in a different venue was hatched.

While George was opting out of Washington, his father was going the other way, announcing that he would run for Congress. Once again, the question was asked of Clooney Jr: would he ever run for office? Once again, the answer was 'no'. 'In the US, they make a big deal out of everything as soon as you run for higher office,' he told *Woman* magazine, referring to his hedonistic lifestyle and the Schwarzenegger election. You can only be successful, he said, if you deny what you did in earlier life. 'It's time we did away with this bigotry in America.' George did find time, however, to side with Mrs Clinton and those pushing for a 211 Bill to provide free emergency telephone advice. The former First Lady became the latest convert to George's charms when they appeared together for a press conference on the subject. 'And George Clooney, what can I say?' she began. 'At least, what can I say in public!' Cue media laughter and an abashed-looking movie star. If only *K Street* could have had more political support like this . . .

George Clooney does not need to work again. According to his accountant, he hasn't needed to since he received the cheque for *Batman*. But he is as busy now as he has ever been. And why? For posterity's sake, for a chance of being remembered after he is gone, for plain old ego. George calls his movies his surrogate children, and it is by them that he wants to be judged by future generations. He worries that if he is knocked over by a bus tomorrow, how will his body of work register in the overall history of American cinema, how will he be thought of? It's the 'guy thing' again: if he refuses to have children then George needs to have made a lasting impression on the world in some other way or what will have been the point? It's what Spencer would do, isn't it?

George also wants to buck the family trend. He wants to become the first Clooney to make a sustained success of his show business career. He has never been driven by money – from his days as the highest-paid unknown on television to his insistence on taking a fraction of what is due to him on movies – but money does give you power and a certain freedom. The production companies, the development work, the collaborations with the most celebrated talents around – it all adds up to an impressive insurance policy approach to work. As he has said, 'The reason why you produce is because there will be a period of time in the not-too-distant future when people will be sick of seeing you.' Can anyone imagine a time when it happens to George? Maybe not, but this is the man who spent half his time during interviews for *Batman* predicting that his only professional lines the following year would be, 'You want fries with that?' That is why he has back-up. There will be no trailer park in his future, nor in the future of any Clooney ever again. And why not? Because he will be calling the shots. Because he will be one of the biggest players in town. Just like he always wanted.

And yet if he had taken his father's advice back in 1982 it could have been so different. 'If my son had listened to me, he would now be the number one disc jockey in Ashland, Kentucky,' Nick Clooney laughs. Ashland's loss is the world's gain.

SOURCES & BIBLIOGRAPHY

In the course of putting together this book I have referred to many sources across several media to support my own research. Some texts or resources have been used for a general overview throughout, others have more specific reference to a particular chapter. The main sources are listed below.

BOOKS
Davis, Francis, *Afterglow: A Last Conversation With Pauline Kael*, Da Capo Press, 2002.

Dougan, Andy, *The Biography Of George Clooney*, Boxtree, 1997.

Keenleyside, Sam, *Bedside Manners: George Clooney And ER*, ECW Press, 1998.

McCabe, Bob, *George Clooney*, Chameleon, 1997.

Strait, Raymond, *This Is For Remembrance: The Autobiography Of Rosemary Clooney*, Robson Books, 1977.

WEBSITES
By George, It's George Clooney! (georgeclooney.org), Clooneyfan.com, Clooneyfiles.com, NBC, CNN, Warner Bros, Fox, BBC, Reuters, Ananova, Amazon.com, E! Online, eDrive's, E-star, Hollywood.Com, Peoplenews.com, Virgin.com and various *ER* sites.

TV AND RADIO
60 Minutes Australia, *Access Hollywood*, *Barbara Walters*, Cannes Press Conference (May 2000), *Entertainment Tonight*, *Film 2000–02*, *Fox News Network: The Factor*, October–December 2001, *Howard Stern Show*, *Larry King Live*, *Late Show With David Letterman*, *Oprah*, *Rosie O'Donnell*, Princess Diana Press Conference, *Radio One*, *Today Show*, *Tonight Show With Jay Leno*, *Under The Bunker: Behind The Scenes Of Three Kings*.

NEWSPAPERS AND JOURNALS
American Cinematographer, *Asian Age*, Associated Press, *Atlantic City Inquirer*, *Big Screen 2000*, *Biography*, *Boston Herald*, *Broadband Monthly*, *Canadian Press*, *Canoe*, *Chattanooga Times*, *Chicago Sun-Times*, *Cincinnati Enquirer*, *Cinefex*, *Closer*, *Creative Screenwriting*,

Daily Express, *Daily Mail*, *Daily Mirror*, *Daily Telegraph*, *Dish*, *Elle*, *Emmy*, *Empire*, *Entertainment Weekly*, *Esquire*, *Essentials*, *Examiner*, *Eyepiece*, *Fangoria*, *Film Quarterly*, *Film Review*, *Financial Times*, *Flicks*, Fox press kit, *George Magazine*, *GQ*, *Guardian*, *Heat*, *Hollywood Reporter*, *Hotdog*, *Independent*, *Independent On Sunday*, *Interview*, Italian *GQ*, *LA Times*, *London Evening Standard*, *Louisville Courier-Journal*, *M*, *Mail On Sunday*, *Men's Journal*, *Movieline*, *National Enquirer*, *Neon*, *New York Daily News*, *New York Times*, *News Of The World*, *Newsweek*, *Now*, *NY Post*, *Observer*, *OK!*, *Orange Country Register*, *Parade*, *Paris–Match*, *People*, *People Weekly*, *Sunday People*, *Playboy*, *Premiere France*, *Premiere*, Reuters, *Roughcut Q&A*, *Scenario*, *Scotsman*, *Screen International*, *Sight And Sound*, *South China Morning Post*, *Splicedwire*, *Starburst*, *Sun*, *Sunday Express*, *Sunday Telegraph*, *Sunday Times*, *Sun-Sentinel*, *Telé-Star*, *Three Kings* script, *Time Out London*, *The Times*, *Times* magazine, *TNT*, *Total Film*, *TV Guide*, *TV Guide Insider*, *TV Zone*, Universal press pack, *US*, *Vanity Fair*, *Variety*, *Variety Weekly*, *Vogue*, *Washington Post*, *Written By*.

INDEX